FLIGHT 7
IS MISSING

To Ray —
"A Pius Amica for life."
[signature]

KEN H. FORTENBERRY

12-23

FLIGHT 7
IS MISSING

THE SEARCH FOR
MY FATHER'S KILLER

FAYETTEVILLE
MAFIA
PRESS

Book designed by Mark Karis
Front & Back design: Mark Karis
Edited by David Bushman

Published in the USA by Fayetteville Mafia Press
Columbus, Ohio

Contact Information
Email: fayettevillemafiapress@gmail.com
Website: fayettevillemafiapress.com

ISBN: 9781949024067
eBook ISBN: 9781949024074

CONTENTS

This work is dedicated to my father, William Holland Fortenberry, a wise and worldly man whom I adored and whose memory I treasure. His romance with the skies took him to the far corners of the earth, but he was never very far from home and the family he dearly loved.

It is also dedicated to those innocent men, women, and children who perished on that unforgettable and dreary November day in 1957, and to their families, who are left with little more than photographs and precious memories.

ACKNOWLEDGMENTS

This work would not have been possible without the advice, support, and encouragement of my partner and awesome wife, Anna Jonas Fortenberry, who has been by my side for nearly every step of the lifelong search for my father's killer and who has patiently put up with me through all of the ups and downs. I also want to thank our five amazing children, Angela Fortenberry Payne, Jonas H. Fortenberry, Benjamin H. Fortenberry, John B. H. Fortenberry, and Leslie Fortenberry Thomas, for having faith in their old man and for their confidence in this project.

Special words of sincere gratitude and appreciation to my colleague author/historian Dr. Gregg Herken, for his immeasurable help and loyal friendship, and to the brilliant David Pawlowski for his unflagging support and belief in both me and this project.

Also, my most heartfelt thanks to Norma G. Clack and the Clack family for sharing their personal and poignant memories of Lee and his family; Bette Anne Wygant and her family for their spiritual encouragement (Amazing Grace, my friends); Dr. Jeff Kieliszewski for his invaluable professional input in helping to solve this mystery; my older brother, Jerry H. Fortenberry, who has grieved in silence for more than sixty years; my running buddy and little brother, Craig H. Fortenberry; the Pan American World Airways family; the Pan Am Historical Foundation; Fred Sohn; the late Frank Garcia Jr.; The Pan Am Museum Foundation; the staff of the Otto Richter Library at the University of Miami; Margaret Stiles Storm and her late father, investigator Russell Stiles; Karen Crocker Derry; Tom Crocker; Dick Ferguson; Lee Gaffrey Jr.; David Lane; Duke Hughes; Tom Hughes; Cynthia Brown Stark; Bill H. Fortenberry; Charles Hatchette; William Nowdesha; Lindsay Newton; Mark Lubiszewski; Stan Rolfsrud; Richard Grossheim; Cathy Davis; Jim Phillips; Elizabeth Blach; Bidney Bozard; Jim and Connie Martin; Brad and Shan McClain; Claudia Allen; Lani Suchicki; Fred Ellis; Kathryn Oplinger; Steve Allen; David Joyner; Harry Hawkins; Bruce Carlton; Georgia Biershenk Wall; Jackson Payne; Harris Payne; Anna Caroline Payne; Jason Payne; Isaiah Foster; Ryker H. Fortenberry; Sarah, Maddie, and Molly Thomas; Ronnie Agnew; David Bushman and Scott Ryan of Fayetteville Mafia Press for giving me the encouragement I needed to complete my search; and my Facebook friends and countless others who have contributed or helped me along the way with information or interviews. If I have forgotten someone, please understand that it is a mistake of the head, not the heart.

Profile artwork courtesy of Mike Machat and used with permission. Cover photo by Bob Whelan.

INTRODUCTION

When I was six years old, I thought my dad hung the moon. More than sixty years later I still do.

My father perished on November 8, 1957, when a Pan American Boeing Stratocruiser flying across the Pacific mysteriously crashed midway between San Francisco and Honolulu. The cause of the crash was never determined, and it is frequently listed as one of the top unsolved mysteries in American commercial aviation history.

Heartbroken and full of unanswered questions, I began a lifelong journey to find my father's killer when I was fourteen years old, and before I said my prayers and went to sleep that night in 1965, I made a promise to him and to everyone who had lost their lives on Flight 7 that I would find out how and why they died, even if it took me the rest of my life.

As it turns out, it nearly did.

More than six decades after the giant four-engine plane, nicknamed *Romance of the Skies*, plunged to the bottom of the Pacific Ocean, this book finally answers some troubling questions about the crash. It puts together many pieces of a puzzle that was left unsolved by Washington bureaucrats including Federal Bureau of Investigation Director J. Edgar Hoover, who seemed to be more interested in saving face and protecting his agency's image than in helping to solve the mystery.

The search for my father's killer has taken many twists and turns through the years and has been a journey of emotions throughout my childhood and into my senior years. From the first "low" in 1965, when my letter to the Civil Aeronautics Board was dismissed by a low-level bureaucrat, to a recent "high" when documents I had been trying to obtain for more than forty years finally were released, I have never given up the search. Through countless frustrating and often fruitless Freedom of Information requests to agencies including the FBI, the Central Intelligence Agency, and the National Security Agency, I kept opening doors. As soon as one was slammed in my face and I was told there were no more records in their files, I would find another door to push open, and I would keep looking.

All the time, the central questions remained: How and why did the plane crash? Three words were always in the back of my mind: possible, plausible, and probable. There is a huge difference. Even if it was possible to bring the plane down by one means, I still had to ask the next question: was that angle plausible? In other words, was that theory believable? Was it credible? And once I determined that the cause was plausible, was it probable? I am neither an aviation scientist nor a psychologist, and only you will be able to decide if my final probable cause is worthy of believability.

As you read this book you will wonder if *Romance of the Skies* was brought down by a mechanical failure, as some federal investigators hinted, and crashed because penny-pinchers at Pan American had cut corners and failed to properly maintain and inspect the plane before it took off on its ill-fated journey.

You will consider if the largest, most luxurious airliner in the world was somehow sabotaged by a crewmember who changed his will the morning of the flight and thought Pan Am was out to get him.

Strange as it may seem, you will consider whether *Romance of the Skies* lost power and simply fell from the sky because of electromagnetic interference from an unidentified flying object.

Perhaps even stranger is the remote possibility that the plane had been targeted by the Communist Chinese as payback for a CIA-foiled plot to assassinate Chinese Premier Zhou Enlai in a plane blown out of the sky by a time bomb.

Finally, was *Romance of the Skies* destroyed by a former Navy frogman and explosives expert who scraped together enough money to buy a one-way ticket to Honolulu and purchased three huge life insurance policies in the days before the crash?

I wrestled with many theories through the years and chased down every lead, no matter how inconsequential it may have seemed. Every time I convinced myself that the plane had crashed because of mechanical failure, the nagging notion that my father and others on the plane had been murdered forced me to reexamine my findings.

Every event in this book is real. No names have been changed. None of the characters have been invented, but in order to tell the story about some of the events I have occasionally created dialogue based on interviews, sworn testimony, documents obtained from federal government agencies, various company records, newspaper reports, and my own research and knowledge of events and circumstances.

Nearly fifty years as a newspaper editor and investigative reporter have taught me many important lessons, not the least of which is to tell the truth and to trust my gut. This story is the truth, and my gut has been gnawing at me for a very long time.

The search for my father's killer begins. . . .

PART ONE

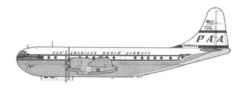

1

STRANGE THINGS OVER PLANET EARTH

FRIDAY, NOVEMBER 8, 1957

IT WAS AN ORDINARY DAY that went straight to hell in a heartbeat.

Two miles high in a cloudless late-afternoon sky over the Pacific Ocean, the navigator and copilot of Pan American Flight 7 to Honolulu senses that the end may be near, and his perfect world has suddenly been flipped upside down.

The hair on his skin bristles and he is overwhelmed by a feeling of impending doom, a sensation that briefly numbs the veteran aviator before he regains his senses. Bill Fortenberry tosses his plastic whiz-wheel flight navigation computer onto the floor, tightens his headset and glances to his right, where the normally calm Boeing Stratocruiser cockpit has been transformed into a frantic scene that looks as if it has been plucked straight out of a Hollywood aviation disaster movie.

But this is no movie, and Fortenberry shakes his head in horrified disbelief, as if that will somehow miraculously end the terrifying scene unfolding all around him.

"What the hell was that? What's going on?" he shouts.

On the flight deck a few feet away, pilot Gordon H. Brown and first officer William P. Wygant wrestle with the controls of the huge four-engine plane and struggle to keep it from plunging into the vast, unforgiving ocean that seems to fill the cockpit windows as the plane begins to lose altitude. Tiny wisps of smoke seep under the closed cockpit door, and the Stratocruiser dips sharply to the left and vibrates violently from cockpit to tail. Their heads shake back and forth as the vibration intensifies, and the groaning sound of bending and stressed metal fills the flight deck.

The blindsided pilots are losing control, and any hope for a successful water ditching is fading fast, but the experienced, war-veteran professionals are not about to give up without a fight—a fight for their very lives and for everyone aboard *Romance of the Skies.*

"Zero 2 fuel flow! Zero 2 fuel flow! Coordinate!" Captain Brown orders. "What about 3 Engine?"

Flight engineer Albert Pinataro is stone-cold stunned. His eyes nervously dart left and right, up and down at the maze of intricate gauges and instruments in front of him. He doesn't have time to wonder what has caused the sudden emergency; he tries to focus on what he can— what he must—do now to help keep the engines running and the plane in the air.

The waves of the Pacific Ocean are closing in at a quickening pace, and *Romance of the Skies* is 10,000 feet high and careening crazily out of control.

Soon, it will all be over.

Just moments earlier the seventy-ton airliner had been cruising across the Pacific and had radioed a nearby Coast Guard vessel that everything was normal and proceeding as planned on the flight from San Francisco to Honolulu. As Flight 7 reached the midway point of its ten-hour flight—the point of no return—the plane's position was charted by the Coast Guard crew and radioed to the Clipper flying overhead.

And now, the once-serene flight has turned into hell, and forty-four souls are hanging in the balance, the odds overwhelmingly against any of them living to see another day. The airliner continues to plummet like an out-of-control missile from the Pacific sky.

Fortenberry shivers and feels powerless.

Lost.

Alone.

Images of his wife and three small sons dash across his eyes as he quickly charts the plane's position and prepares to send out a distress call on the radio.

For reasons that remain unexplained, his message is never heard.

A panic-stricken couple kiss their last kiss, grasp each other's cold and shaking hands, then bow their heads and pray aloud. Hard-sided makeup bags, ladies' leather purses, and men's felt hats tumble from the overhead compartments and rain down on the seats and cabin floor eight feet below as the big airliner jerks back and forth.

"Our Father, who art in heaven, hallowed be thy name. Thy kingdom come. Thy will be done . . . "

Their prayer becomes a quiet united communion of hearts and souls as other passengers join in.

Five hours ago, they were mere strangers. A moment ago, they were reading magazines, enjoying before-dinner cocktails, thinking about tomorrow, and dreaming of the sugar-white sandy beaches and turquoise-blue waters of Waikiki.

Now, they are unwilling partners in an unfolding tragedy.

The familiar words of the Lord's Prayer are chanted rhythmically, and for a few brief moments there is a strange peace and calm aboard Flight 7 to Honolulu.

" . . . but deliver us from evil, for Thine is the kingdom, the power, and the glory forever. Amen."

Suddenly, there is the ear-deafening roar of crunching and ripping metal as the Stratocruiser's long starboard wing smashes into eight-foot waves and breaks in two. Tons of water gush into a huge, gaping hole that just moments ago was part of the luxurious passenger cabin, and what's left of the aluminum fuselage cartwheels in the sea and splits in half.

Screaming passengers are yanked from their seats, heads jerking violently left and right. Bones are crunched and snapped like pretzels as they are tossed and turned in a salty hell and knocked unconscious by the ferocious crash.

Then, silence. Total silence as *Romance of the Skies* is slowly sucked into the bottom of the Pacific Ocean.

Flight 7 has ended.

FRIDAY, NOVEMBER 1, 1957
SANTA CRUZ, CALIFORNIA

Oliver Eugene Crosthwaite is on a collision course with the devil.

His whiskey-bloodshot brown eyes dance around the puke-green room, bouncing from wall to wall. They search frantically for something—anything—to focus on, to rest on, to hide behind. The tiny office inside the annex of the Santa Cruz County Courthouse is closing in on him, just like everything else in his go-to-hell world, and he can't take much more. He *won't* take much more.

For a split second, his eyes fix on a cheap dime-store landscape picture on the cement block wall, but just as quickly they flit away. They are dancing again. Moving again. Shifting again. Just like the story of Gene's forty-five-year-old life. He tugs at his left shirt sleeve, and then nervously twists the cuff between his thumb and forefinger.

Back and forth. Back and forth. Twist. Twist.

Gene is about to explode. Last night's double shot after double shot of whiskey hasn't helped, but he needs the booze to cope these days, and whose business is it anyway if he likes to take a drink?

Gene has spent much of the last week visiting old friends, friends from his early days with Pan American World Airways, friends of his recently deceased wife, and just about anyone who will listen to him bitch about Pan Am, the stepdaughter he despises, and his miserable life in general. And now here he is, bitching again, this time to Santa Cruz County Juvenile Officer Sergeant Herbert G. Johnson, a retired Navy chief warrant officer and professional polygrapher, who is trying to make sense of it all.

Sergeant Johnson leans attentively forward in his chair and fights back his growing impatience with the strange man sitting across the desk from him. What is this guy saying? What is his problem? Why isn't he making any sense?

"Hold on now, Mr. Crosthwaite. I don't have any idea what you're talking about. Just slow down and start from the beginning. Now, what exactly is the matter? Give it to me slowly this time."

"What's the matter? What's the matter? I'll tell you what's the matter—Tania. That's my daughter. Not my real daughter, my real daughter is Billie JoAnn. She lives with my ex-wife."

"How old is Tania?"

"Sixteen. She graduated from Holy Cross High a couple of months ago. Didn't I tell you that already? I travel a lot with Pan Am—that's my job—and even her grandmother says she can't control her. She can't find a job, and I don't know if she even really wants one."

"Slow down, Mr. Crosthwaite. I'm trying to take notes and understand what you're saying at the same time."

"OK. I'll slow down, but I ain't gonna repeat this no more. I've already told the sheriff and he didn't do nothing. Not a damn thing. He sent me to you. Tania's my adopted daughter. She's not my real blood, and I told her so a couple of months ago. Her real father was some Italian-Russian sailor who died in China during the war. She's the matter. You've got to do something with her!"

Crosthwaite rubs his temples and clamps his eyes tightly shut.

"Look, now I've got another one of those damn headaches. Had 'em ever since I was a kid."

"Just slow down, Mr. Crosthwaite, and tell me the problem. Everything's going to be OK, but I can't do anything until I understand what this is all about. It's very confusing right now. Please, just start at the beginning."

For the next few minutes Crosthwaite weaves an improbable tale of paranoia and persecution, centered on his stepdaughter and Pan Am. He believes both are out to get him. He is against the world; the world is against him. Something has to give.

Soon. Very soon.

"And I'll tell you another damn thing, too. She killed my wife, just worried her to death. The doctor says it was stomach cancer, but Tania caused it. I know she did, staying out all hours of the night, refusing to do what I told her to do. Me and her, we just don't get along. Look, this is crazy. I've already told the sheriff. Do I have to tell it all again?"

"I'm afraid so, Mr. Crosthwaite. You're doing just fine. Go ahead, but please slow down."

"I just can't get her to do nothing. She just sits around the house and never lifts a damn finger. I've tried to help her get a job. I've even driven her from here to San Francisco and back so she can put in applications everywhere, but she don't ever get a callback."

"Well, now, Mr. Crosthwaite. That's not really unusual. She's just sixteen years old, you know, and with no experience."

"When I tell her to do something, she refuses," Crosthwaite interrupts. "She really thinks she's something. Ever since her mother died back in August, all she does is give me trouble."

"Most teenagers seem to give their parents trouble, Mr. Crosthwaite."

"Not like this one. Not like Tania. She does it all the time. Trouble oughtta be her middle name."

"What does she do?"

"She drives me up a wall. Right up a wall. She's a demon, I tell you."

Crosthwaite neglects to tell Sergeant Johnson that his job as a Pan American purser takes him away from home for weeks at a time, denying Tania both the love she craves and the parental guidance all teens need. Instead, he focuses on what he sees as *her* faults, *her* shortcomings, and what he considers her blatant attempts to drive him crazy.

If driving him crazy is Tania's goal—and Sergeant Johnson doubts that it is—she obviously is succeeding. Crosthwaite's neuroses are plain to see; he is a certifiable nutcase.

"As long as she lives in my house, she'll do what I say when I say it. And I'll tell you another damn thing. If Pan Am thinks they're gonna fire me, they'd better think again."

"*Fire* you? What's Pan American got to do with this?"

"Everything! They want to fire me. They've been on my damn back ever since I had tuberculosis. Hell, that was more than a year ago, but some of them hotshots in the office say it's not safe for me to breathe around passengers in an airplane. Confined in an airplane is what they say. That's just a bunch of crap, and the union told 'em so. I had to force Pan Am to let me go back to work. I'm the best purser they've got, but they're still on my back. I filed a workman's compensation claim against them, but they've got me over the barrel with all their attorneys. Between Tania and Pan Am, I've had it up to here. You've got to do something with her. You've just got to! She needs to be locked up. Behind bars, I tell you. Can't you put her in some kind of juvenile detention place? I'm sure she's breaking the law staying out all hours of the night. Can't I sign something that says she is out of control?"

Johnson scribbles some notes on a legal pad, leans back in his seat and briefly closes his eyes attempting to make sense out of all this madness.

"Julia tried. God knows she tried. But Tania wouldn't listen. Julia died in August in the hospital in San Mateo. Did I tell you that? Yeah, I believe I did. My God, she wasn't but thirty-two years old. Anyway, I've had it with Tania. She's the reason Julia is dead, and no one can tell me otherwise."

"People don't cause cancer, Mr. Crosthwaite."

"Well, I know that's what they say, but I ain't so sure. Julia was only sixteen when Tania was born, and she just about died bringing her into the world. I've heard people say that having a hard childbirth can cause all kinds of female problems later on in life for some women, and I think worry has a lot to do with it, too. Tania worried Julia to death. Just worried her right to her grave. Haven't you heard of people worrying themselves sick? That poor woman was just sick with worry about Tania. She worried so much it made her stomach hurt all the time. All the damn time."

Crosthwaite puts his face in his hands and begins to softly cry, but quickly regains his composure and continues rambling, almost incoherently at times.

Sergeant Johnson makes some more notes on his pad, but he makes some mental notes, too. This man Crosthwaite is trouble. Big trouble.

He just doesn't know how big.

"Tell you what I'll do, Mr. Crosthwaite. I'll look into this and I'll talk with Tania, too. After that, we'll get back together and come up with a plan that will be good for everyone. OK? Let's make an appointment for Tania to come and talk with me."

Crosthwaite isn't impressed, but he doesn't have much of a choice.

"I'm flying to Honolulu next Friday, but I guess that'll have to do for now. But I'm not kidding, sergeant. Something bad's gonna happen, I just know it. Tania needs to be straightened out. She won't even listen to her grandmother. She's from Russia, did I tell you that? She don't speak much English."

He reluctantly shakes Johnson's hand and walks outside, fumbling for his car keys.

"Who's that son of a bitch trying to fool, dammit?" he asks himself as he unlocks the door to his Ford sedan. "He's not going to do anything to Tania. He's just like the rest of them. No one believes me. Not a single damn person! Well, if he won't do something about her, I will. I'll have the last word."

Crosthwaite hops into his car and drives south to his home on Hillside Drive in Felton, but not before stopping off at Green's Service Station for a bottle of his favorite whiskey, which he tucks reassuringly at his side on the front seat. He resists the temptation to open the bottle and take a small sip for comfort. He's been trying to cut back on his drinking since his bout with tuberculosis, but he isn't having much success.

Crosthwaite spends much of the rest of the afternoon in private, tinkering with God knows what in his basement workshop, and later that night he barks again at Tania as she tiptoes into the living room on her way to bed.

It's becoming a sick and predictable routine.

He demands that she pay room and board.

"Fifteen dollars a week or out you go!" he shouts. "You need to find a job. And I mean right now!"

She ignores him, not because of a lack of respect but because she is terrified of the gloomy, angry man he has become in the past couple of years. He wasn't much of a father before her mother died, but he's been even less so since. He's never shown her any love, even as her mother was passing away, and his tough, my-way-or-the-highway parenting is leaving both of them miserable.

Without a word, Tania backs away and tiptoes quickly to her bedroom. She's seen and heard enough of her angry stepfather for one day.

Crosthwaite sits down in his oversized chair in the living room and stares out the second-story bay window. He sits there for the rest of the evening, seething inside with all sorts of crazy ideas that are fighting for attention in his mixed-up head. He speaks to no one, but angrily glares at Tania when she passes by on her way downstairs to talk with her grandmother. She can see the hatred in his cold eyes and feels his anger from across the room but doesn't have a clue what she has done to make him so mad, and isn't about to ask.

Sitting. Staring. Brooding.

Crosthwaite finally reaches his boiling point—that hellish moment where liquor, depression, paranoia, and anger crash together—and he gets out of his chair, stumbles over to an antique Chinese desk, and pulls some papers from a drawer. Then, like the madman he has become, he tosses them into the fireplace and contentedly watches them go up in flames. Seconds later, he goes on a tear, yanking everything—legal documents, personal letters, photographs—from other drawers in the red desk and throws them into the fire. He stares in strange satisfaction as they shrivel up and disappear into ashes.

As he is about to return to the desk for another round of fire fuel, his mother-in-law, Russian-born Katherina Stub, walks into the room and is frightened by what she sees.

"What are you doing, Gene? What is wrong?" she pleads, wondering not only why he is burning the papers, but also what has become of the man she used to know.

Crosthwaite ignores her and continues to toss documents into the fireplace.

"Gene! No, Gene! Not those!" she screams, and grabs Tania's adoption papers from his hands, stashing them behind her back for safety. "Please, not those! Why are you doing this, Gene? No more, Gene. No more! Please stop!"

Briefly interrupted in his moment of insanity, Crosthwaite storms away, slams shut the door to his bedroom, and locks it. Tight.

Tough man Oscar Eugene Crosthwaite climbs into bed and quietly cries himself to a restless sleep.

SATURDAY, NOVEMBER 2, 1957
LEVELLAND, TEXAS

"Good God Almighty! What the hell is that?"

Pedro Saucedo and Joe Salaz are frozen in fright. Their eyes wide open, they stare in disbelief as a mystery as old as the ages unfolds in front of them. They think they might be seeing things in the clear, cool Texas night sky, and in fact, they are.

What the petrified farmworkers are seeing about four miles west of Levelland ultimately will send nearly everyone in this ranching town of about 10,000 into a frenzy and make headlines all over the world. Before the sun rises tomorrow, one of the most active weeks in the history of UFO sightings will be well underway, and across the planet dozens of unexplained sightings by ordinary citizens will be reported to government bureaucrats.

The bureaucrats will promptly kiss off the UFO reports as everything from mirages and imaginations gone wild to weather balloons and meteorites. But Saucedo and Salaz are not imagining things; what they are seeing is real. Exactly *what* it is, however, is another matter. Right now, they aren't worried about how scientists and bureaucrats might react tomorrow and how their skeptical friends might laugh and talk about them. Right now, they are just crouching low to the ground in utter, fearful silence.

Moments earlier, as they had cruised along Texas Rural Road 114, a long, runway-like stretch of asphalt in the middle of nowhere, a brightly lit, cigar-shaped object about 200 feet long suddenly appeared out of the dark sky and headed directly toward their vehicle.

"When it got near, the lights of my truck went out and then the motor died. I jumped out of the truck and hit the dirt because I was afraid," Saucedo, a thirty-year-old Korean War veteran declared later. "I called out to Joe, but he didn't get out. The thing passed directly over my truck with a great sound and rush of wind.

"It sounded like thunder, and my truck rocked from the blast. I felt a lot of heat. Then I got up and watched it go out of sight toward Levelland."

The UFO disappears with an ear-deafening noise and a wild rush of wind, and Saucedo and Salaz restart the truck and race to nearby Whiteface, where Saucedo stops at a roadside Southwestern Bell phone booth. He swats away the annoying bugs that cluster near the overhead light, plunks a nickel into the slot, and dials the operator, who connects him with the police

Levelland police officer A.J. Fowler politely listens to his improbable tale, dismisses the men as a couple of Saturday night drunks, and hangs up. Until the call from Saucedo, it had been a routine night for the officer, but things are about to change—in a big way.

A few minutes later, the police department phone rings again. This time the call comes from the tiny town of Whitharral, about four miles north of Levelland, and once again officer Fowler listens to a story that is simply too improbable to believe. The caller tells him that he has just encountered a brightly lit egg-shaped object in the middle of the road. The caller reports that he got out of his car and cautiously approached it but was too afraid to get very close.

Seconds later the object slowly lifted off the ground and disappeared into the night. His vehicle, like that of Saucedo and Salaz, had been immobilized by the object, but as soon as it was gone, he was able to restart his car and quickly made his way to the closest phone booth.

One call becomes two. Two calls quickly become three.

At midnight, a man driving about eleven miles north of Levelland encounters a UFO hovering over the roadway. His vehicle is suddenly disabled, and he sits in shocked silence, staring at the unidentified object on the roadway. A few minutes later, the UFO swiftly flies way, disappearing like the others into the big, wide Texas night. The caller tells the police dispatcher that his car fired up immediately after the UFO was out of sight.

Ten minutes later, nineteen-year-old Texas Tech freshman Newell Wright is driving about nine miles east of Levelland when his car engine abruptly stops. Wright gets out of the car, opens the hood, and checks to see if an electrical problem has disabled his vehicle. Suddenly he sees a weird, bluish-green object about 120 feet long land on the pavement just down the road from him. Then it quickly rises into the sky and disappears.

What in the hell is going on in Hockley County, Texas?

At 12:15 a.m., just five minutes after Wright's call to the cops, another driver near Whitharral comes across something unusual in the middle of the road. Like the other vehicles, his is totally disabled. By this time police officer-dispatcher Fowler realizes that something is going on—something so incredible that he can't begin to fathom it—and he urgently calls out on the radio for all patrol cars in the Levelland area to be on the lookout for a UFO. He feels a little silly, but he can no longer ignore the truth. Something is happening out there.

The calls keep coming. A ball-like object changes color as it lands on a highway. A truck driver reports a 200-foot object floating in the sky. His vehicle has been disabled. Another vehicle is stopped by some weird object. Thunder-like sounds emanate from floating objects. By 1:30 a.m. it is no longer just civilians reporting the unknown objects in the sky. Two cops, about three miles out of Levelland, report that a large, glowing object passed directly in front of them as they drove along a highway. A fire chief driving about seventeen miles north reports a glowing object in the night, and even the county's respected sheriff sees something he can't begin to comprehend.

During a two-and-a-half-hour span this evening, at least fifteen frightened people—neither crackpots nor Saturday-night drunks—will report mysterious objects in the skies above Levelland.

And this is only one night in one little Texas town in early November 1957.

MONDAY, NOVEMBER 4, 1957

The overnight flight from Porto Alegre to São Paulo, Brazil, is on schedule and perfectly routine as Captain Jean V. de Beyssac, chief pilot of the Varig Airlines Curtiss C-46 airfreighter, commands the twin-engine plane to a height of 7,500 feet and maintains his altitude above the thin clouds.

At 1:30 a.m. the routine flight turns into a real-life nightmare.

Captain de Beyssac notices a strange red light below and to the left of the aircraft and asks his copilot to lean over and see if he notices a flying saucer. They both joke for a second or two, but not for long. Moments later, the fast-moving object approaches the aircraft, and before the startled pilots can change course, a strong, strange smell of something burning enters the cockpit. The red UFO moves closer to the plane, then suddenly dashes away.

No fire detectors are activated, and as the UFO fades into the distance, the pilots realize that their radio transmitter, the magneto of the right engine, the right-engine generator, and the radio goniometer have all mysteriously been fried to a crisp by whatever just occurred. They turn the plane around, return safely but frighteningly on one engine to Porto Alegre, and make a complete report to authorities about the event.

As it turns out, it is the second time in less than ninety days that a Varig Airlines crew has had a close encounter with a UFO. On August 14 another crew was flying above the clouds on a route to Rio when the pilots saw a brilliant, disk-shaped object dash by at superhuman speed. The engines failed, the radio quit, and the plane began plummeting to the earth. As the pilots struggled to regain control of the plane, the UFO vanished, and electrical power suddenly was restored. It was a near-death experience—and a close encounter they would never forget.

A continent away, near Alamogordo, New Mexico, retired Navy man James Stokes is driving along an isolated desert stretch of Highway 54 in his late-model Mercury when the radio begins to crackle and fade away. He reaches down and tries to turn up the volume, and that's when the engine falters and dies. Frightened nearly out of his mind, Stokes gets out of his car and notices other vehicles stopping nearby. One motorist steps out of his car and points excitedly to the sky.

Stokes gazes skyward. There it is! A mother-of-pearl, egg-shaped object coming toward him at an amazing speed out of the northeast sky.

It quickly disappears, then reappears on the same path. No noise. No smoke. No vapor trail. Nothing but the unexplained object from God knows where. By this time the engines of at least six other cars nearby have conked out, and their passengers are standing outside peering in amazement at the mystery in the sky.

Stokes, a missile engineer working on an upper-air classified research project at nearby Holloman Air Force Base, feels a burning sensation on his face and is suddenly warm all over. A severely sunburned Stokes later estimates that the object was flying at Mach 1 or Mach 2 at an altitude of 1,500 to 3,000 feet.

Military and other government officials publicly dismiss the sightings and ridicule the people who report them. It is standard operating procedure; ridicule is a powerful tool in dissuading citizens from reporting similar events. Officials say flying-saucer reports from coast-to-coast are simply the result of mass hysteria, the byproduct of Russia's recent launch of the satellite Sputnik. The flying objects that perfectly sane people are seeing in the skies above them simply don't exist. They laughingly label it Sputnikitis.

Case closed.

Meanwhile, United Press International reports that the US Air Force is confidentially warning its radar network to be on alert for strange objects in the sky and instructing Air Force jets to shoot them down if possible. At the same time, the US Coast Guard in New Orleans, reeling from a twenty-seven-minute, carefully documented UFO sighting by one of its own cutters off the Louisiana coast, is alerting ships to be on the lookout for unidentified flying objects.

Hysteria or not, something strange is happening in the skies over Planet Earth in November 1957, and other strange things are occurring down below.

* * *

Thirty-five miles south of San Francisco, in rapidly developing suburban Santa Clara, my parents, Bill and Ronnie Fortenberry, cuddle on the living room floor of our newly built three-bedroom ranch-style house on Loyola Drive in the Junipero Gardens subdivision. For years they had scrimped and saved to make the down payment on a new home, and just eleven months earlier they moved with my two brothers and me from a rental house in nearby San Mateo.

They listen and sing along as they often do to Ezio Pinza's rendition of "Some Enchanted Evening" on their new "South Pacific" 33 1/3 LP album.

Some enchanted evening, when you find your true love,

When you hear her call you across a crowded room,

... Once you have found her, never let her go.

(By Rodgers, Hammerstein)

They had found each other more than a decade earlier, growing up dirt-poor in rural South Carolina, they fell in love and vowed to never let each other go. They love music, especially Rodgers and Hammerstein, and after an exhausting day of yard work, it is time to relax and be together, a rarity given my dad's recent flying schedule with Pan Am.

"I'm really going to miss you, Bill. You will be home for Thanksgiving this year, won't you? Promise me. I won't even ask about Christmas. You're never here for Christmas," she pouts.

"Wouldn't miss it for the world, honey."

"Which one? Thanksgiving or Christmas?" she teases, knowing that his Pan Am seniority never seems to be high enough for him to be home at Christmas.

"It never gets easier, Bill. I miss you so much when you're on a trip, especially the long ones. Where did you say you were you going this time?"

"We're flying a fifty-nine-L pattern on a Stratocruiser."

"You know I can't understand that pilot talk."

"Well, first it's Honolulu, then on to Wake Island. Then we're off to Tokyo and back to Wake, Honolulu, Los Angeles, and home! Nothing to it. A piece of cake."

"It's not a piece of cake to me. I worry about those Stratocruisers, Bill. They're so big and fat. I just don't understand how they even get off the ground. They don't seem safe to me."

Both are keenly aware of the history of Stratocruisers and their safety records. Last year's successful mid-Pacific ditching and a fatal crash in Oregon not long before that are occasionally on their minds, but they don't talk about those things.

"Well, one of these days I'll take you and the boys to Honolulu on a Strat and you can see for yourself. Now, there's an idea. How about Christmas in Honolulu this year? Wouldn't that be nice?"

"The boys really would like that."

"And how about you?"

"It would be nice once we got there, but you know how I am about flying, and flying in a Stratocruiser just scares me to death."

"Don't worry about it now, honey. We can talk about it when I get home. Right now, let's not talk about Stratocruisers, Honolulu, Christmas, or anything else. I don't leave for three more days anyway, so why don't we just listen to the music and relax?"

Daddy rolls over on the floor and teasingly pulls my mother into his arms.

He is the happiest man on earth.

My father's journey from a miserable childhood to becoming the happiest man on earth was not an easy one.

William Holland Fortenberry was born in Spartanburg, South Carolina, a small textile mill town, on January 29, 1922. His mother, the former Lillie Mae Hembree, was barely sixteen years old and totally unprepared for either marriage or parenthood. His father, Thomas Jefferson Fortenberry, was nearly twice as old as his mother, and was a noncombat veteran of World War I. An hourly waged textile-mill worker and a part-time tenant farmer, he had nothing in common with his young wife. They were an unlikely couple, and their marriage lasted less than six tumultuous years.

Daddy and his only sibling, younger brother Raymond, were abandoned by their parents during the Great Depression when the boys were six and four years old respectively, and my father was taken in by a farm family in nearby Campobello, who raised him until he went to a local junior college. He and Raymond didn't see each other for another twelve years.

Daddy was an able-bodied male in a family of two girls, and he spent hours in the sizzling hot summer sun plowing the red clay dirt behind an old mule, studying at night, and planning for a career as a Methodist minister. He preached a few sermons at small churches here and there, but his eyes were always on the skies.

After non-combat Navy service in World War II, he worked as a carpenter, obtained his pilot's license, and operated his own small construction company in Miami—a place he always loved. He called Miami the Garden of Eden, and it was in Miami that he got his big break. Not long after he and my mother married, he joined Pan American World Airways as a flight navigator, and an exciting new world opened for them both.

He was a compassionate man with deep faith and a special place in his heart for others, especially those less fortunate, perhaps because of his own childhood. I remember that my brother Jerry and I were riding our bikes one day in a plum orchard along Saratoga Creek near our house in Santa Clara when we came upon a homeless Spanish-speaking family with several very small, very dirty children with sad, hollow eyes, and dressed in tattered clothing.

We tried to talk with them, but their English-language skills were poor, and our Spanish-speaking abilities were nonexistent. We did, however, realize that they were desperately in need of help, so we raced our bikes back home and told Daddy. Without hesitation, he asked my mother to empty the cupboard, and we all went back to the orchard and gave them a helping hand. It felt like Thanksgiving Day for everyone. The homeless family was joyously grateful, and our family was reminded of just how fortunate we were. It was a life lesson I never forgot.

My father was a well-rounded man who read the classics, studied philosophy, inhaled world history, treasured German waltzes, and had a wonderful sense of humor. He was full of love for all people, places, and things and truly had a romance with the skies. He was passionate about

19

photography and developed his own prints and slides in his garage darkroom. He loved the outdoors, primitive camping, and especially landing a feisty rainbow trout on one of his special lures as he fished in a cold, rushing mountain stream.

Most of all, he loved his family.

THE CONDADO BEACH HOTEL
SAN JUAN, PUERTO RICO
TUESDAY, OCTOBER 5, 1954

"Dear Mom & Boys:

"I'm back in San Juan. I spent Saturday night in the air, Sunday night here, and Monday night at Antigua, British West Indies. Tonight, we start the long flight to Rio and Sao Paulo. It has been pretty easy until now, but from now until I come home, I will practically live on the airplane—the Pan American kind.

"I went swimming yesterday and today and got just a little bit sunburned. It sure is nice here now. I hope I can have time here on my return to get some avocados. They are really nice now, big, fat, golden yellow jobs.

"You boys be good and above all take care of yourselves. You have a wonderful life ahead of you. I hope you will learn to love this great green earth of ours as much as your father does. Just flying over it and seeing it, I sometimes almost laugh out loud with joy. Only a great omnipotent God could have ever thought of such a perfectly wonderful world for man. I don't think man was ever cast from the Garden of Eden; we are still in it.

"Yes, you boys have it pretty nice. The closest love your old dad ever knew before your mother came along was that of my devoted dog, June. The only security I ever had was my own stubborn youth and

faith in my personal abilities. There are, of course, many things that you might need that we can't give you, but your mother's love and your Dad's devotion are the greatest assets you can ever have in this world—until your own dear wives come along.

"Your mother is to me the greatest thing on earth, the base on which all my hilarious happiness is built. She has enabled me to have just about everything I have ever wanted. Now it is time for her to have some of the things she wants, if I can get them for her.

"If all else should go, while I have you, I'll be happy and able to make it. I love you boys, and I love you, too, Mom. Your old Dad is the happiest, most contented soul on earth because of you.

"Love, Dad

"See you Saturday."

WEDNESDAY, NOVEMBER 6, 1957

After another night of restlessness and self-pity, Gene Crosthwaite almost welcomes the morning California sun.

Almost.

The nights since Julia's death are becoming increasingly harder to bear, and he begins to curse the darkness when he locks his bedroom door at night. The nighttime loneliness deepens his depression; only daybreak seems to ease his suffering. But now he is beginning to hate even the sunlight. All that means is another day. Another day without Julia. Another day with Tania.

Another day. Dammit. Another day.

Why did Julia have to die? He almost shuts out of his memory the arguments they had had after his release from the TB sanatorium in Redwood City. Sure, he was drinking a lot of liquor. Yes, he had gained weight. More than fifty pounds, to be exact. But what the hell did she expect? He had been locked up in that damn place for six months. Still,

21

he wasn't any different otherwise. So why did Julia keep telling him he had changed?

"You're different, Gene. Something's wrong. I don't know what it is, but you've changed."

"You've changed. You've changed. You've changed," that's all he seemed to hear. Even Tania sometimes got into the act.

Bullshit. He wasn't any different, and he was tired of hearing otherwise. Just because he didn't want to go out for dinner, did that mean he had changed? Just because he didn't want to take Julia dancing or to parties, did that mean he had changed? He never did like to dance anyway. She knew that. Besides, she always seemed to prefer other men to him at parties, and he couldn't help it that he had been impotent since his hospitalization. Did she have to pester him all the time about it? It made him wonder what she had been up to all those months he had been confined to the sanatorium.

Tania was even worse. Whenever she and Julia got into a rare disagreement, Gene would step in and try to help Julia out. But it never worked. Instead of helping Julia, he found both of them teaming up against him. Everybody and everything these days seems to be teaming up against him. His stepdaughter. Pan American. Even that damn TB and those drugs he still needs to take.

"You've changed! You've changed! Why do you have to be so angry all the time?" they would chant, and Gene would get pissed off again.

Everything was Tania's fault. Always had been. Always would be. She wouldn't listen to anybody, and always wanted to do as she damn well pleased. She really thought she was something special with that strawberry blond hair, slim ballet figure, and sneaky smile that he was convinced hid something. If only he could figure out what it was.

Julia wasn't perfect, but he had loved her. Oh, how he had loved his beautiful little Russian. And now, all he has is her daughter, Tania, a teenager he can't control.

But that will end soon.

Very soon.

Gene goes back to work in his basement workshop.

"Now, where did I put that goddamn blasting powder?"

William Harrison Payne parks his banged-up sedan outside the Pan American World Airways terminal at San Francisco International Airport and kicks a badly worn left front white sidewall tire, reminding himself that nearly all of them need to be recapped or replaced. He shakes his slightly balding head at the predicament and walks briskly inside to the ticket counter.

He is a man on a mission and can't be distracted by simple things today.

The forty-two-year-old former Navy frogman and demolitions expert is in deep trouble and is being buried alive with debts and howling creditors who want money, and they want it now. A mortgage note on the hunting and fishing lodge he and his wife, Harriet, own in the mountains of remote Scott Bar is nearing foreclosure, and if he doesn't come up with some big money soon, they will lose not only their real estate, but also their dreams.

A judge in Siskiyou County recently ordered him to pay the county $450 in fines for damages he caused to a county road, and he's still fuming about that. Not only does he not have the money, and is unlikely to have it any time soon, but he doesn't think he owes the county one damn penny. He's had a long-running feud with both loggers and county officials over the use of that road, and he's determined to stand his ground. Sure, he may have torn up the road. Yes, he has been forcing people to pay him cash tolls to use it. But dammit, as far he is concerned it's his road—not the county's—and he can do damn well as he pleases with it.

On top of all of that Harriet has been on his ass for weeks now, insisting that they do some inexpensive repairs to the main lodge, but both of them know that their checks drawn on Scott Valley Bank in Fort Jones are bouncing all over Siskiyou County and there is simply no money left to keep the place up. They have recently listed the property for sale with Stout Realty Company in nearby Weed and are asking twice what they paid for it two years earlier.

He has managed to scrape together enough money for what he intends to do today, but after that, well, that's why he came here in the first place. That's the plan he has been working on since he left

Harriet and his boys in Scott Bar a few days ago and drove with his baby daughter, Kitti Ruth, to his mother's house in Stockton. He needs a base to put his plan into action, and Stockton is perfect. He's always been a mama's boy, and Mama always seems to understand him when no one else even bothers to try. And Mama can take care of Kitti Ruth until he returns—if he returns.

As a retired Navy noncommissioned officer, he is entitled to fly standby from San Francisco to Honolulu on a Military Air Transport plane for less than ten bucks, but that is not part of his plan. He must be on a commercial airliner for his plan to work. Nothing else will do.

Although troubled by his mostly self-imposed financial misfortunes, the hardheaded Payne isn't going down easy, and he thinks he has come up with a way to reverse his family's fortunes. Although he never bothers to share details of it with his wife, his doting mother, or anyone else, it supposedly involves something as simple as an airline flight to Honolulu, where he plans to collect money owed to him by two unknown men for an unknown reason or—or, if they don't pay, "blow them up."

Pan American agent C. H. Huang pleasantly greets the round-faced, no-neck Payne at the ticket counter.

"Yes, sir. How may I help you this morning?"

"Honolulu on Friday," Payne crisply replies as he glances at the static timetable on the wall behind the ticket agent.

Huang is momentarily taken aback by the cold-talking Payne.

"Yes, sir, just a moment, please." Huang checks some papers, makes some notations with his pencil, then smiles and looks Payne in the eyes.

"Our Flight 7 leaves at 11:31 a.m. Friday. It's a Stratocruiser, and I know you'll love it. It's a magnificent plane. Would that be OK?"

"Yeah, fine. How long a flight is it?" Payne nervously glances around the ticketing area for something else that is pressing on his mind.

"About ten hours, sir, but you'll be very comfortable on the Stratocruiser. It's a roomy, luxurious plane and even has a downstairs cocktail lounge. You'll be very pleased. Would you like me to book you in the President section? That's what we call first class on the Stratocruiser."

Payne is growing impatient. He knows full well about the Stratocruiser. He knows about its history, how long the flight is to

Honolulu, and how much an economy-class ticket will cost. He knows everything. Just ask him.

"No. I don't want first class. Just book me on the lowest fare to Honolulu, will you?"

"And when will you be returning?"

"Not sure when I'm returning. Just book it one-way."

"One-way?"

"One-way. I said one-way, didn't I?"

"Yes, sir, you did. And your name please?"

"Payne, William Harrison Payne. Address, Scott Bar, California. I own a lodge up there."

A few minutes later Payne confidently struts away with a $175 one-way economy-class ticket to Honolulu aboard *Romance of the Skies*, departing late Friday morning.

Huang thinks it is a bit unusual that Payne does not want a return ticket, but it is none of his business, and he greets the next customer in line as Payne fades away into the busy crowd.

Payne tucks Pan Am ticket number 261-211662 into his coat pocket, stops momentarily to light up a cigarette, and looks around the ticketing area until he spots what he most needs next: a trip insurance vending machine.

"Airline Trip Insurance. Follow These Simple Steps . . . $62,500 Coverage. Only 10 quarters."

Payne buys two policies with twenty quarters and strolls away with $125,000 in accident life insurance.

Life is going to get better very soon for the Payne family.

Halfway across the country, business executive Hugh Lee Clack and his wife, Ann, herd their four children through the busiest airport in the world—Chicago's Midway International. Their United Airlines flight from Midland, Michigan, has just arrived, a few minutes late, and they have walked out of the airplane into a cloudy, cool Illinois morning. The roar of arriving and departing aircraft deafens the chatter of the excited children as they enter the busy terminal and head to the gate for their flight to San Francisco, where they will spend a few days before flying on *Romance of the Skies* to Honolulu and ultimately to their home in Tokyo.

Clack adjusts his glasses and clutches two-year-old Mariko between his left arm and his chest as he rushes toward their gate. He holds a navy-blue Pan American carry-on bag in his right hand and walks briskly past the newspaper racks, without even noticing the front-page story in the *Chicago Tribune* about the mysterious egg-shaped flying objects seen by dozens of people in Texas, or another page-one story, about the Russian launch of the Sputnik 2 satellite and its canine passenger into space.

He urges Ann and the children to hurry; they must make it to their gate on time, and there's not a minute to spare. It's been a nice vacation, but it's time to get back to work.

Arroyo Drive in Santa Clara is a quiet, straight asphalt-paved street with a few new houses in a rapidly developing subdivision in what recently was farmland and plum orchards. It's perfect for what I am trying to do, made even more perfect by the fact that my father's right hand is on the back fender of my Schwinn bike to guide me and keep me safe.

"You're doing fine, Kenny. Just keep pedaling. Don't worry. Keep your eyes straight ahead," he urges as I pedal a little faster now, swerving less and feeling more and more confident.

I turn my head slightly around and see Daddy fading away in the distance, clapping his hands in the air and smiling proudly.

"You're doing it, son! You're doing it!"

Daddy's right. I am doing it.

I am flying on my own now and it feels wonderful.

2

A PERFECT DAY TO FLY

FRIDAY, NOVEMBER 8, 1957 7:30 A.M.

PAN AMERICAN MASTER MECHANIC Norvin B. Fortune arrives at San Francisco International Airport and is assigned to perform a predeparture walk-around inspection of N90944, *Romance of the Skies*. The gigantic, double-decker airplane has been parked at a Pan Am maintenance base wash rack station about two miles from the main terminal since it arrived from Honolulu on Wednesday afternoon.

For some reason the graveyard shift has not yet serviced the aircraft, and only the number three main gas tank has been fueled. This perturbs him, because Friday mornings are always busy for Pan American, and this one is not only shaping up to be busy, but is putting an extra strain on the morning ground crew to prepare the plane for an on-time departure, something their very jobs depend on.

It's the thirty-one-year-old Fortune's responsibility to methodically check everything on the inspection list before the plane is taxied to the new passenger terminal area for its late-morning flight to Honolulu. He finds that all items are normal except for the right nose gear tire, which has gone flat, and he orders that the tire and the entire wheel assembly be replaced. Ground crewmen Lewis Mucca and Joe Alamorong take care of that duty, then fill the Stratocruiser with fuel and oil.

Flight servicemen Hugh P. Greene and Bo Bowen join several other ground crewmen and begin to load overseas airmail and cargo, which includes two heavy pieces that pose an unusual problem. After several failed attempts, they are unable to fit one piece of cargo—a huge IBM 305 RAMAC computer with 3.75 megabytes—through the cargo door, so it is finally carted away to be shipped by sea to Japan. The world's first hard-drive computer, it weighs more than a ton. The other IBM computer, weighing a whopping 600 pounds, takes a lot of effort but is eventually stowed away in the forward cargo compartment near barrels of movie film.

"Good morning, San Francisco! It's forty-nine degrees here at the 'World's Greatest Radio Station' and there's a soupy morning fog outside, but the weatherman promises a nice day with cloudy skies and a high near sixty-four. So, get out of bed, grab a cup of coffee, and get on with the day! Up and at 'em. Thank God, it's Friday!"

KSFO radio morning man Don Sherman continues to chirp mercilessly as Gene Crosthwaite rolls out of bed.

He looks at the beige, plastic RCA Victor alarm clock radio beside his bed, shakes the previous night off, then mentally plots the rest of his morning. He has so much to do and there is not a minute to waste. He pats himself on the back for having had the foresight to pack his bags last night, even though the booze had made it hard for him to focus.

The five-foot, eight-inch Crosthwaite takes a quick shower, squeezes into his Pan American purser's uniform, and downs two prescription pills with a cup of ink-black coffee. As he is about to walk out the front door, stepdaughter Tania crosses his path, and he makes it a point to ruin her day with an angry, crinkled face and some hateful, worrisome words—words that will haunt her for the rest of her life.

He is bullying her again and he loves it.

Tania shakes her head and nervously darts away, wondering again what she has done to make him so mad.

He knows his cruel words are inflicting pain and worry, and that gives him a weird, sadistic satisfaction. He doesn't hug her. He doesn't bother to say goodbye. He never does. He's going to have the last word and this little bitch will just have to live with the consequences.

He walks outside, sucks in a breath of the fresh hillside air, and remembers those early dreary days in the TB sanatorium, when getting a decent breath of anything was hard as hell. But that was then; this is now. Oliver Eugene Crosthwaite is in charge today and that brings a slight smile to his otherwise gloomy face

He gets behind the wheel of his sedan and drives north on Highway 9, past Green's Service Station, then turns right onto Mount Hermon Road and ultimately enters the busy Santa Cruz Highway. He weaves in and out through the morning traffic and about an hour later parks his car along San Mateo's Fifth Avenue, feeds a nickel into the parking meter, and walks briskly into the law office of Hugh Mullin. He checks his watch: 8:45 a.m. This will have to be quick or he will be late for the mandatory flight briefing.

"I'm Gene Crosthwaite, and Mr. Mullin is supposed to have my will ready. Him and me already worked it out," he says to the receptionist.

"Yes, sir, Mr. Crosthwaite. I remember you. Just a minute, please," she says pleasantly, ignoring his atrocious grammar.

A few minutes later the secretary returns with some legal documents that she hands him to review. She points to a nearby couch.

"Why don't you sit over there and look these over, Mr. Crosthwaite, and see if everything's in order? I believe you'll find that we've taken care of everything requested. If anything is out of order, I'll get Mr. Mullin. If not, all you have to do is sign and I'll notarize it. Then you can be on your way."

Crosthwaite nervously checks his watch again. Time is becoming an obsession, and he has only an hour until check-in for his flight to Honolulu. If there are any problems with the will, it could throw his timing off.

Crosthwaite sits down on the couch and begins to read:

"LAST WILL AND TESTAMENT OF OLIVER EUGENE CROSTHWAITE

I, Eugene Crosthwaite, being of sound mind and body . . . "

A few minutes later Crosthwaite walks over to the secretary, places the will on her desktop, and steps back.

"This looks good. Want me to go ahead and sign it?"

"Sure, I'll witness it and then we'll be done. Do you have a flight today?"

"Yeah, I'm off to Honolulu in a couple of hours."

"Lucky you. I wish I were going. I've always wanted to visit Hawaii, especially this time of year."

"Yeah, I guess it's OK, but it don't do much for me anymore. It's just a job. It kinda gets old after a while."

Crosthwaite pulls a Paper Mate ballpoint pen from his pocket and scrawls his signature. His hand slightly shakes as he dots the "i," and he stuffs the pen back inside his uniform coat. The secretary walks away and returns a few minutes later with a warm, Thermofaxed copy of the will inside an oversized envelope.

Crosthwaite mutters a half-assed "thank you" and walks outside.

"There, that'll let her know who's the damn boss," he mutters to himself as he puts the envelope containing his last will into the glove compartment and slams it shut. He pulls out into traffic and heads north on Bayshore Freeway. Minutes later he parks his car at Beacon Storage on Broadway Avenue in Millbrae before taking a taxi to the San Francisco International Airport, less than a mile away.

10:30 A.M.

Romance of the Skies is taxied to spot thirty-two in the main terminal area, where master mechanic Fortune and flight engineer Albert Pinataro begin their joint inspection of the blue-and-white-over-silver aircraft. Pinataro has logged 1,596 hours in the air, all of them in Boeing 377 Stratocruisers, or "Super Strato-Clippers," as Pan Am has recently begun calling them, and he has flown on this particular plane many times prior to today. He loves his job with Pan Am, and although he is the youngest of the cockpit crew, he goes about his job with the kind of methodical professionalism of much older, more seasoned engineers. Pinataro celebrated his twenty-seventh birthday a week ago and recently told a relative that if he died tomorrow, he would die a happy man because he enjoys his job so much.

Pretakeoff procedures are already thirty minutes behind schedule because of the IBM cargo problem, but Pinataro and Fortune cut no corners in ensuring that the plane is airworthy. Pinataro, a former US Air Force mechanic, soon discovers that the number one engine turbosupercharger is down about a half-gallon of oil from its capacity and orders that it be filled to the brim. Pinataro rechecks the oil level after it is filled, then he and Fortune climb onto the wings to check the fuel level of each gas tank. The tanks are measured with a long dipstick, and each has the specified level of fuel required for the flight. Pinataro also removes all the oil caps and ensures that each engine has the maximum twenty-seven gallons of oil. Oil is the lifeblood of any engine, and although the plane has a fifty-six-gallon oil reserve system in its belly, Stratocruiser engines are notorious for guzzling and dripping oil. Many Stratocruiser captains are so concerned about the oil problem that they personally watch as oil is added at each stop along a flight path.

After examining each of the sixteen propeller blades, and the exterior inspection is complete, Pinataro thanks Fortune for his assistance, enters the flight deck from the lower-right cargo door, climbs up into the cockpit, and begins his engine prestart checklist at the engineer's station. While every member of the crew has an important role to play today, Pinataro realizes that the finicky Stratocruiser engines will require his full-time attention, and he will have to monitor everything from engine temperatures and fuel consumption to the intricate electrical and cabin pressurization systems. Although the engines are precisely crafted, experts agree that they seem to have minds of their own, and flight engineers like Pinataro need to "think like an engine" to keep them operating efficiently.

While Pinataro runs through his checklist, Captain Gordon Herrick Brown conducts the required emergency briefing for the rest of the flight crew that has gathered inside the base. Using a paperboard mock-up of the Boeing 377 that depicts the interior layout, Brown issues paper "tags" to each crewmember. The tags list emergency equipment on the plane, and he requires every crew member to show where their tags and equipment are located on the plane. Brown then briefs the crew on details of the flight and asks them to recite their duties in case of an emergency. It's all routine, but everyone realizes the importance of the briefing, especially considering that just a year earlier a sister Stratocruiser had ditched mid-Pacific and that the military version of the planes are having troubles in flight.

Flight dispatcher James Murray then conducts a weather briefing with Captain Brown and his cockpit crew—a briefing that includes forecasted weather conditions not only in the air but also for the airport in Honolulu.

"You'll encounter some moderate frost immediately off the California coast, but the weather on into Honolulu is clear for the entire route," he informs the crew. "It's a perfect day to fly."

Copies of the forecast are stapled to the plane's flight paperwork, and after signing off on the documents, Captain Brown puts on his cap, cocks it slightly to the lower left of his forehead, and walks outside to board the aircraft. He immediately takes in a whiff of the distinctive exhaust of aviation fuel that drifts across the tarmac and, like many of his colleagues, considers it an almost addictively fine smell.

Purser Crosthwaite boards immediately after the briefing and ten minutes before passengers begin to take their assigned seats. He checks to see if sufficient food, snacks, and booze—especially booze— have been loaded for the flight. As purser, he is the senior cabin manager, responsible for supervising the stewardesses and ensuring that passengers are safe and comfortable. He's also in charge of the below-deck horseshoe-shaped cocktail lounge, his favorite duty.

He is aware that service supervisor Jack King is on today's flight, but that really doesn't bother him. Crosthwaite has never let a supervisor rattle him up or make him nervous. King, a last-minute addition to the crew, volunteered to fill in for a sick colleague. However, he might also be on the plane to keep an eye on Crosthwaite because of recent complaints about his work performance and lingering allegations that he may have been stealing liquor from the airline. Crosthwaite also is unaware that Pan American has suspected him in the past of smuggling goods from Hong Kong but has never been able to prove it. And one more thing: crews have been complaining recently about the abrasive, irritable purser. They say he is a "blowhard" and a "braggart" and not well-liked by either employees or passengers.

Crosthwaite knows his job is in jeopardy, but he shrugs it off. Today, he is in his element and he won't let anything, or anyone, bother him. He loves to criticize others, but criticism has no effect on him. He always makes up an excuse for his failures at work and at home. That's just who he is. He really doesn't give a damn what others think of him, and he's quick to let everyone know that, even more so since he spent those six miserable months in the TB sanatorium.

He is known as a prickly man who walks around with what seems to be a permanent chip on his shoulder, but today he has a different attitude. Today, he is the man in charge of what happens next in his life.

The passengers on today's flight are a cross section of a rapidly shrinking world. They range from hourly wage workers and enlisted military men to senior corporate executives, high-ranking government and military officials, and highbrow socialites. There are housewives, missionaries, doctors, and entire families on the flight manifest. One passenger is a Free French Air Force ace from World War II. It is the "Golden Age" of American aviation, and the men are dressed conservatively in coats and ties; the ladies in fashionable dresses.

Their reasons for boarding today include impending marriages and recent family deaths, business trips and vacations.

Before the day is done, they will have one common purpose: to stay alive.

Recently promoted US Navy Commander Gordon Cole of Alexandria, Virginia, is among those boarding the Stratocruiser for the trans-Pacific flight. Cole is about to realize his lifelong dream of commanding his own destroyer and is headed to Hong Kong, where he will become executive officer of the *USS Lenawee*. He is scheduled to take command of a destroyer within six months, and the thirty-five-year-old father of one is well suited for the task.

Cole already has led an adventure-filled life, and has the scars, aches, and pains to prove it.

He spent a year as a second mate on a tramp steamer on a New

York-to-South America run before serving as a navigator on an attack carrier in the Pacific during World War II. After the war he returned home to Michigan, where he opened a record shop in Muskegon and commanded the local naval reserve unit on the side.

In 1950 he made headlines when he crossed the Atlantic in a forty-five-foot sailboat with four other men. The perilous thirty-one-day voyage from New York to Bergen, Norway, was full of challenges and daily hardships, from drift ice off the Grand Banks to a four-day gale off the coast of Scotland. The 3,697-mile journey made the tough, determined Cole even better prepared for life ahead.

Cole was recalled to active service during the Korean War and while serving aboard the destroyer *USS Frank Knox* in the Sea of Japan was severely injured during a violent storm. A twenty-foot wall of water slammed Cole into the ship's steel infrastructure while he supervised securing the ship and its depth bombs. He suffered leg and shoulder fractures, a severe cut on his leg, and a dislocated shoulder.

Cole is not only mentally and physically tough, he is also a man of deep faith, the superintendent of his Sunday school at St. Paul's Episcopal Church in Falls Church. He is a devoted husband to his wife, Rosemary, and dedicated father to his five-year-old son, Gordon Jr., both back home in Virginia.

He is no stranger to the sea, and he respects both its beauty and its fury.

Commander Cole, directed to Seat 16A in the first-class, Rainbow section, is the perfect seatmate for Harold Sunderland, who is boarding behind him.

"You're in Seat 16B, Mr. Sunderland," twenty-six-year-old stewardess Yvonne Alexander smiles, pointing to an aisle seat in the left rear section of the luxurious cabin. Alexander, impeccably dressed in her sky-blue uniform with white blouse and blue pillbox hat, was driven to the airport this morning by her father, Albert, who is visiting from New York. Although originally from San Francisco, the confident stewardess had relocated less than a year ago from New York, where she worked Pan Am's New York-to-Frankfurt run for several years before requesting the transfer to the West Coast to be closer to her divorced mother, Lucille, who lives in Larkspur and is fearful for her daughter's safety in the air.

A former travel agency secretary, Alexander loves her stewardess job and recently told her mother, who had emigrated from Germany in 1926: "Mommy, as a matter of fact I feel safer up there than I do down here."

Working the flight today with Alexander is the bright-eyed twenty-six-year-old Marie McGrath, a popular substitute teacher in San Mateo when she is not flying with Pan Am. A New York native who has traveled on five continents, McGrath was snow skiing in Austria this time last year with Pan Am colleagues. She is a graduate of Keuka College in upstate New York, where, as an English major, she edited the college's literary magazine and dreamt of one day flying for Pan Am as a stewardess. Her dreams have come true.

Both stewardesses flash the famous "Pan Am (no-gums, all-teeth) smile" as they greet the passengers. They are perfect fits for Pan Am stewardess requirements: extroverted, trim, beautiful, fluent in English and at least one other language, culturally aware, able to walk down an aisle in heels without wobbling, witty, and bossy but not bitchy.

They are well trained to treat passengers like royalty, and they pass out postcards with color pictures of the Stratocruiser as their guests board the aircraft. The stewardesses will pick the postcards up shortly before arrival in Honolulu, and they will be mailed gratis by Pan Am, just another perk of flying on the finest airline in the world.

As he is seated, Sunderland is pleasant but isn't saying much. That's his style. An Air Force officer stationed with the 1134th Special Activities Squadron at Travis Air Force Base just northeast of San Francisco, he is off on a secret intelligence mission to Burma. Sunderland places a briefcase in the overhead compartment, quietly takes his seat, and settles in for the long flight. Sunderland is a spy, a listener, a man who covertly and sometimes overtly gathers information for the highest levels of the US government, and his destination is a hot spot for spies like him. He has been visiting his fiancée, Jean Spear, in Sacramento for the past few days.

Passenger Louis Rodriguez is in a state of shock and is on a sad mission today. He has been crying. Anyone can plainly see that. His eyes are red, and his face has that cried-out look. The fifty-five-year-old St. Luke's Hospital surgical orderly is traveling to Honolulu for the funeral of his mother on Monday. It is his first time on an airplane, and the father of three is terrified.

Rodriguez, normally an outgoing, helpful machine technician for the Monroe Calculating Machine Company, had been working in his backyard garden when he received word that his mother had died.

Thirty-three-year-old US Navy Commander Joseph Jones confidently walks down the aisle, his uniform pressed sharply, as he sits down in Seat 6A, the window seat next to Rodriguez.

"Good morning. I'm Joe Jones. Looks like we'll be sitting next to each other," he says as he extends his hand, smiles, then scoots in front of Rodriguez and sits down.

Rodriguez nods politely and shakes the officer's hand.

"Good morning to you, too, sir. I am Louis Rodriguez."

Jones, a veteran of Pacific fighting in World War II and now commander of the Seventh Navy Mobile Construction Battalion on Long Island, New York, is on his way to Honolulu, where his fiancée, twenty-nine-year-old Navy Lieutenant Mary Ann Collins, plans to pick him up at the airport that evening. She will be accompanied by his mother, Katherine, who has been in Honolulu for a week helping her soon-to-be daughter-in-law with wedding arrangements.

Collins is a New York engineering school graduate serving as a personnel officer at Pearl Harbor. Tomorrow, she and Joseph's mother plan to drive down to the Honolulu ports to meet the ocean liner *Matsonia*, whose passengers include her mother and rock 'n' roll superstar Elvis Presley. Little does she know that by the time the *Matsonia* docks at Pier 10 it will have been involved in a huge air-and-sea search for her fiancé and forty-three others lost at sea.

Edward T. Ellis is another busy man with a lot on his mind this morning, not the least of which is a speech he is scheduled to make at a meeting of the Society for the Advancement of Management at the Hawaiian Village Hotel. Ellis is known in corporate circles as not only a visionary executive, but also an excellent public speaker, so it is not unusual for him to be away from home for meetings and speaking engagements.

Ellis is the type of person who seems to do everything right all the time. He has a golden touch in the business world; some might call him an overachiever. He is a meticulous planner, but also an excellent people person. He has never met a stranger, and he always makes those around him feel comfortable, whether a senior executive, a congressman, or an hourly production worker. In twenty-six years, he has risen through the ranks of McCormick & Company, the nation's major spices-and-condiments seller, and is now a director of the company and vice president of its Schilling division. Colleagues believe the forty-five-year-old is in line to become president of McCormick upon the retirement of John N. Curlett.

The married father of three beautiful girls—Suzanne, Marilyn, and the recently married Joan—the executive settles into aisle Seat 10C and introduces himself to seatmate Robert L. Halliday, an Australian businessman, who booked this flight to get home to his family earlier after his scheduled flight on another airliner was delayed.

Ellis reaches into his coat pocket and hands Halliday one of his business cards, and the men begin chatting to get to know each other before the flight takes off. Ellis plans to stay with Colonel Howard H. Cloud Jr., director of manpower and organization with the Pacific Air Headquarters at Hickam Air Force Base, during his trip. Cloud is scheduled to speak tomorrow at the same conference as Ellis. The seatmates hit it off immediately.

Passenger Ruby Quong is a twenty-nine-year-old registered nurse who just two days ago resigned her job at San Francisco's Kaiser Foundation Hospital for a temporary move from her home in Chinatown to Hong Kong, where she will assist her ailing mother. She sits down in window Seat 5D and is joined moments later by Bess Sullivan, a microbiologist whose husband of thirty-three years, Philip, a State Department executive, will be seated in the first-class section. Philip, a former missionary to China, has been in San Francisco for several days on official government business. Bess recently flew in from their home in Washington, D.C., and plans to visit their daughter in Kyoto, Japan, while her husband travels on to New Delhi for an important international conference.

The noise level in the cabin increases slightly as four excited children and their immaculately dressed parents board the aircraft and head for their seats in the first-class section. The Clacks are one of two entire families boarding this morning, and the Clack children soon will make friends with the Alexander children, David and Judy, who will be seated behind them. David and Judy's father, thirty-eight-year-old Robert, and their mother, Margaret, a school PTA leader, are taking the kids on a vacation to Hawaii. Margaret and the children have just gotten over bouts with the flu. Robert is an experienced Pan Am copilot, and his skills and experience may come in handy before the end of the day.

Dow Chemical Company executive Hugh Llywelyn (Lee) Clack, his college-sweetheart wife, the former Ann Mae Carter, and their four children have been on a three-month stateside working vacation, reuniting with family and friends in Michigan. Their family has grown in the past two years with the addition of their adopted Japanese-American daughters, Kimi, seven, and Mariko, two, and the Clacks enjoyed showing off their newest children during their visit to the United States—a place they told the girls was "The Promised Land."

The Clacks already had two children, Bruce, nine, and Scott, six, and the boys quickly embraced their new siblings. Lee and Ann had always wanted daughters, loved Japanese children, and told family members they felt they should do their part to make amends for Japan's war orphans.

Lee is general manager of Dow International in Tokyo and successfully opened Dow's first Far Eastern office just two years ago. The World War II Navy veteran did graduate work in chemistry at Harvard and the Massachusetts Institute of Technology and is considered not only brilliant, but compassionate as well. While home in Michigan he and Ann spoke to several civic clubs and enjoyed telling about life in Japan, and sharing the history and customs of the Japanese people.

Lee is a rising star in Dow Chemical, and the Clacks seem to be the perfect American family. They love America but are eager to return "home" to Japan.

Marion Florence Barber takes window Seat 9A about midway in the aircraft, and immediately fastens her seat belt. She flips nervously through a travel magazine as the other passengers settle in, but she is not really interested in reading anything as the plane is readied for takeoff.

She has been waiting so long for this day that nothing else seems to matter.

A Shaker Heights, Ohio, housewife, the forty-nine-year-old is flying to Honolulu, where she plans to meet her husband, Army Colonel Keith H. Barber, who is returning from duty in Vietnam—long before Vietnam becomes a household word. They plan to vacation for a few days in Honolulu and then fly back together to the US mainland, where he will take on a new assignment at Fort Hood, Texas, a sprawling post where armored tanks crawl the mesquite-covered hills and rule the day.

William Deck, like Commander Jones, has love on his mind this morning. The twenty-four-year-old former sailor met Masako Sasaki while stationed with the US Navy in Japan two years ago, but they haven't seen each other in the eleven months since his discharge. Deck left his home in Radford, Virginia, yesterday, and it seems like he has been on an airplane ever since. A former student at Virginia Tech, he is flying to Japan for his wedding, and then plans to return to the US mainland and enter the Milwaukee School of Engineering. Masako, who is finishing college in Japan, will join him later in Wisconsin. Before leaving Virginia, he sent this telegram to his sweetheart:

"Meet me at Kyoto Station, 6:30 a.m. Monday."

Deck checks his watch. This plane can't get off the ground fast enough for him. His heart races with just the thought of his bride-to-be. He walks up the ramp steps and smiles to himself as he notes the name lettered on the side left of the aircraft: *Romance of the Skies.*

"It sure is," he says. "It sure is."

He takes a seat beside Tokyo-bound twenty-five-year old Melih Dural of Ankara, Turkey. Dural is returning to Ankara to serve a two-year stint in the Army after studying engineering at the University of Illinois and Florida Southern University. He plans to visit a friend in Tokyo before proceeding on to Turkey.

Thomas McGrail of Dover, New Hampshire, is en route to

Rangoon, Burma, for his new assignment as cultural attaché at the US Embassy. He celebrated his fifty-second birthday yesterday and is looking forward to his new position. He'd been in Washington, DC, for the past several months after serving in Tel Aviv and Tokyo. A former English professor at the University of New Hampshire, he has worked for the US Information Agency for seven years and is eager to leave the backstabbing bureaucracy of Washington behind.

Soledad Mercado has already settled in to window Seat 12D by the time McGrail arrives at his seat, next to hers. The petite and impeccably dressed Mercado is a widely known dress designer and manufacturer who lives in Phoenix, where she is known as Soledad of Arizona. She is bound for Tokyo to visit her son, Andy, and then on to Manila, where she plans to see long-lost relatives. Finally, the fifty-three-year-old designer will board another Pan Am flight to Hong Kong, where she will buy merchandise for her clothing line.

Mercado has had a lot on her mind lately. Just eight months ago the Arizona Supreme Court ordered the estate of a wealthy socialite, Mary Louise Anderson, to pay her $20,000 for taking care of the elderly spinster. It has taken two years to get to this point, and the legal battle has been not only emotionally exhausting, but bitter as well. A flight to Asia is just what she needs to get her mind off all the hassle.

Six years after arriving from her native Philippines in September 1933, Mercado met Anderson and became her cook, housekeeper, laundress, maid, and nurse. She later married her employer's chauffeur, Emilio Ray Mercado, and in 1949 started sewing for extra money in a small cottage at the rear of the Anderson mansion in Biltmore Estates. Sewing was second nature to Soledad, who learned the skill a child and was designing and making her own clothes by the time she was in high school.

By 1950, her sewing business was beginning to boom, but Anderson insisted that she not leave her side.

"'Soledad, I am getting too old now. I can't live without your help,'" Anderson told her, according to testimony Soledad had given in a lawsuit she brought against the estate. 'I'll pay you well in my will if you will just stay with me.'"

When Anderson died in 1953, she didn't leave Soledad Mercado a single penny. Instead, she left the bulk of her $350,000 estate to Vassar College for Women in Poughkeepsie, New York. Strangely, however, she left her 1953 Lincoln, $3,000 in cash, and all of her household belongings to Soledad's husband and business partner, Emilio.

By this time the Mercados really didn't need the money from the estate; her sportswear line was prospering, and she not only was manufacturing clothing in Phoenix, but also had retail shops in Estes Park, Colorado, and Scottsdale and Chandler, Arizona.. Her fashionable line of clothing was making headlines all over the country, and the beautiful and vivacious Soledad was on top of the world. No, it wasn't the money that drove the hardworking Soledad to file a lawsuit; it was the principle of the thing. After all, she had worked for Anderson for nearly twenty years without any direct compensation.

Soledad has other matters on her mind this morning as well. She is about to open a new shop in Prescott, Arizona, and things have been a bit tense with Emilio in recent months. Still, Emilio accompanied her to San Francisco and kissed her goodbye before she walked up the staircase to the big Stratocruiser a few minutes earlier.

World traveler Helen Rowland of Springfield, Vermont, has just completed a visit with her aunt in Palo Alto, and is boarding the plane today out of necessity. She doesn't like flying but knows that the most convenient way for her to reach Tokyo for a lengthy luxury cruise is on an airplane. The sixty-year-old is in the business of restoring old houses and loves to travel the world as a sideline. She takes window Seat 7A and straps her seatbelt tightly.

Cassiqua Soehertijah VanDer Bijl is a history teacher on her way home to Jakarta, Indonesia, after a conference in Rome. She's spent the past several days sightseeing in San Francisco. She is in aisle Seat 6C.

Tomiko Boyd is excited about seeing her husband and family as she takes window Seat 6D. There is no one seated between her and VanDer Bijl. Boyd's husband, US Army Master Sergeant Robert Boyd, is stationed in Korea, and after visiting family in Japan she plans to reunite with him for a brief time before returning home to Baltimore, Maryland.

Mrs. Boyd looks out the window as the ground crew loads baggage into the airliner's big belly. She wonders how they keep track of all those bags and hopes that hers is among those being put aboard.

Toyoe Tanaka and assistant plant supervisor Hideo Kubota of Tokyo are returning home after a hectic business trip in the United States. The fifty-year-old Tanaka is executive director of Koa Oil Company. They are in Seats 14C and 14D in the President section, directly in front of the Clack children.

The cheapest seat on today's flight is reserved for the troubled lodge owner William Harrison Payne, and he squeezes in to Seat 7, a middle seat between machine mechanic Frederick B. H. Choy and Army Sergeant David Anderson Hill, both of whom have been aboard for several minutes. The thirty-one-year-old Choy, married and the father of two sons, is headed to Honolulu to visit his bedridden father, Harry, whom he hasn't seen in six years. After receiving word last night in his San Mateo home that his father was gravely ill, he bought a last-minute ticket and hopes to arrive in time to visit his father before he dies.

A bachelor, the twenty-one-year-old Sergeant Hill has been on leave in North Carolina and is returning to Hawaii, where he works for the Army Security Agency at Helemano Radio Station.

Payne, who arrived a few minutes late, seems annoyed that he must take a middle seat. Neither Choy nor Hill is interested in talking, and that suits Payne just fine. He has other things on his mind, too.

It's combination work/vacation time for several passengers, including Robert and Nicole Lamaison. Mr. Lamaison has spent much of this year flying across the country promoting his company and its low-priced, high-efficiency cars. Detroit is worried because imports have quadrupled in the past three years, and Lamaison's company is one of the domestic automakers' biggest concerns.

"Why buy a car that gives you only fifteen miles to the gallon when you can buy one that gives you forty?" Lamaison, vice president and general manager of the French-owned Renault, Inc., loves to tell audiences. The economy-car market is booming, and suburbanites in postwar America are beginning to buy second cars.

The tall, blue-eyed and handsome forty-one-year-old Lamaison is the perfect spokesman for his company. He won numerous meritorious awards for his daring aerial exploits with the Free French Air Force in World War II and was a star rugby player while growing up in France. The Lamaisons make their home on prestigious Park Avenue in New York City. Today, he and his wife, a part-time model, are setting off on a well-deserved vacation to Honolulu. Their three children are being taken care of by relatives, and the Lamaisons are looking forward to a relaxing week on the islands after the executive makes a final decision on a Hawaiian distributor for Renault. They are seated in Seats 9C and 9D.

Louisville community activist and Cumberland College trustee Norma Jeanne Perkins Hagan and her surgeon husband, Dr. William H. Hagan, are directed to first-class Seats 11A and 11B. Mrs. Hagan, the daughter of a well-to-do coal mining executive, takes the window seat as Dr. Hagan settles into a wide, comfortable reclining aisle seat that Pan Am says resembles a "soft, flying, foam rubber cloud." No one is behind them; they are seated in front of the plane's entrance and near the winding stairs leading to the below-deck cocktail lounge.

Dr. Hagan, a thirty-seven-year-old Harvard Medical School graduate, plans to attend the Pan-Pacific Surgical Association conference in Honolulu. He is the medical partner and son of Dr. Harbert Hart Hagan, one of Louisville's leading surgeons, and he already has established himself as a respected medical professional. The Hagans, who live in a large two-story colonial home in an exclusive area of Louisville, are one of the city's most promising young couples. They have left their ten-year-old son, William Jr., in the care of relatives.

The plane is quickly filling with passengers. In less than twenty minutes they will be airborne.

Waiting anxiously to learn whether they will be able to board the flight today are eighteen-year-old college freshman Sandy Nelson and her twelve-year-old brother, Bobby, of nearby Menlo Park. Their father, Bob Sr., has been a Pan Am employee since the end of World War II, and he and his wife, Edna, a kindergarten teacher at James Flood Elementary, have decided that it's time for their children to see a bit of the world beyond the mainland of the United States.

Bobby and Sandy's parents have taken the children out of school for a two-week vacation to Hawaii, and the family is on the standby list to Honolulu. Their chances of getting on this flight are not very good because it is nearly full, but just a few minutes before the scheduled departure time a gate agent tells them that a couple whose car has broken down on one of the bridges into San Francisco may not make it to the airport in time and that those seats might be available. The family decides that if only two seats become open, the children will travel on to Honolulu and the parents will catch up with them on the next flight out. Bobby is especially excited because his father knows Captain Brown, and the youngster has been promised a visit to the cockpit once the airliner is in the sky and everyone has settled in.

Minutes later the agent gives Bobby and Sandy their tickets and they excitedly walk through the open wooden concourse toward the waiting Stratocruiser, waving to their parents as they leave. Just as they are about to board, the late-arriving couple come running into the gate area, and the Nelson siblings are bumped from the flight.

As fate will have it, they will not be flying to Honolulu today on *Romance of the Skies*.

11:20 A.M.

Flight engineer Pinataro completes his prestart checklist and gives the "Ready to Start Engines" report to Captain Brown, who has been running through dozens of items of his own that must be checked off before starting the big air-cooled engines. Starting the four powerful Pratt & Whitney Wasp R-4360 engines requires the full attention of Flight 7's flight crew; Stratocruiser engines need constant attention. If the crew doesn't follow the prescribed starting procedure exactly, there is a very real possibility that all fifty-six spark plugs will be fouled and the flight will be delayed, something that Pan Am considers unacceptable.

At 11:25 a.m. lead ramp crewman Coraino Carvahalo closes and secures the forward cargo door and Daniel Hernandez signals Captain Brown to start engine three. It thunders to power and comes alive with the expected flume of belching, oily smoke, and engines four, two, and one follow. The pretaxi checklist is read aloud and Flight 7 is ready to leave on the first leg of its around-the-world flight.

"Pan American 7, this is San Francisco Tower. You are cleared to taxi to runway two-eight right"

"Roger, San Francisco Tower. This is Pan American 7 acknowledging taxi to runway two-eight right."

Just as the plane begins to pull away from the terminal, a cargo representative excitedly runs onto the tarmac and notifies the ground coordinator that Flight 7 is thirty-two kilos overweight in the forward compartment. Captain Brown is immediately notified, and to save time, only the number three engine is shut down. Cargo crewmen rush to the plane, put the wheel chocks back in place, open the forward cargo door, and hastily remove company mail from the cargo compartment. Just as they are about to close the cargo door again, an alert coworker notices that the thirty-two kilos of company mail had not been included in the cargo weight in the first place, so they reenter the cabin, remove some more cargo, and close the door.

Captain Brown restarts engine three, but this has been a bit unusual. The morning already has been anything but routine, for three reasons: 1) the rare stopping of the engine to remove cargo because the plane is overweight; 2) the heavy IBM machine in the forward hatch; and 3) cargo being loaded into an upstairs, unused cabin area, something that seldom occurs.

At 11:35 a.m. Captain Brown eases the giant airliner away from the terminal and scans out the broad cockpit windows for any obstructions on the ground. The late-morning fog dances off the aluminum fuselage, portions of which reflect the sun that occasionally reveals itself from behind the clouds.

For a moment, it looks as if *Romance of the Skies* is on fire.

In a fenced-in observation area near the departure gate, two little boys wave wildly at the departing plane. One of them, in a straw cowboy hat shouts excitedly.

"Bye-bye, Daddy! Come back soon! We'll go fishing, OK?"

The younger boy, his brown hair peeking out from around the corners of his Davy Crockett cap, waves both hands in the air and blows kisses at the departing plane.

"We'll be waiting for you, Daddy! Hurry home!"

The children's mother holds a curly-haired toddler tightly in her arms, but he takes a cue from his older brothers and gets into the act, too, waving and shouting for Daddy to come home soon.

My mother pulls my little brother closer for warmth. She feels an icy cold chill that sends ripples of nervous waves from the top of her head to the tips of her toes. Blaming it on the cool, foggy San Francisco morning, she tries to shrug it off.

Still, something is bothering her. Something she can't explain.

"San Francisco Ground Control, Clipper Nine-Four-Four, taxi clearance, please. IFR to Honolulu."

"Clipper Nine-Four-Four cleared to Runway Two-Eight Right via the south taxiway and Runway One Right. Wind calm."

A few minutes later the flight crew is given clearance to cross Runway 28 Right and is told to taxi into position and hold. Captain Brown receives the "all-secure" report from the cabin crew, noting that all passengers' seatbelts are fastened and the cabin is secure. He sets the parking brake, then runs through a list of pretakeoff engine checks.

The tower then radios Flight 7 its takeoff instructions.

"ATC clears Clipper Nine-Four-Four to the Rainbow Intersection. Climb northwest bound on northwest course of the low frequency range via the San Francisco Gap, direct Pedro. Maintain four thousand, Balboa direct Rainbow. Maintain altitude for a left turn at the Gap, one thousand five hundred feet, and contact departure control 120.5 immediately after takeoff."

This is the normal departure route for the San Francisco-to-Honolulu route, and Captain Brown repeats the instructions.

"Tower, Nine-Four-Four is ready for takeoff."

At 11:51 a.m., Captain Brown looks down the runway from the eighteen-window flight deck, positions *Romance of the Skies* on the white center line, releases the parking brake, and pushes the four throttles to 2400 RPM as the giant, somewhat ungainly airliner roars down the runway toward the green threshold lights. Brown pulls back on the stick, and the plane slowly lifts into the California sky.

"Clipper Nine-Four-Four, off at fifty-one, climbing."

Moments later Captain Brown orders the landing gear to be retracted, the flaps are raised, and Flight 7 is on its way. He then gently applies the brakes to slow the wheels that are still rotating from takeoff.

Romance of the Skies heads northwest for the routine ten-hour flight to Honolulu, and passes over south San Francisco, San Bruno, and Daly City. The Golden Gate Bridge quickly fades away below the right-side cockpit windows, and in less than three minutes there is no land in sight. It climbs to 4,000 feet and Captain Brown requests, and is granted, clearance to climb to the cruising altitude of 10,000 feet.

Captain Brown, like the rest of the Flight 7 crew, knows the cockpit of this plane like the back of his hand. He has logged more than 12,000 hours of flying time, including 756 hours in Stratocruisers like this one, and is filling in for a sick colleague today. The son of a Boston investment banker, Brown joined Pan Am after earning his bachelor's degree from Northeastern University in Boston. He and his family have been in the United States only since last December, when they moved to nearby Palo Alto from Germany, from where he had piloted Pan Am aircraft throughout Europe. He has five children: Edward, nineteen; Aminta, eighteen; Cynthia, eight; Gordon Jr., five; and Nancy, two.

A calm, confident man known by his colleagues as a "pilot's pilot," Brown stands nearly six feet tall and is certified to fly not only the Strats, but also DC-3s, DC-4s, and Convair 240s. Within the previous three months he has taken refresher training courses in all aspects of flying Stratocruisers, including wet ditching drills, something that has had even more meaning to aircraft crew members in the past year.

The forty-year-old Brown has had eleven days off before today's flight and is well rested for what is expected to be a routine run.

Second in command today is the very capable William Purdy Wygant of Redwood City, a veteran World War II Navy pilot who participated in the bombing of Iwo Jima and Okinawa. The Oregon native was a premed student at the University of Oregon when he enlisted in the Navy Air Corps just a few weeks before the Japanese attacked Pearl Harbor. The thirty-seven-year-old Wygant has been with Pan Am for eleven years and has logged more than 4,000 hours in Stratocruisers, including *Romance of the Skies.* He has three children from a previous marriage to the former Berneice Erickson: William, seven; Bette Anne, four; and Brenna, two.

Wygant plans to meet his current wife, twenty-seven-year-old Pan Am stewardess Betty Sue, for a fifteen-minute reunion when their flights cross paths at the Honolulu airport later this evening.

Flight 7's navigator, radio operator, and relief pilot is my father, William H. Fortenberry, who has more than 2,680 commercial flight hours, more than half of those in Stratocruisers. Like Captain Brown and first officer Wygant, he has completed all regular and special courses, including those on emergencies and ditching. All his certificates and ratings are current.

Romance of the Skies is a giant maze of metal and sophisticated electronics equipment. A flying Boeing-built marvel, she has been in continuous use since her purchase by Pan American in 1949. A descendant of the World War II B-29 Stratofortress bomber, she is one of fifty-five Boeing Stratocruisers and is considered the most advanced airliner ever made. It is a mammoth airplane, thirty-eight feet tall with a wingspan of 141 feet and a length of 110 feet. It is the first "jumbo" commercial aircraft ever built, and although it is often referred to as "Tomorrow's Aircraft Today" its days are numbered.

Mechanically, its electrical generating capacity is sufficient to operate all the appliances and lights in fifty eight-room houses. Boeing boasts that creating and building the Stratocruiser required nine acres of blueprints and three years of the most advanced engineering, fabrication, construction, and testing of any aircraft to date, including 5 million hours of design and development, before the aircraft was put into commercial use.

Stratocruisers can fly farther, faster, and more comfortably than any other passenger plane built, and they are luxuriously equipped with wide aisles and cushy and comfortable seats, and each has a cocktail lounge that is reached by descending a winding staircase to the airplane's belly. The lounge includes leather and rich fabric seating for fourteen, a snack bar, five sightseeing windows, hot- and cold-running water, and an ice compartment.

Stratocruisers are considered the aviation wonder of the age, and passengers love them. They are roomy enough for passengers to stroll about in the main cabin, and Boeing claims the "flying hotels" offer the "smoothest ride in the sky."

They are also notoriously unreliable, especially among pilots, despite claims by Boeing and Pan American that they "offer the ultimate in both comfort and safety."

Some pilots joke that Stratocruisers are the "best three-engine airplanes ever built."

Romance of the Skies is no stranger to the news. On January 20, 1956, the plane was on the same route as it is today—San Francisco to Honolulu—when pilot Captain Henry C. Kristofferson (father of music and film star Kris) was informed that a passenger, Lelia Henderson of Asheville, North Carolina, was about to give birth, 400 miles out in the Pacific. The baby had not been expected for another two months, and Marine Sergeant Robert Henderson and his wife had no clue that it was to be premature. The Hendersons and their small daughter, Patricia Ann, had left their home a few days earlier en route to his new duty station in Hawaii.

Flying at an altitude of 12,000 feet, Captain Kristofferson immediately turned the giant airliner around and raced the stork back to San Francisco. Baby Henderson, however, did not wait for the Stratocruiser to land and was delivered at 3:04 a.m. with the assistance of Honolulu-bound passenger Frances Norton, who used fingernail scissors and sterilized tape in the delivery. When the plane landed in San Francisco the Hendersons and their new baby, wrapped in a Pan Am-blue blanket, were met by Dr. Frederick Leeds, an airline physician, who pronounced that mother and baby were in fine shape. Shortly thereafter the plane left again for Honolulu, and the onboard birth made headlines around the world.

Romance of the Skies made news again about a month later when the airplane developed engine trouble about halfway between San Francisco and Honolulu and was forced to return to California. That may have been a sign of what was to come.

Pilots often say they would rather fly a Stratocruiser through a thunderstorm than any other plane, and they love its spacious cockpit with its numerous, abnormally large windows.

Because thirty-six passengers are on board today and because there is so much mail headed for Honolulu, the front right portion of the cabin has been transformed into a cargo area. At liftoff, *Romance* weighs 197,000 pounds, the maximum allowed by safety officials. It has enough fuel to stay aloft for thirteen hours.

As soon as Daddy's plane is out of sight, my mother piles us into our 1955 two-tone blue Ford and heads back home to Santa Clara, a forty-minute drive south of the airport.

"Where's Daddy going this time, Mama?" Jerry asks.

"Honolulu."

"Where's that?"

"You know. Where they have beautiful beaches and flowers . . . "

"And hula dancers," I inform him.

"That's right, honey."

"Will he be home for Thanksgiving?" I ask.

"Sure."

"Will we have a turkey?"

"The biggest, juiciest turkey you ever saw."

"And pumpkin pie, too, Mama?"

"And pumpkin pie, too. Your daddy loves pumpkin pie."

My mother drives south on US 101, past the Moffett Field Naval Air Station on her left, with its huge Navy blimp hangar towering nearly 200 feet in the sky. A Navy Constellation—very similar to airplanes Daddy has flown in the past—takes off just ahead of us, and Mom shudders again with that unexplained chill.

"Maybe I'm coming down with the flu. Wouldn't that be great? Bill on a trip and me sick with three boys to take care of," she says to herself.

She tunes the radio dial into a Palo Alto station and listens to The Duprees sing about a lonely heart:

Fly the ocean in a silver plane
Watch the jungle when it's wet with rain
Just remember 'til you're home again

You belong to me."

The cold, the chill again.

Something is bothering her, and it is getting worse by the minute. If only she knew what it is.

Meanwhile, Flight 7 of the "World's Most Experienced Airline" heads out over the Pacific.

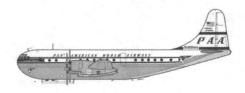

3

THE POINT OF NO RETURN

TWENTY MINUTES AFTER TAKEOFF, Flight 7 is at its planned cruising speed of 226 knots, and its passengers are settled in for the ten-hour flight. Stewardesses McGrath and Alexander begin serving a light lunch and pouring freshly brewed coffee from a five-gallon urn in the huge and well-equipped galley in the rear of the plane.

After lunch, the soft, steady hum of the plane's engines provides a soothing background noise as some passengers drift off to an early-afternoon nap. Others chat with their seatmates, play card games, and flip through the latest edition of *Clipper Travel*, Pan Am's colorful highbrow travel magazine. The front cover features a photo of a young couple riding bicycles near Mont St. Michel, an island off the northwest shore of France. Inside are feature stories, Hollywood gossip, and advertisements for expensive wines and liquors. One ad encourages passengers to ask the Pan Am crew for anything they may need to make their flight more comfortable, including complimentary Benson & Hedges cigarettes. Pan Am encourages smoking "to your heart's content" while on board. Other ads promote everything from "Kitten-Soft" pure-cashmere sweaters and cardigans from Swan & Edgar of London to promotions for some of the most famous restaurants and nightclubs in the world.

Page two is a full-page advertisement urging passengers to look at the Pan Am timetable inside their seat pouches and dream of exploring the new horizons in eighty-one countries on all the continents—"all within the spread of Pan Am's wings."

Other passengers read "Flying Clipper Wise," Pan Am's brochure designed especially for the Stratocruiser. The brochure assures passengers that Pan Am is not only the most experienced airline in the world, but also one of the world's safest, and today's plane has "at least two direction finders" that will provide "continuous two-way communication with ground stations, ships and other planes." It also offers this comforting statement: "And on trans-Pacific hops, LORAN [a long-range radio navigation system] gives us an immediate radio fix at any point in the flight."

In midafternoon, the stewardesses make their way up the aisle with silver trays overflowing with freshly cut pineapple, honeydew melon, grapes, other assorted fruits, and cheeses for the pampered passengers. In the downstairs, horseshoe-shaped lounge, purser Crosthwaite dutifully pours free cocktails and listens to the melodious banter of passenger small talk before heading back up to the main cabin deck to assist with the evening meal.

Shortly before 5 p.m. an elegant seven-course dinner is being prepared in the galley ovens, and the tantalizing smell of prime rib begins drifting into the passenger cabin from the "highest flying kitchen in the world." A call chime is occasionally heard, and one of the stewardesses rushes to see what the passenger wants, always with a smile on her face, always eager to please. The Pan Am way.

As the Stratocruiser glides across the Pacific skies and chases the setting western sun, the cockpit crew momentarily relaxes and prepares for the second half of the journey. Soon stewardesses McGrath and Alexander tie on their aprons as they prepare to serve dinner, first to the passengers in first class, then working their way up the aisle to economy.

So far, the flight from San Francisco has been uneventful. Captain

Brown and his able crew understand that the Jet Age is on the horizon, but for now the celebrated, but expensive-to-operate, piston-engine Stratocruiser is still master of the skies.

Brown looks out the wide cockpit windows to the blue-green sea far below him and the horizon ahead and concentrates on getting his plane and passengers safely into Honolulu. The crew knows full well that the giant Stratocruisers have had problems during the past couple of years. But so far this year the giant airships have been safe.

In addition to the two near disasters that made the news, there was a close call just four months ago that didn't make headlines when fifty-eight passengers aboard a Honolulu-to-Wake-Island Stratocruiser were warned to be ready to "ditch at any moment." Captain Fred Walts had radioed for help after one engine died and another momentarily lost power. He immediately ordered passengers to don life jackets and to take off their shoes as a precaution, but the Stratocruiser miraculously made it to Wake Island and landed safely.

But that flight doesn't cross Captain Brown's mind as he prepares to make a routine radio report a few minutes from now.

In many ways this has been a banner year for Pan Am, with record-breaking passenger loads and increased cargo driving revenues up. A Pan Am Clipper lands or takes off somewhere in the world every two and a half minutes, and more people fly Pan Am internationally than any other airliner in the world. President and founder Juan Trippe, always the optimist, says the best is yet to come.

However, in reality operating costs are outpacing revenue and squeezing Pan Am's profitability. *Aviation Week* reports that profits have declined every quarter for the past two years, and earnings are likely to be 50 percent less than two years earlier. This trend cannot continue if Pan American is to remain number one in worldwide commercial aviation.

The net operating income of the Pacific-Alaska Division is expected to drop from $3.6 million in 1956 to $2.8 million this year. The Civil Aeronautics Board has rejected requested fare increases since the end of the war, and Pan Am is hard-pressed to find new sources of capital to buy high-priced jetliners—the future of aviation. Less than two weeks earlier the first 707 rolled out of Boeing's factory in Seattle. It will be Pan American's first jet, and the first jet in commercial aviation, but Pan Am must find ways to simultaneously increase revenue and decrease operating costs in order to remain first in commercial aviation—and to pay for the new jet fleet.

Nowhere is the financial pinch felt more than in the Pacific-Alaska Division, where Pan Am has been cutting corners, particularly in the maintenance and inspection of its flying fleet, a move that mechanics and the Transportation Workers Union claim is putting passengers' lives at risk. Pan Am officials reject the claims as "union talk."

5 P.M.

About midway in the Pacific between Honolulu and San Francisco, the *USS Minnetonka*, a 225-foot-long US Coast Guard cutter, is on duty as Ocean Station November. Positioned about 1,200 miles from either city, the ship is one of five Coast Guard cutters that are alternately assigned for three weeks at a time to provide weather observations and serve as a position checkpoint for airline traffic. The crew also is available for search-and-rescue duties if needed.

It is normally a boring assignment, but the crewmen understand the importance of their mission.

The Combat Information Center (CIC) is the focus of the cutter, and it is here that the monotony of life at sea is broken by crewmen keeping an eye on radar, plotting contacts, and communicating via radio with every aircraft that passes in the skies above them. The CIC crew calculates the course, speed, and position of the passing planes and relays that information to the pilots. The contact with the airplanes is a welcome break from the humdrum of normal duty on the sea.

These are the days long before satellites and sophisticated mapping-and-tracking technology, and both the crew in the air and the crew on the sea welcome the contact with each other. The crew in the air is always grateful that the Coast Guard is down there.

It is 5:04 p.m. Pacific time and *Romance of the Skies* is flying just a few miles west of the location that pilots call the point of no return, where the plane must proceed to its destination because it does not have enough fuel to return to its point of departure. Captain Brown radios the floating *Minnetonka* and asks for a routine radar fix to confirm the plane's exact location.

"This is Clipper Nine-Four-Four on 121.5. Over."

"This is Ocean Station November. Read you loud and clear. Standing by to copy flight information."

"This is Nine-Four-Four. Departed San Francisco at 1915Z. Estimate Honolulu 0549Z. Cruising 10,000. On track 245. True ground speed 212. Air speed 225. Fuel remaining eight hours."

Captain Brown then asks the ship's radioman for a continuous radio beacon, radar fix, and ground-speed check.

"You are forty-three miles west of Grid Oscar Juliet. We have you tracking on a course of two-four-four degrees true, making good a ground speed of two-one-five knots. Did you copy? Over."

"Roger, November. Copied it OK. Thank you. Nine-Four-Four listening out," Brown replies.

"Roger, Nine-Four-Four. If there is nothing more we can do for you this afternoon, wishing you a pleasant flight on into Honolulu. This is station November listening out, Nine-Four-Four."

It is 5:05 p.m. and Flight 7 is about twelve miles ahead of schedule.

The Coast Guard radioman carefully notes the time in his log, but doesn't realize until later that he is the last person on earth to talk to anyone aboard *Romance of the Skies*.

The radio report complete, Captain Brown relinquishes control of the cockpit to First Officer Wygant and begins to put on his hat and uniform coat to make the customary PR walk through the cabin before dinner is served.

We may never know for certain what happens during the next twenty minutes, but Captain Brown and the crew are well trained, and they know that the first thing they must do if anything goes wrong is to send a radio message to Pan Am and to Ocean Station November. Survival after a forced landing at sea depends to a great extent on rapid rescue, and the captain knows that it's absolutely critical that all stations be advised as soon as any incident occurs that might develop into an actual emergency. Pilots know they may not have time to send an SOS after an emergency develops and are encouraged—even when in doubt—to call it an emergency, in an overabundance of caution.

There is no doubt about what is happening now on Flight 7; this an emergency of the worst kind.

Smoke slowly begins to fill the passenger cabin, and the Stratocruiser suddenly careens left, right, out of control at 10,000 feet, and quickly begins an accelerating descent to the ocean swells below. Even before the flight crew has time to notify the cabin crew, apron-clad stewardesses Alexander and McGrath realize that something is desperately wrong and immediately prepare the passengers for the trouble ahead.

Passengers are ordered to remove their shoes and any sharp objects and to put out any cigarettes.

"Loosen your belts and neckties. Tighten your seatbelts and put on your life jackets."

Brown has now rushed back into the pilot's seat, and he struggles with the flight controls to keep the crippled Stratocruiser in the air. He sets his altimeter and considers dropping fuel from the Stratocruiser, but there isn't time. There isn't even enough time for him to put on his life jacket, and Wygant is too consumed with the emergency to think of saving his own life.

The pilots brace their bodies against their seatbacks for stability and strength as they fight to keep *Romance of the Skies* from crashing into the Pacific. Brown locks his fingers around the control wheel as a cold sweat begins to drip on his face. An ocean ditching now seems the only option, because the plane is quickly losing altitude and Brown's feverish attempts to keep it in the air are failing. He forces the plane slightly to the right and the descent accelerates.

Brown glances to the left and below the cockpit and sees widely spaced, eight-foot ocean swells coming from the southwest. He convinces himself that if he can put the plane down in the middle of those swells he might have a chance to save some of the souls aboard. He remembers that the radioman on Ocean Station November had reported just a few minutes earlier that some of the waves were coming as far as thirteen seconds apart, and that gives him hope.

But reality quickly gobbles up hope, and as the seconds tick by, the sinking airplane seems to have a mind of its own, acting like an out-of-control rocket. Captain Brown realizes that the afternoon sun setting in his face is creating a glare and will make an ocean ditching even more risky and complicated.

But there is no alternative.

"We've got no choice; we're going in!" he shouts.

Captain Brown speaks into his microphone the words that no pilot ever wants to utter:

"AM DITCHING FLIGHT!"

Engineer Pinataro is horrified. He studies his main instrument panel gauges and shouts the desperate situation to the pilots, who already are painfully aware that the plane is going down and there is little they can do about it. Pinataro turns on the plane's emergency lights and begins to depressurize the aircraft.

Fortenberry's face turns pale, his body consumed by waves of fear. He prays for a miracle as the plane bounces up and down on its race to the ocean. It leans sharply. Left, then right. Vibrating violently now.

Vacationing Pan Am pilot Robert Alexander is one of the first to notice the impending catastrophe. He attempts to rush from the rear of the plane to the cockpit to see if there is anything he can do to assist his colleagues.

He staggers for balance, grabbing seat backs for support, and alerts his family and passengers along the way to prepare for ditching.

"Tighten your belts! Put your heads in the pillows! It looks like we're going down."

He never makes it to the cockpit.

Stewardesses Alexander and McGrath, who have been trying to keep panic from spreading throughout the passenger cabin, know that their words have brought little reassurance to anyone, including themselves. Training is one thing. Real life is another.

"If we are given the order to ditch, lean forward, put your head in your hands."

Passengers in the first-class section of the plane—in the rear of the aircraft—rush to put on their life jackets, but the task is nearly impossible, as the cabin has become an airborne roller coaster.

In the forward, tourist section, Louis Rodriguez, who has been thinking about his dear mother and her impending funeral, now realizes his own life may be about to end. A life jacket is the last thing on his mind.

"Holy Mary!" he shouts, but he is drowned out by those around him.

He sinks his head, makes the sign of the cross, reaches into his pocket, and pulls out his crucifix. He kisses it, then holds it tightly as he closes his eyes and prays softly:

"Please forgive me, Lord, for all I have done . . . To you, Lord, I lift up my soul. . . . Lord Jesus, receive my spirit. . . ." He repeats the words again and again as his seatmate, Commander Joseph Jones, tightens his safety belt and refuses to give in. He's been in tough situations before—nothing like this, of course—but he tries to convey confidence.

"We're going to make it," he tries to reassure Rodriguez. "We're going to be OK."

Rodriguez smiles the slightest of grateful smiles but knows in his soul that the end is near—so near in fact that before he takes another breath the seventy-ton airliner plows into the brick-hard Pacific with such incredible force that only tiny bits of mangled metal and broken, ripped bodies remain.

What's left of *Romance of the Skies* gurgles to the bottom of the ocean.

It is 6:04 p.m. and Flight 7 should be making a position report to Aeronautical Radio, Inc. (AIRINC), a communications network maintained by the scheduled airlines, but there is no word from the plane. Despite several attempts, AIRINC is unable to contact the crew, and informs Air Traffic Control in Honolulu:

"For your information, we haven't been able to raise Clipper Nine Four Four. His last contact time was at 5:04."

Air Traffic Control in Honolulu isn't particularly concerned, because airplane crews occasionally get busy with other chores and check in a bit late. Nevertheless, ATC notes that a Japan Air DC-6B is near 944's flight path and asks AIRINC to see if the pilot can make contact on VHF. While ground-to-air communications sometimes fail, plane-to-plane communications nearly always are successful.

The pilot of Japan Air 23 tries to reach 944. Again and again. Nothing. He advises AIRINC, which dutifully notifies Pan American operations in Honolulu that 944 is overdue in making its position report.

At 6:35 p.m.—about ninety minutes after the Coast Guard radioman had wished the Flight 7 crew a "pleasant flight" on into Honolulu—air traffic control sends out an urgent alert notice through Honolulu International Air Traffic Communications:

"Clipper Nine Four Four, a Stratocruiser en route from San Francisco to Honolulu, last heard Honolulu AIRINC position two-nine-two north, one-four-one-three-five west 5:04. Primary frequency one-seven-nine-zero-six-point-five, secondary one-three-three-four-zero-four-point-five AB."

The alert notice goes out to all aircraft and all Navy, Air Force, and Coast Guard communications. Planes flying near Flight 7's last reported position are asked to try to contact the missing plane on emergency frequencies. Approximately forty other aircraft are en route both ways between San Francisco and Honolulu and six are in the general radio range of *Romance of the Skies*. All are immediately asked by San Francisco and Honolulu ground stations for their assistance in locating the missing airliner.

By now, everyone is keenly aware that something is wrong. This is no longer the case of a careless flight crew forgetting to make a position report. This is trouble.

Still, there is no panic. The plane could be having radio problems, rendering it unable to transmit messages. If that is the case it won't be long before all air traffic in Honolulu is shut down to clear airspace for a disabled aircraft.

US Coast Guard reservist Dick Ferguson is on the mess deck of the

Minnetonka playing cards with about ten other crewmembers when the men are ordered to the bridge and informed that N90944 has disappeared and that Honolulu has been unable to establish radio contact. Ferguson and several others are given binoculars and ordered to search the horizon for flares, but the only thing they spot is the Russian Sputnik crossing the early night sky.

At 8:50 p.m. a Pan American dispatcher at Honolulu Airport passes word of the missing airliner over the company radio. His voice is calm and matter-of-fact:

"Pan American Flight Seven is missing and overdue on a flight from San Francisco, California. There has been no radio contact with the pilot since 3 p.m., but the plane carries enough fuel to last until 1 a.m."

Ticket agents and ground crew at the Honolulu airport quietly circulate among those who have been patiently waiting at the gate for the arrival of Flight 7. Friends and family are calmly and professionally notified about what they already know: the flight is overdue, but they are encouraged not to worry. These things happen sometimes. Strangely, there is no immediate panic. No tears. No crying. But smiles fade instantly into tight faces, and worry grips everyone in the gate area. Within minutes the tenseness will turn to utter fear and then into dread and helplessness.

About the same time, the phone rings in our Santa Clara home, where my mother has just gone to bed but is not yet asleep.

Reluctantly, she picks it up and instinctively knows who is on the other end.

"This is Pan Am calling, isn't it?"

"Yes, it is, Mrs. Fortenberry, it is. I'm afraid that Bill's plane is overdue in Honolulu. It may be nothing but a radio problem, but I wanted to let you know."

"Oh my God! I felt like something was going to go wrong all day."

"Don't worry. We'll keep in touch, and I'll let you know just as soon as we know something. It may not be anything but a radio problem."

"I'll be here, right by the phone."

"Oh, one other thing: If I don't call by 3 a.m. you'll know that the plane's gas supply has been exhausted and the plane is down."

What a cold, heartless thing to say, she says to herself, then freezes like an iceberg. That chill. That late-morning chill is back again. Now she knows what it was all about when Daddy left the airport this morning.

"Oh God. What now? What will I tell the boys? Please, God, don't let anything be wrong."

"I am so sorry, Mrs. Fortenberry, but we'll keep you informed. Someone will call in an hour or so."

She phones some of our neighbors, who rush over. They spend the long, worrisome night with her.

It is the longest night of her life.

A contact from Pan Am calls every hour with an update, but the news is never good.

"This is Pan Am again, Mrs. Fortenberry. I'm afraid we haven't found Bill's plane yet."

"Have you heard anything?"

"No, I'm afraid not, but we're still hoping that it's just a communications problem. Their radio might just be out."

"I hope so, but that's what the other fellow told me a couple of hours ago. What is Pan Am doing to find them? A big plane like that can't just disappear, can it?" she asked.

"We have every available plane and ship in the area searching their route. Everyone's doing everything we can. We'll stay in touch."

At 10 p.m., Honolulu Air Traffic Control sends a message "in the blind" to Flight 7, broadcasting in hopes that the plane's crew can hear radio transmissions but for some unexplained reason is incapable of sending them. The tower gives Flight 7 clearance for a standard instrument approach to the Honolulu International Airport, and every ship in Pearl Harbor turns on its searchlights for twenty-five minutes. The sky comes ablaze with bright lights, beacons for the missing plane.

Again, nothing. Moments later, all approaches to the Honolulu airport are cleared of all other aircraft just in case *Romance of the Skies* needs to make an emergency landing.

My mother paces the floor, wringing her hands behind her back. From the kitchen to the family room. From the family room to her bedroom. Back to the kitchen and on to the family room. Again and again. When the phone rings shortly after 3 a.m. she knows what she will hear.

"They're definitely down now, Ronnie, but we have to keep the faith. We have our planes in the air, the Air Force is helping us, and the Coast Guard is sending out ships. Every plane—commercial and military—along the route is being told to be on the lookout for our plane. Bill's plane has survival equipment—rafts, radios, and such— and we just have to be hopeful that we'll find them soon."

Mom tries to be hopeful, but she has keen instincts, and those instincts tell her the news won't be good from here on out.

A Quantas airliner is flying nearly the same route as *Romance of the Skies* when Captain Max Bamman gets the word to be on the lookout for the missing airliner. He immediately descends from 15,000 feet to 5,000 feet and follows along the route of the missing plane's last reported position.

The weather is clear. There is a full moon. All aboard are asked to look out the windows for any sign of the plane.

They see nothing.

We are on a long family camping adventure, somewhere in Oregon on our way to Canada, when Daddy suddenly pulls the car off the two-lane road near a high steel bridge that crosses a river. We're not sure what's on his mind, but when he opens the trunk and takes out our fishing gear Jerry and I get excited. This isn't just going to be another stop to pee; it's going to be a fishing adventure!

I grab my rod and reel and remember to keep my thumb slightly on the reel as I let the line down to the slow-moving river below and hope for a bite.

It's not long before I grow bored.

"Patience, son. Patience," Daddy urges, and I keep staring down at the red-and-white floating plastic bobber below.

Then it happens!

A tug like I had never felt before, and I instantly start reeling the line in.

"That's my boy. You're doing fine," Daddy encourages as he rushes over, pats me on the back, and looks below.

"Keep reeling, son. Steady now. It's a whopper, Kenny. A dad-blamed whopper!"

I can barely contain my excitement but somehow manage to pull the fish in as Daddy grabs the line to secure the catch.

"It's a crappie. The biggest crappie ever!" he says proudly.

I break into a huge grin as Daddy tells me to open my hands and to hold the fish tightly so it doesn't get away.

He's right; it is the biggest crappie ever.

I'm a real fisherman now. Just like Daddy.

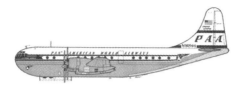

4

A NEEDLE IN A HAYSTACK

IT IS SATURDAY MORNING, November 9, and there has been no word from *Romance of the Skies* since the routine position report nearly twelve hours ago, and there is no doubt now that the giant airliner is down somewhere in the middle of the Pacific. The plane had enough fuel to stay in the air until 3 a.m., and the urgent questions now are: where did it go down, and is anyone alive?

"We are now past the gasoline endurance point and the aircraft must be presumed to be down somewhere in the Pacific," Pan Am executive vice president Robert B. Murray Jr. tells reporters. "The crew is experienced and well trained and we are still hopeful."

In the gloomy predawn morning at Pan American's San Francisco base, a Boeing Stratocruiser and a DC-7C are parked nose to tail on the ramp outside the dispatch office. The aircraft are surrounded by trucks and service vehicles as ground crewmen prepare them for missions that might last more than twenty hours in the air.

Pilot Cliff Pierce, who had been asked at 10:30 the previous night to join in the morning search as "extra eyes," slowly walks into the briefing room. Today, there is none of the usual good-humored banter.

No conversation or light jokes among crewmembers. Pierce knows there is nothing to laugh about.

On this morning, a Pan American plane is missing; six of Pierce's colleagues have disappeared.

Forty-seven-year-old Captain Don Kinkel, a Pan Am assistant chief pilot who flew the Korean air lift with Captain Brown six years ago, will command the Stratocruiser; Captain Sam Peters, the DC-7. When they reach the search area, they will drop down to 200-300 feet and fly patterns covering 200 square miles of ocean. They really don't expect to find the plane, and they realize that even if it made a controlled landing and had not broken up there is little chance it will still be afloat.

They are, however, hoping to find people in life rafts, and the pilots are desperately praying that they will be found alive before they perish at sea. But even that seems unlikely. Pierce and the other Pan Am employees understand that if the plane had been able to make a safe landing the crew would have had time to report the problem, like Captain Dick Ogg had done a year ago, when he successfully ditched N90943 in roughly the same area with no loss of life.

Still, they hold out hope.

By 5:30 a.m. the search planes are in the air, each with two pilots, two flight engineers, and four observers. It will take them four and a half hours to reach the search area, about 1,106 miles east of Honolulu. None of the searchers have had breakfast, but once aboard their planes they check out the galleys and are surprised to find bacon, eggs, toast, and piping-hot coffee for all. It takes a slight edge off the stress.

At about 10 a.m. they rendezvous with the Coast Guard weather ship *Minnetonka*, stationed halfway between San Francisco and Honolulu. The ship was the last known contact for the missing airliner, and the search commences from that point.

There is plenty of junk floating on the ocean this morning, and observers quickly jump at everything they see. It doesn't take them long to become accustomed to the floating garbage, and the novice observers become veteran searchers within an hour. The area is saturated with military aircraft, cargo vessels, the passenger liner *Matsonia,* even a submarine. Everyone is searching within hundreds of miles in all directions for anything that might provide a clue to the missing airliner.

As morning breaks, the house at 1338 Loyola Drive in Santa Clara is being held captive, tossed and turned by hope one minute and despair the next

"Is the paper here yet?"

"I don't know, Ronnie. Here, why don't you have a cup of coffee?" Dr. William Schaffer urges, as he hands Mom a white-and-gold China coffee cup from a set Daddy had bought on one of his overseas trips. "I just made it fresh. You haven't slept a wink all night."

Dr. Schaffer and his wife, Marjorie, across-the-street neighbors, are a sweet elderly couple who love children and occasionally invite my brother Jerry and me over for root beer floats and a game of Parcheesi.

"Thanks, Dr. Schaffer. I'll get some in a minute, but I want to see the paper first," Mom replies as she opens the front door and walks outside. The first thing she notices is the sweet smell of the cedar siding on our almost-new house. It smells so fresh, so alive. My mother picks the newspaper up from the sidewalk, rips off the rubber band, and opens the front page with its big headline. It seems to scream off the page at her:

SF Airliner Overdue With 44 On Board

HONOLULU - A Pan American Stratocruiser, last heard from at 5:40 p.m. yesterday and due to run out of gas at 3 a.m. today, was presumed down in the West Pacific Ocean, somewhere between here and San Francisco.

This is no longer a terrible nightmare to be shaken out of. This is real. She feels that bone-chilling cold again, and now she knows for certain why she had felt that way yesterday morning. She scans the names of passengers and crew and shakes uncontrollably when she finds what she is looking for and still hoping not to see:

Second Officer William H. Fortenberry, 35, 1338 Loyola Drive, Santa Clara.

Her eyes flood and she begins to weep. She has always known that flying an airplane carries with it certain risks, but she has tried not to think about something like this ever happening. But there it is, in black and white, and it can't be denied anymore.

Bill may be dead, and she will be left all alone in the world to raise three little boys, more than 3,000 miles from any relatives back in South Carolina. It is a thought she quickly erases. Bill is still alive. She just knows it. The phone will soon ring and someone from Pan Am will tell her that Bill and all the others have been found safely aboard life rafts floating in the ocean.

Walking back into the house, her head buried between the pages of the newspaper, she nearly trips on a cracked piece of sidewalk.

"Bill said he was going to fix that when he got home," she mumbles and starts to cry.

I meet her at the front door. There will be no Saturday morning cartoon watching today; Dr. Schaffer has broken the news to Jerry and me that our father's plane is overdue in Honolulu and that a big search is underway.

"Did they find him, Mama? Did they find Daddy?"

My mother pulls me close and her tears overflow onto my face.

"Not yet, honey. Not yet. But they're still looking."

"They'll find him, won't they, Mama?"

"Oh, Kenny. Let's hope and pray they do."

"Daddy's a good swimmer, Mama. He'll be OK. I know it."

The families of the other crew members of Flight 7 spend most of Saturday fielding questions from reporters, talking with friends and relatives, and praying for some good news.

They remain hopeful that the plane has successfully ditched in the ocean and everyone is safely aboard life rafts awaiting their imminent rescue.

The telephone rings in the suburban Detroit, Michigan home of Wynne and Barbara Clack just as Wynne begins to fix breakfast for their children, Norma and David. His wife, calling from her job at J. L. Hudson's in Detroit, tells Wynne she has just heard part of a radio newscast about a missing plane and thinks she heard the report mention Wynne's brother, Lee.

Wynne, a teacher at Van Dyke Junior High School, immediately turns on the AM radio, tunes in the 9 a.m. news, and calls Norma and David into the kitchen to listen while he continues to fix their breakfast. The next words shatter his life:

"A Pan American flight from San Francisco to Hawaii is overdue and is presumed to be down at sea. Among the passengers is a Michigan resident—Dow International executive H. L. Clack and his family."

The thirty-two-year-old Wynne freezes, and for a few moments tries in vain to answer his children's questions, then is consumed by grief. He asks Norma to finish breakfast, then goes into his bedroom and closes the door. He kneels by his bed and begins crying, his face buried in the covers. The unfolding tragedy is so overwhelming that his mind can't grasp what is happening. A decorated Navy veteran who served in the South Pacific during World War II, he has seen some terrible things in his life, but nothing—nothing—has prepared him for a moment like this.

He grows numb and, like others who are getting the awful news this morning, cries until he can cry no longer.

In the Los Altos home of Captain Brown, thirty-nine-year-old Emily speaks briefly and tensely with reporters who have gathered for news of her husband's overdue plane. The house is packed with concerned neighbors and friends who are trying to comfort the family, but there is nothing they can say, nothing they can do, to ease the near hysteria of Mrs. Brown and her five children.

Her eldest son, nineteen-year-old Edward, hovers over his mother and tells her that everything will be OK. She runs her fingers through her hair, smiles weakly, and speaks softly as her eldest daughter, eighteen-year-old Aminta, sits reassuringly by her side.

"I pray to God everything will turn out all right," Mrs. Brown says.

"We are hopeful it will be turning out all right, and the next thing we hear is that they're fishing from rafts," Hal Gillespie, a former Pan Am pilot and friend of Captain Brown's, answers.

She looks around and asks no one in particular:

"How much gas did he have? How long can he keep it in the air?"

In midafternoon, my mother walks to her bedroom, opens a closet door, and pulls out a Buster Brown shoebox—once containing a pair of size-four shoes for either Jerry or me. It is now her treasure chest of letters from Daddy. The letters are postmarked from places like Berlin, Beirut, Frankfurt, Wake Island, Tokyo, and Sydney. They always comfort her when he is away on a flight. Now, she fears, they are more than just letters.

She sits on the edge of their bed and opens the first letter she comes to:

HOTEL MONOPOL-METROPOL
FRANKFURT, GERMANY
8 P.M., TUESDAY, NOVEMBER 9, 1954

"Dear Mother and Boys:

"Last night when I got home from Beirut there was a letter from my dear Mom and my boys. Gosh! It was good to hear from you!

"You are a wonderful and beautiful wife, Darling, and I know it. I knew you would be. That is why I married you. You have been everything to me and I love you more and more each day. I know that home is where I grumble most and am treated best. In this business, I have to be sweet whether I like it or not and it is great to be able to come home and grumble a little. When I get home I don't think I will ever grumble anymore. I'm going to spend all my time giving you all the love I have been saving for you. . . . "I can't say that I'm sorry I came here, but I sure do miss you. It will be good in several ways: this will be the longest we have been apart since we were married, and you will have time to decide whether to keep me or not! I think the boys will keep me and maybe you will, too. You could do better, but you might do worse!

"I'll write more tonight.

Love, Daddy"
Mom falls face first on the bed, grabs a pillow, and covers her head.
"Oh, God, grumble for me again, Bill. Please, grumble for me, Bill!!"
Minutes later she regains her composure and walks back into the family room, where more people have joined the vigil. She notices a newspaper on a coffee table. It's the afternoon final edition of the *San Mateo Times*, and its big, bold headline strikes even more fear and dread in her heart:

AIRLINER HOPES FADE
44 Aboard Lost For Over 22 Hours

She picks it up and doesn't even notice the main picture and the other headline on the page. It's a remarkable story about a mysterious blazing unidentified fireball—"as bright as a searchlight"—that fell at an angle from the sky over nearby Hillsborough last night and smashed into a field.

By 4 p.m. the 1,600-crew aircraft carrier *USS Philippine Sea*, docked at Pier E in the Long Beach Naval Shipyard, about twenty miles north of Los Angeles, is being readied to join the massive search-and-rescue mission for the missing plane. Navy shore patrol trucks and police cars are roaming the streets of San Diego, contacting sailors and ordering them back to the ship. Sailors strolling arm in arm with their girls are stopped dead in their tracks and told to report back to the ship at once.

Switchboard operators at the Long Beach Naval Station begin making phone calls to the ship's key personnel, and in San Diego the same scene is being repeated, these calls being made to crewmen of Squadron VS21, an antisubmarine outfit equipped with propeller-driven Grumman aircraft, and to crewmen of HS6, a helicopter squadron. The crews from both units are ordered to fly to Long Beach, and by late afternoon a steady caravan of cars begins pulling up to the big gray flattop carrier as other crew members report for duty.

"Now hear this, now hear this," the ship's loudspeakers blare on the public-address system. "This ship is being made ready to join the search for the airliner that is missing at sea. You will be notified of further developments as they are received."

Trucks loaded with supplies for the big ship, which had just returned from deployment in the Far East, begin arriving at shipside, and promptly at dusk the first of twenty-eight helicopters from San Diego roars over the carrier and lands on the flight deck.

Unaware sailors attending the Stanford-University of Southern California football game are alerted by loudspeakers to immediately return to the carrier, and by 8 p.m., when officers of the Shore Patrol bring two AWOL sailors aboard the ship, departure preparations are well underway.

The officers and crew of the *USS Philippine Sea* are about to participate in the largest air-sea search-and-rescue mission in history. It is extremely rare for a commercial airliner to just disappear, and not since the search for famed aviatrix Amelia Earhart twenty years earlier has such an effort been organized.

There is still hope for survivors. *Romance of the Skies* carries four twenty-man life rafts and extra life vests. Each raft has enough rations for twenty people for one day. With some conservation measures, the food can last a couple of days as stranded survivors float in the Pacific awaiting rescue. The rafts are also equipped with Victory Girl emergency radios, low-frequency transmitters that automatically emit distress signals when the manually cranked generators are actuated. They also can send automatic SOS signals as long as the crank is turned. Signals can be heard for hundreds of miles, so there is still hope, even though the odds are increasingly mounting against a successful rescue.

In Alma, Michigan, the Reverend and Mrs. Robert W. Clack wait for the phone to ring with the good news that their son, Lee, and his family have been rescued at sea. They have been waiting all day for a call that will never come.

The Reverend Clack, a Congregational minister and former YMCA missionary in China, has recently retired as a math and astronomy professor at Alma College. He conducted the wedding ceremony that united Lee and Anna in 1943.

"We just can't believe they are gone," he tells a newspaper reporter. "We're praying that their plane is floating or that they are safe in rubber boats and will be rescued soon."

It has been less than thirty-six hours since Daddy kissed her goodbye, but Mom is fighting to remember what he looked like, what he felt like, how he smelled. She still can see his smile, and that gives her some comfort.

She opens the shoebox again and reads another letter sent by Daddy when he was in Germany several years earlier:

FRANKFURT, GERMANY
8 P.M., FRIDAY, NOVEMBER 26, 1954

"Dear Mom and Boys:

"Your Dad is sitting here thinking of how much he loves you and misses you. It seems that it has been much longer than five weeks since I left you angels in the terminal.

"I've told everyone here about my Kenny-Bo flying our 'Buddy-Seat' plane. I hope he can learn to fly it one day. That's one of the reasons I bought it, you know, so our boys could someday learn to fly like their daddy. Everyone over here thinks it's funny that Kenny calls the plane his 'Buddy-Seat' plane. Today, one of the fellows saw a plane overhead and told me to wave to it because it was probably that 'Buddy-Seat' plane and in the right Germany, too. I thought it very funny, too, but I could see more than a laugh in such a statement. I could see the big ideas that run through that beautiful head of his and the brightness of his thinking that he wasn't sure of where I was. This Germany is a big place as European nations go and I'm sure you can find it, Son. Some of these days your dad will show you the way here and a lot of other places, too. You just grow big and strong and care for yourself and you'll find much happiness in this world.

"I believe Jerry is going to have little lust for any adventure, but God bless your little dickens, I love you both. I hope I can make your home so happy you won't want to roam, but I believe the whole world is going to be Kenny's playground, or possibly even beyond our good earth.

"In everything sweet and beautiful I see you, Dear Mom, and while I loved you as much in '47 as anyone possibly could love anyone, I have managed somehow to love you a little bit more with each passing day. I know I fail to tell you, but I try to show it in my own clumsy way. I often wonder how I rated you in the first place.

"Love always, Dad"

Mom sequesters herself in a corner of the kitchen as neighbors field questions from reporters. She is an emotional woman, but speaks publicly just once:

"Why do they want his picture? He isn't dead. My God, he isn't dead!"

Later that evening I am facedown on my bed, my pillow literally soaked in tears, crying, begging for Daddy to come home.

"Oh, please, Daddy, don't be dead. Please, God, bring my daddy home!"

Jerry sits up his bed and glances over at me. He seems annoyed by my crying, but he is really angry with God. How could God let his daddy die? How could he?

In an adjoining bedroom. Craig is sound asleep in his crib, unaware of the unfolding tragedy that is consuming his family, unaware that his daddy will never hold him again, unaware of almost everything, as two-year-olds are when they clutch their favorite blankies in sleep.

There is still some daylight left over the Pacific, and dozens of planes and ships continue to look for any sign of the missing plane. As the *Philippine Sea* makes its way from port, two knife-nosed Navy submarines—the *Cusk* and the *Carbonero*—join two Gearing-class destroyers—the *John R. Craig* and the *Orleck*. Before the night ends, freighters, tankers, a troop ship, numerous Coast Guard vessels, and a luxury passenger liner are in on the hunt. It is the largest fleet ever assembled for a peacetime search. At least thirty planes, fourteen surface vessels, and two subs are now involved.

A Coast Guard spokesman remarks that the search "includes everything that'll float or fly that we can put our hands on."

Overhead, commercial airliners are diverted from their normal courses to fly low over the ocean; military bombers and transport planes fly as low as they safely can while crew and passengers peer out the windows.

Each plane and ship has an assigned search sector, but they are looking for a needle in a haystack. The search area is more than 150,000 square miles of Pacific Ocean loneliness, but even as night falls, the searchers don't give up hope, looking for a light, a flare, anything that will lead them to the missing plane.

Les Snipes, a reporter for the *Oakland Tribune*, has spent the day skimming the whitecapped Pacific aboard the Pan American DC-7 flying at 600 feet. He and other newsmen are joined by Pan American employees who are stationed along each side of the plane, peering out the windows in a dawn-to-dusk quest.

"Everyone is wondering. Everyone is waiting. Everyone is hoping," he reports to his newspaper. "The whitecaps, the cloud shadows, the birds, even flying fish confuse searchers. We can see thirty miles in any direction—thirty miles of sky and water."

The searchers report seeing some yellow square objects that may be lifejackets, but it is impossible to tell at 600 feet above the water. The plane makes numerous passes above the objects, but they can't be identified, appearing as small as postage stamps in the wide Pacific.

An Air Force pilot radios the location—28 degrees 11 minutes north latitude 142 degrees and 45 minutes west longitude. Nearby ships will be asked to check out the objects, but they will not be found.

Another glimpse of hope fades.

Reporter William Mackey of the *San Francisco Examiner* is also doing double duty as a searcher. He stares at the sea for hours. Always hoping. Rubbing his burning eyes, he looks for what is not there. From time to time he sees things floating on the water and he shouts to the crew. The locations are plotted and transmitted to other searchers, including veteran pilot Kinkel. Mackey is flying aboard a Boeing Stratocruiser, a sister ship of the missing *Romance of the Skies*. He notes that for Kinkel, this is more than just a search for a missing plane; he has friends on the crew of the missing airliner.

At 11:51 a.m.—more than six hours after the search plane left Honolulu — Kinkel's voice is heard over the intercom:

"That smoke curl to the port . . . another aircraft has sighted debris and dropped a flare. . . . There goes the weather ship towards it!"

Fifteen minutes later his voice crackles on the speakers again:

"A mirror flash—a possible mirror flash to the port! Focus as we circle."

It turns out to be sunlight reflecting off an oil slick, likely from a passing ship.

At 12:27 Captain Kinkel again alerts the searchers:

"An object under the starboard wing. Please scan there with your binoculars."

Everyone moves to a starboard window and focuses binoculars on the ocean below.

"There it is again. It's very bright orange. Get a sighting on it, somebody!" Kinkel orders.

The sightings are radioed to surface ships, along with those from other aircraft. The vessels speed to where they are directed to hunt. A Coast Guard cutter arrives fifteen minutes later.

But again, nothing.

At 2:11 p.m. Kinkel gets back on the intercom:

"We've sighted a white object. Try and keep it in view. We need it. Bad!"

Nothing.

Reporter Mackey is dead tired, as is everyone else aboard the Stratocruiser, when, in late afternoon, a discouraged and weary Kinkel walks into the cabin.

"Sorry, but we have to call it quits, folks. We're heading home," he grimly announces, then heads back to the cockpit. The Stratocruiser's huge wings dip gently toward the ocean—seemingly in tribute to its missing sister plane—and seconds later the DC-7 joins the Strat in the long trip back to San Francisco.

The first full, heartbreaking day of searching is coming to an end.

Strange things flash through reporter Mackey's mind. Things he wishes he hasn't seen. Things like a bright orange strip of some kind of material floating on the water. Things like a mail sack. Things that resemble an aircraft hatch door.

In the morning, Mackey will board the same plane and repeat the process. Hopefully tomorrow's search will have better results.

University of Southern California grad student Douglas Clack has been trying to study but is feeling nothing short of miserable. It's just been confirmed that his big brother Lee is aboard the missing Stratocruiser. By now the entire Clack family has heard the heartbreaking news and is trying to come to grips with what is happening midway across the Pacific.

Douglas decides to take a bath before bed, and just as he settles into the bathwater the missing Lee is suddenly in the room with him. He has appeared from out of nowhere, with no sound, no words, but he is there.

"It is all right," he tells Douglas in a positive, reassuring voice, and a feeling of comfort surrounds him.

No matter what has happened to Lee and his family, Lee has reassured him that they are all right, out there somewhere.

As commercial and military aircraft continue to crisscross the Pacific on Sunday morning, November 10, all eyes not actively involved in operating the aircraft are directed on the seas below, and all ears are focused on monitoring the radios for any hint of the missing airliner.

US Air Force Lt. Donald Lang of Pocomoke City, Maryland, is copiloting a Military Air Transport Service flight from Travis Air Force Base near San Francisco to Hickam Field at Pearl Harbor when the first sign of hope appears in the form of an SOS signal. Lang reports a "clear and strong SOS signal" in about the same position as the last radio report from *Romance of the Skies*.

For at least forty-five minutes the SOS signal is heard loud and clear by the Air Force search flight crew, and Lang says it is definitely from a "Gibson Girl" hand-operated radio, the kind that is standard equipment on all the missing airliner's life rafts.

"The SOS was followed by a series of numbers. I could not make out all of them clearly, but I do know definitely the last number was four, and I think the next-to-last number was four," he later recalls.

The missing Stratocruiser was number was N90944, and Lang says he had no idea about the plane's number when he heard the distress call.

Halfway across the world, in Sydney, Australia, Ruth Halliday has not yet told her four children — Lindsay, nine; Julia, six; James, five; and Margaret, three months — that their father's plane is missing. Weeping and red-eyed, she is holding out hope that her husband, Robert, a thirty-six-year-old executive with a Sydney printing company en route home after a four-week business trip to England, Canada, and the United States, will be found alive.

"He's been on two previous overseas trips, both to Europe," she tells a reporter. "I have been listening to the radio and been in touch with Pan American ever since I first heard the plane was missing.

"Until something definite is found, I will never give up hope."

There is a sharp rap on the front door, and a telegram is delivered to 1338 Loyola Drive shortly after noon. It is sent with love, but the message is clear: There is really no hope; Bill Fortenberry is dead.

"Dearest Ronnie. Sorry about Bill. Wish we could be with you. With love, Hazel, O'Neal, Wayne."

The telegram from her siblings in far, far away South Carolina is a reality check. My mother faces the cold, hard truth that she may now be alone—a young widow with three little boys and her closest family members thousands of miles away. If Daddy is gone, what in the world will she do now? Sell everything and move back to South Carolina, a place where my father did not want his children raised? Move back to Miami, the place they both dearly loved but still far away from family support? Stay where she is, in Santa Clara, and somehow cope with the agony of loneliness, and memories of him in every corner of the house?

She folds the telegram and takes it to her bedroom, where she places it in a dresser drawer, sits on the edge of their bed—*her* bed now—and cries.

"Bill is still alive." She says it over and over in a feeble attempt to convince herself, but in her heart she knows he is gone.

While the search for the missing plane continues throughout the afternoon and evening, the world goes on as if nothing happened. At Honolulu Stadium, 15,000 frenetic and screaming fans are showing the world why Elvis Presley is the King of Rock 'n' Roll. The crowd, mostly teenage girls, is oohing, bouncing, and shrieking to his beat and soulful Southern sound, and is enthusiastically joined by the mothers in the audience in idol worship. A missing plane out there in the ocean is the furthest thing from their minds.

On Monday morning the phone rings in Pan American's San Francisco office. An anonymous caller has a simple question:

"Was William Payne of Scott Bar on that missing plane?"

"Yes, as a matter of fact, he was. Are you a relative?

"No. Just curious."

"Why is that?"

"Because it couldn't have happened to anyone more deserving," the caller replies, and then hangs up.

Fortune seekers have panned for gold and mined for precious metals in the granite mountains and swift-moving streams of Northern California's Siskiyou County for nearly 200 years, and it was here in the summer of 1955 that William Harrison Payne went to strike it rich, first as a lodge owner, then as a miner.

He was an unlikely prospector, a recently retired Navy machinist's mate with no experience in either mining or his new career—owning and operating a hunting-and-fishing lodge—but he was a hardheaded man and determined to make a go of it. The odds were stacked against him, but after two decades in the military following orders that he often thought were stupid, Payne was eager to be his own boss, to determine his own destiny, and to order others around for a change.

His risky first venture into the business world was poorly financed and not very well developed. But the Paynes managed to make the down payment and swung the deal to buy the Roxbury Lodge and the 200 acres it was situated on, about three miles upstream from the tiny gold-mining ghost town of Scott Bar.

The lodge had been built in the early 1900s on a bluff near the confluence of the Scott and Klamath rivers, close to the site where huge amounts of gold were discovered during the California Gold Rush. Wealthy Boston capitalist H. P. Nawn constructed it as a guesthouse for friends, family, and business associates and had nicknamed it The Bungalow, but it was much more than that. It featured sixteen rooms with all the modern conveniences of the time, and guests lounged in comfortable high-back rocking chairs on a spacious veranda while enjoying a panoramic view of the river rushing over boulders and bright-red coho salmon jumping and splashing before their eyes. Their dinners were prepared by a seasoned gourmet chef and served in rustic elegance surrounded by a vast, rugged, but stunningly beautiful wilderness. Diners enjoyed fresh fruit and vegetables from Roxbury's own gardens and orchards, and fresh dairy products were delivered from neighboring farms.

This outdoorsman's paradise had once attracted notables from far and wide, including Herbert Hoover prior his inauguration as president of the United States. But that was long ago, and Roxbury Lodge's glory days had long since passed by the time the Paynes took it over.

Unrestrained post-World War II logging was causing massive soil erosion, and the rivers were filling with silt. Local mills were cutting more than 40,000 board feet of timber every day, and fishing was on the decline. Even deer hunting was becoming less popular, as more farms were being carved out of the valley and newcomers moved in.

Payne's only civilian employment since retiring from the Navy on June 3, 1955, had been as a coremaker for Augustine Brass Casting of Stockton. He found the work—creating molds to produce metal castings in a ship-building foundry—not only boring and beneath his dignity, but even worse distracting from his real goal: owning a resort lodge. One of his former supervisors at Augustine recalled that Payne was not at all interested in his work and talked frequently about consummating a deal to buy Roxbury Lodge. His job at Augustine lasted less than two months.

On July 4, 1955, Payne met with brothers James J. and Charles H. Brown, who had owned the property since 1946, and began to negotiate the purchase. His only income was his $160 monthly Navy pension, but his wife, Harriet, a twice-married hairstylist, owned their small house in Manteca, worth about $5,000, and she came up with enough money for them to make the $5,000 down payment. Harriet, or "Hap" as she was called, wore the pants in the Payne family, and her husband took a back-seat role as she worked out the final details with the lodge owners during the next few weeks.

The Paynes agreed to pay the Browns an additional $25,000: $10,000 in six months and the remaining $15,000 six months later. Where they figured to come up with that kind of money is anyone's guess, because the lodge had come upon hard times in recent years, and even when business had boomed it never generated the kind of cash flow necessary to make the mortgage payments, but the Paynes convinced themselves they could make a go of it.

They were dead wrong.

The impetuous Payne moved with his wife and their two sons into the tight-knit community, and many suspicious residents thought the outsiders might be running away from something back in the city. Most of the residents of Scott Bar and nearby Happy Camp (once called Murderer's Bar) had deep roots in the area and were fiercely independent and wary of city folks. They were hardworking people who fished, hunted, logged timber, and mined for gold like their ancestors before them, back when bloody fistfights over gold claims often ended in gunfire and death.

Scott Bar was unlike any place the city-slick Paynes had ever lived, and that was part of the attraction. Thy were blind to the fact that fools had been created here ever since indigenous Karuk tribesmen had roamed the wild land thousands of years earlier, decapitating their enemies and proudly taking their heads as trophies.

The bullheaded and shortsighted William Harrison Payne was a foolhardy man and business was slow from the beginning, but it got even worse in the ensuing months. There was little cash to keep the place afloat, and a once-in-a-lifetime flood in December sent the swollen Klamath and Scott rivers over their banks. Local residents remember Payne standing with his dog on a collapsing bridge as the lodge owner snapped pictures of the swelling river and avoided death by jumping to safety moments before the structure collapsed, its supporting timbers rushing down the raging river.

Payne returned to the lodge minutes later and ignored the family's two whinnying palomino ponies that were trapped in a small, fenced corral near the rapidly rising river. The corral was becoming a death-trap pond. They beat their hooves feverishly on the ground in an attempt to get someone's attention, but the water continued to rise.

Payne ignored them; the horses were left to drown.

Nineteen-year-old logger Tom Crocker, who rented a small trailer from the Paynes at the back of the lodge property, came by and was incredulous at Payne's heartless indifference. He jumped into the emerging pond and opened the gate, and the horses ran free to higher ground.

His reward for saving the horses?

"Why don't you come inside and buy yourself a drink?" Payne told Crocker.

"A real bastard, an asshole," Crocker recalled.

Tuesday, November 12, 1957
CIVIL AERONAUTICS BOARD
Washington, D.C.
November 12, 1957
TO: Members of the Board
FROM: Associate Director (Investigation)
Bureau of Safety
SUBJECT: Missing Aircraft—Preliminary Notification
Pan American Flight 7, Boeing 377, N 90944, en route
San Francisco to Honolulu, November 8, 1957

Pan American Flight 7, a Boeing 377, N 90944, enroute from San Francisco to Honolulu with 36 passengers and 8 crew, has been unreported since 1704 P.S.T. November 8, 1957. An extensive Search and Rescue activity has thus far been unsuccessful in locating anything that can be identified with the flight.

Flight 7 departed San Francisco at 11:31 P.S.T., estimating arrival at Honolulu 9 hours and 56 minutes later. Gross weight at departure was 147,000 pounds, the maximum allowable, and included sufficient fuel for approximately 13 hours of flight. The flight plan called for cruise at 10,000 feet, true airspeed 226 knots; the equatime point was estimated to be reached 5 hours 17 minutes out of San Francisco. Good weather was forecast for the flight. Captain Gordon H. Brown, First Officer William P. Wygant, Second Officer William H. Fortenberry, Flight Engineer Albert Pinataro, Purser Eugene Crosthwaite, Stewardesses Yvonne Alexander and Marie McGrath, and Flight Supervisor Jack King comprised the crew.

The flight made routine position reports as it progressed westward and reported over the ocean station vessel "November" (the equatime point) at 16:40 P.S.T., only one minute later than its estimated arrival there. A weather analysis was given the flight at this point reflecting substantially the same information as the original forecast out of San Francisco; the flight made no revision of flight plan or estimates.

The last contact with Flight 7 was a routine position report at 17:04 P.S.T. There was no indication of any emergency at any time and all transmissions were normal. No significant weather had been forecast and none was reported.

Search and Rescue operations began one hour after the flight was unreported and the most extensive search ever conducted in peacetime is continuing.

Air Safety Investigators from the Board's Oakland and Santa Monica offices began an immediate check of the aircraft maintenance records and operational aspects of the flight. William S. MacNamara,

Flight Operations Specialist, and Allen B. Hallman, Airworthiness Inspector of the Washington Office, are being dispatched to San Francisco today.

—Leon H. Tanguay

By now all sorts of theories are circulating about what might have happened to the airplane. A propeller tore loose and flew into the fuselage. An engine caught fire and could not be extinguished before it consumed the plane. A madman planted a time bomb. There is even talk that a mysterious "death ray" operated by enemy agents might have seized control of the plane, silenced its radios, and landed the Stratocruiser on some island. That idea is abandoned when searchers scrutinize a map of the Pacific and discover no land other than the Hawaiian Islands close enough for the plane to have reached with its fuel load.

Nothing else is being ruled out, but more important than figuring out what happened are two pressing questions: Where is the plane? Is anyone alive?

The search goes on.

It is Wednesday, November 13 — six days since *Romance of the Skies* departed San Francisco and there is still no sign of the missing airliner.

US Coast Guard Rear Admiral Stephen H. Evans notes that the search is the "most massive ever mounted in this ocean" and states that the huge armada of ships, planes, and submarines is "combing an ocean area much larger than the state of Texas." Surface vessels alone have cruised more than 30,000 miles in their search for the missing plane in a carefully plotted "area of the greatest probability."

The search is indeed massive. The Coast Guard has provided eight cutters and three long-range aircraft; the Navy, one carrier with forty-one aircraft and two destroyers, two submarines, one transport ship, and thirty-one long-range aircraft. The Air Force has put twenty-four long-range planes in the area, and Pan American has had two DC-7s and two Stratocruisers involved since the morning after the plane disappeared. Even Britain's Royal Air Force has entered the search, with five long-range Shackleton bombers in the air.

"Seldom in all time has such a tremendous effort been made to save so small a group of people from dire distress," the admiral tells the media.

Back in Washington, FBI Director J. Edgar Hoover receives the first of what will become many confidential memos about the missing airliner. Chicago Special Agent Raymond J. Driscoll tells Hoover that Pat Tighe, retired chief of police in Aurora, Illinois, has been contacted by a local attorney who states that he has a client with information about the missing Stratocruiser.

"The unknown client said that one of the deceased on this plane was a Soledad Mercado who operates some dress shops with (name redacted) in Phoenix as well as in the State of Colorado. According to the client, (name redacted) would have a possible reason for wanting to get rid of (name redacted) . . . According to the client (name redacted) would not necessarily cause her death for the purpose of getting insurance."

The memo further states that the client is "acquainted with other individuals who might be able to shed light on this matter."

Stunningly, the memo-telegram ends with this:

"No further action being taken by the Chicago Division."

Is the attorney's client implicating Mercado's husband in some kind of plot to have her killed? We'll never know the answer to that question; the FBI never follows up.

Out in the vast Pacific the sun is setting, but the searchers are not giving up. *Los Angeles Times* reporter Deke Houlgate, who has made friends with some of the sailor radiomen, is filing reports back to the newspaper, but there is nothing much to tell.

The ocean is large.

The search is massive.

The plane is still missing.

By 6 p.m. darkness covers the ocean and the search planes are returning to the flight deck of the *Philippine Sea.* By 6:15, six airplanes and four helicopters have been secured, and the carrier maneuvers are on a course to be refueled by the *USS Navasota* shortly before midnight.

Tomorrow will be another day. But will it be another day of finding nothing?

By 3:40 a.m. the *USS Navasota* has pumped 741,723 gallons of fuel into the *Philippine Sea,* and at 5:30 a.m. the carrier sounds flight quarters, awakening pilots and searchers for what they all hope will be a day of discovery.

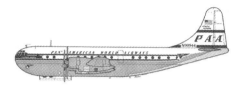

5

SHARKS AND BODIES

BEFORE THE SUN RISES on Thursday, November 14, five Grumman S2F antisubmarine airplanes and four helicopters are in the air, and by the time the *Philippine Sea* turns off its navigational running lights, at 6:57 a.m., the airmen are methodically working their search patterns in what has become a desperate, seemingly impossible task.

At 7:35 a.m. radar operator F. T. Kingsley suddenly picks up a small and intermittent contact on his screen and immediately notifies the flight's commanding crew, Lieutenant Commander Paul G. Cowan and Lieutenant Lee J. Gaffrey. Moments later Cowan sights something unusual floating in the water and takes his twin-engine plane down to investigate. He orbits the object twice and determines that it is a small piece of silver or white wreckage from the lost aircraft. About the same time another S2F team, this one commanded by lieutenants Earl E. Carlovsky and John N. Stanley, discovers a second piece of wreckage— and the gruesome sight of a lifeless body, arms and legs fully outstretched, floating in the sea.

The search for *Romance of the Skies* is no longer the search for a missing aircraft; it is now a search for survivors, wreckage, and more bodies.

Cowan circles his aircraft and keeps an eye on the wreckage while Carlovsky climbs high enough in altitude to radio the aircraft carrier about what they have found. Rear Admiral T. A. Ahroon, the search commander, immediately directs all ships to proceed to the area, and minutes later two other aircraft arrive on the scene and mark the debris and the first victim with smoke bombs to assist recovery teams.

Aboard the carrier, *Los Angeles Times* reporter Deke Houlgate makes a deal with Jerry Warren of *The San Diego Tribune* (later press secretary to presidents Richard Nixon and Gerald Ford). Warren, who has a journalism degree from the University of Nebraska, has been a reporter for only a year, having joined the newspaper after serving as a Navy pilot for three years. What he lacks in reporting experience he more than makes up for in aviation knowledge and Navy ship smarts. The Houlgate-Warren reporting team turns out to be a perfect combination.

"Jerry, you stay on deck and let me know what's going on and I'll set us up sort of a bureau down below and file reports back to our papers," he tells Warren, who quickly agrees and starts taking notes of everything he sees, smells, and hears. By the end of the day they will have filed twenty-eight takes, or story updates and revisions. Warren does what Houlgate calls the "dirty work up on deck" while Houlgate gets the dispatches out.

By 11:40 a.m. the *Philippine Sea* and the *USS Epperson* have arrived, and the search zeroes in on where the body and wreckage have been spotted. Other ships arrive and the crews lower smaller boats into the water; with the assistance of hovering helicopters they begin the grim task of recovering victims and debris.

1:53 p.m.

"HONOLULU (UPI)—The Coast Guard reported today nine bodies of victims of the downed Pan American Stratocruiser were found 75 miles west of the patrolling carrier Philippine Sea.

"One of the bodies was strapped in a plane seat, the Coast Guard said. The bodies were located approximately 128 miles northwest of

the last position report from the vanished plane.

"A pilot from the carrier radioed at 7 a.m. (noon EST) 'highly probable wreckage sighted.' A few minutes later he sent word that nine bodies were sighted, one of them strapped in an airplane seat."

"Damn, look at that crazy bastard! He's ripping the body to shreds!" a sailor screams as he maneuvers the small rescue boat around a lifeless, floating body.

"If we don't get rid of these damn sharks, we won't have any bodies to recover," another sailor yells as he struggles to pull the badly mangled body of a stewardess, still in her serving apron, into the boat.

The shark is not giving up easily. He opens his wide, hungry jaws, and his sharp teeth rip away more flesh, yanking it clean from the bones.

"Shoot him, dammit! Shoot him! That's the only way we're going to get her into the boat."

Seconds later, the disabled shark swims away, trailing blood.

Nearby, the *USS Philippine Sea* has been turned into a floating morgue. Since the early morning sighting, nine bodies have been found floating on their ocean graves. Although autopsies won't be conducted until the ship returns to port, the bodies are carefully examined for any presence of beta and gamma radiation because a package of radioactive medicine was in the plane's cargo. No radiation is found, and the bodies are packed in ice and awaiting identification—if anyone can identify what is left of them.

Meanwhile, VS-21 aircraft spread out over a new search area, this one based on the wreckage sighting, prevailing winds, and ocean currents. They find nothing in the expanded grid, but the search-and-rescue mission, now clearly a recovery mission, continues until darkness begins to set in.

Houlgate, who has emerged from his below-deck reporters' bureau several times during the day to collect his own observations, says that what he has seen is nothing short of "depressing and grisly." (Houlgate later will be nominated for a Pulitzer Prize for his reporting on the crash and search.)

Coast Guard reservist Ferguson, who used binoculars to search the night sky for flares several days ago, watches as the *USS Minnetonka's* small-boat crews pile bits of wreckage on the cutter's forward deck before they are transferred to the *Philippine Sea.*

One item catches his eye and will stay in his memory for the rest of his life: a little boy's blue jacket with a baseball stitched on the left front with the words "Lil' Slugger."

When daylight and luck run out on November 15, nothing much remains of the once-magnificent airplane: nineteen shark-eaten bodies, 400 pounds of mail, and about 500 pounds of twisted wreckage plucked from an area that stretches eleven miles long and three miles wide.

The wreckage is carefully labeled and transported to a warehouse aboard the carrier. Included are charred foam rubber; damaged clothing; bits of luggage; food trays; scraps of cloth and pillows; a step in the stairway from the main deck to the cocktail lounge, where purser Crosthwaite had been serving drinks; and bits of cardboard and insulation.

Three metal scraps are retrieved: light, buoyant doors to lavatories and a piece of engine cowling that for some reason was stuck in a pillow. Nothing of the main airframe of the aircraft is recovered.

Not much left of a seventy-ton aircraft—and precious little for investigators to go on.

"Only small litter and chaff are known to remain," the Coast Guard reports.

Interestingly, the only body recovered from the cockpit crew is that of Captain Brown, suggesting that he might not have in the cockpit when the tragedy occurred, or that the bodies of the other crewmen had been ravaged by sharks or trapped in wreckage at the ocean bottom.

Why would Brown leave the cockpit other than to attend to an emergency involving a passenger or a crewmember?

If a mechanical problem had developed with the plane itself, Brown would have remained in his seat, using his experience and leadership to resolve the problem and keep the plane in the air. If, however, a crewmember had become involved in an issue with another crewmember or a passenger, it would have Brown's responsibility—as captain of the ship—to intervene.

Reporter Houlgate sends a dispatch to his newspaper before he calls it a day and turns in for the night:

"Coast Guard Capt. Donald B. MacDairmid, a search-and-rescue expert, says that the wreckage and condition of the passengers indicate that the plane definitely went into the water in a bad or uncontrolled ditching with the passengers warned of a state of emergency."

He also says the Navy has catalogued the recovered debris, which is now laid out in a fifty-foot square on the carrier's hangar deck under Marine guard. Among the catalogued items that will later be thoroughly investigated Houlgate notes these:

- A piece of yellow sheet metal reading "944 FW-R-SIDE COCKPIT" in grease pencil

- A wide seat "ravaged by flames" that is "blackened and grooved

- A ladies' washroom door with printing in English and some Asian language

- An emergency-exit sign and light fixture, probably from the cabin

- Pillows, some with white covers

- Several gas tank floats

- A snapshot of a man

- A cabinet that might have been used to hold glasses or paper cups

- A woman's wool suit

- A paper sack marked "Rubber Gloves"

- A white toy dog made of fabric with a ribbon around its neck

- Three cases for thirty-five-millimeter slides

- An orange squeezer

- A gray-and-black-checked wool suit

- Three oil-splotched serving trays

- Half of a blue suitcase and one side of another

- Two leather, fur-lined gloves

- A woman's white purse and a green one, both smudged with oil

- Several pieces of a cigarette flip box

- A Christmas card reading "Greetings from our house to your house" with a picture of a baby (likely a card my father had recently made in his garage darkroom with a picture of my baby brother, Craig)

- A notebook charred on the edges, with Asian writing in pencil.

There are several packets of mail that later will be dried out and sent on to the recipients.

Also found floating in the sea is a paperback version of James Agee's best-selling book *A Death in the Family*, the tragic tale of his alcoholic father's death in a car accident shortly before Agee's sixth birthday.

At 5:18 p.m. Friday, November 15, Ensign H. T. Lawson posts this on the deck log of the *USS Philippine Sea*: "Completed search operations, having recovered 19 bodies and various mail and debris from Pan Am Stratocruiser 944. Underway for Long Beach, California."

As the carrier begins the return trip to its home dock in Long Beach, the FBI already has assembled a team in California to help identify the bodies, and has put together a log of all available facts on each person that might aid in the process. The team has gathered available fingerprint records, medical and dental reports, military records, information about special body markings, even information from relatives about the clothing and accessories the victims were wearing and what they might have had in their pockets when the plane went down.

The recovered bodies have already been identified, simply as Victims 1 through 19.

When plucked from the sea, Victim 1 was wearing a sweater by Pringle of Scotland; a suit by Bonwit Teller, tailored by Sloat & Company of New York; a St. Christopher bracelet and three others; and a pearl necklace. She is identified as Nicole Lamaison.

Victim 2 is described as an Asian woman wearing a Japanese obi, an aqua-colored sash for the red print skirt she was wearing when the flight went down. She is still wearing her wedding ring. Victim 2 is identified as Cassiqua Soehertijah VanDer Bijl.

Victim 3 is a white male wearing a blue shirt, a bow tie and red-checkered underwear. He is shoeless, but has on black-and-white argyle socks, and is also wearing his wedding ring. He has gold fillings in his teeth and is identified as vacationing pilot Robert Alexander.

Victims 4 through 19 are identified by clothing and personal items. A red sweater and gray skirt. A bra, size 36B. A female wearing a suit from the Town Shop in Saginaw, Michigan, and a bracelet with jeweled balls. A little boy in a blue-and-brown plaid shirt. A male adult in a gray suit with a black tie and gold-filled teeth.

The remains of Victim 5, identified as Australian businessman Robert Halliday, are among the easiest to identify. Inside his suit are his Pan Am ticket, his British passport, his driver's license, a pocket comb, an auto club card, traveler's checks issued in his name, and his personal exercise notebook. His watch — stopped at 2:20 — is still on his wrist.

Investigators also find a business card in the name of Edward T. Ellis, the corporate executive who sat next to him on the flight.

Another passenger whose identity will be easy to confirm is that of Commander Gordon R. Cole. Among the items recovered with him are his US Armed Forces identification card, his swimming-pool pass, his Virginia driver's license, a District of Columbia library card, his Pan Am ticket, and his brown leather wallet with a gold initial "C." Inside the wallet are four one-dollar bills, seven twenty-dollar bills, and three blank checks from his account at Union National Bank in Muskegon, Michigan.

My father's body is not among those recovered from the sea.

When this day ends, the search will be over. There will be no survivors of the crash of *Romance of the Skies*.

PART TWO

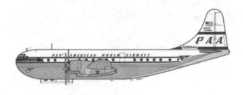

6

FIT TO FLY?

AT 6:28 A.M. ON MONDAY, NOVEMBER 18, the sun rises on the California coast and the navigational lights on the USS *Philippine Sea* are turned off as the giant carrier moors portside to Pier E at the Long Beach Naval Air Station. As the carrier/funeral ship docks, a section of its deck is covered with what is left of the giant airliner now packed in fourteen cardboard cartons, two small wooden crates, and eight half-filled sacks of airmail that searchers fished from the ocean.

At 7:40 a.m. officials from the Civil Aeronautics Board, the Civil Aeronautics Administration, the Federal Bureau of Investigation. and Pan American are permitted to board the carrier to begin their investigation of the bodies and debris recovered from the salvage area. Ten minutes later reporters and newsreel photographers board the carrier for a press conference on the flight deck.

Shortly before 8 a.m. the first of the white-shrouded bodies is removed from the refrigerated locker where they have all been kept since being plucked from the sea a few days earlier, and are sent above deck. Ship bells announce the arrival of the first elevator, with three bodies in basket stretchers—one of them a child's.

A Marine honor guard stands in tribute as the bodies are removed one by one from the carrier and placed into ambulances and hearses, then escorted by police vehicles to Mottell's and Peek Mortuary, where dozens of experts await. The *USS Haven*, a Navy hospital ship, has loaned a portable X-ray machine to the effort, and special telephones have been installed in the mortuary so that the team can communicate with sources anywhere in the world.

The mortuary, known as one of the five most beautiful in the world, with its old Spanish architecture and park-like gardens, has been transformed into an efficient, modern investigative unit, where authorities will attempt to determine not only the identifications of the victims, but also how they died and what may have led to the mysterious crash.

Security people lock down the mortuary area and are under strict orders to let no one in while the grim work is underway. FBI men wear white coveralls and white caps with the agency's emblem, while everyone else has paper signs pinned on their backs that identify what jobs they are there to perform. They take fingerprints and record all of the belongings, and anything else they see. They X-ray the bodies from head to toe, and then pathologists and medical examiners conduct detailed investigations, hoping they may learn more about the accident. No definite evidence of burning is found in any of the bodies, and they agree that the minimal external injuries suffered by the victims may have been the result of the "cushioning effect" of the water. They also note a "significant finding" concerning what they believe might be seatbelt marks on the bodies of purser Crosthwaite and Captain Brown, meaning that both may have had seatbelts on at the time of the crash, or the marks may have been caused by something else. If Brown had his seatbelt on, that might negate the speculation that he was not in the cockpit when the plane went down. They also determine that there is no indication that many others whose bodies were recovered were wearing seatbelts. Why were some passengers ready for ditching and others not? That is a question that will never be answered, but the fact that most of the recovered wreckage and most of the recovered bodies were from the rear of the plane might indicate that the forward section was where an explosion or some other incident occurred to bring the plane down.

A few miles away, in Los Angeles, family members gather at the luxurious Biltmore and Wilton hotels and await news from the mortuary about whether their assistance will be necessary to help identify the bodies.

NEW YORK CITY

Philip Deutsch, co-owner of the renowned Hotel Lexington in Manhattan and fourteen other hotels on the East Coast, tells his secretary that he feels a little silly dictating a letter to FBI director Hoover this morning but that after having talked with Pan Am he feels it necessary to share his thoughts with the agency. The forty-three-year-old hotelier and world traveler tells his secretary that he's willing to risk personal embarrassment on the slim chance that what he has to say might be helpful in determining why the plane went down.

His letter reiterates what is already publicly known: the plane was on schedule and having no problems at the time of its last radio contact, but something catastrophic happened suddenly thereafter, within minutes of reaching the point of no return.

"My guess is that there was an explosive on board which put the plane out of commission," he states. "Furthermore, I would surmise that the explosive was so placed strategically that it would knock the radio equipment out at once, making it impossible for the pilot or copilot to report the difficulty. It seems to me that if such a bomb was placed aboard it could not have been placed aboard haphazardly, and must have been placed aboard by someone who was familiar with: 1) flight schedule; 2) approximate time of reaching the point-of-no-return; 3) knowledge of time bombs and detonators; 4) knowledge of radio equipment aboard the plane; and 5) access to the plane before flight time."

Deutsch speculates that a disgruntled employee or perhaps one needing psychiatric treatment might be the culprit, and suggests that a search of the homes, cars, and garages of all employees connected with the crash might lead to a solution.

Hoover sends a polite thank-you letter to Deutsch a few days later and, after having Deutsch checked out as "clean" in the agency's records, dispatches a memo to his staff dismissing the suggestions as simply information for background.

Seventeen-year-old high school senior Dave Kaiser is at his home in Manila, the Philippines, where his parents work for the US State Department. He considers himself to be a very lucky young man today. Less than a week ago, as he and his family had been flying from San Francisco to Honolulu aboard *Romance of the Skies*, he was invited to visit the cockpit when the crew learned that he was interested in aviation and a possible appointment to the US Air Force Academy. Kaiser quickly noticed that both wings of the Stratocruiser were thickly coated with engine oil and wondered why.

"The flight engineer admitted there was a lot of oil and looked in an aircraft maintenance manual onboard the plane. He said the engines had a lot of hours on them and that the aircraft was due for a major maintenance period, perhaps when it returned to Honolulu. We were shocked to learn on our arrival in Manila that the plane had been lost between the mainland and Honolulu as we were flying on to Manila," Kaiser said years later in an interview.

The slim remains of N90944 and the shark-ravaged bodies of nineteen humans have barely been plucked from the sea when a skeptical media and angry members of Transportation Workers Union 505 in San Francisco pounce on the safety record of Boeing Stratocruisers and the maintenance standards of Pan American.

A column in the Tuesday, November 19, 1957, morning edition of the *Redlands Daily Facts* newspaper raises the question of whether Stratocruisers are even fit to fly, and a union newspaper claims a few days later that Pan Am has been gambling with human lives by curtailing critical inspections.

"When the Civil Aeronautics Board attempts to learn why the Pan American Stratocruiser tragically crashed into the Pacific Ocean enroute to Honolulu they won't go back far enough in their inquiry," the Redlands newspaper columnist stated. "They will try to determine, merely, if a propeller came off. Or was there was a fire, followed by an explosion? Or was there was some immediate cause of disaster?

"But we think the question goes much further back than that. The real question is: Was the Stratocruiser ever fit to fly across oceans?

"For years this column has been saying that anyone who sets out across the ocean in this particular kind of an airplane does so at his own risk. The Stratocruiser's record has been too poor. There have been too many engine fires, too many engine failures, too many forced turn-backs short of the point-of-no-return.

"Pan American will gloss it over with the frosting of beautiful statistics. They will tell you that the airplane has flown a certain number of miles without a fatality and in the very same statement omit an explanation that one Stratocruiser did go down at sea before. It was not the dependability of the aircraft to which these passengers owed their lives. It was a skillful crew and a prompt rescue.

"It is doubtful that the CAB will ever reach a finding that the Stratocruiser was unfit for cross-ocean flying. After all, they have been licensing these craft for years. There is, however, no rule that a person buying an airline ticket has to agree with them. There are more dependable aircraft in the sky."

On November 25, an article published in *Organized Labor* and circulated to 15,000 readers in the San Francisco Bay Area suggests that mechanical failure resulting from Pan Am's decision to reduce the number and quality of inspections may have caused the crash. The double whammy of bad publicity is quickly met with the expected counterattacks and denials from Pan Am's massive PR apparatus, but the articles have struck a nerve.

Organized Labor reporter Jeff Boehm points out that his newspaper began documenting and publishing charges of dangerous inspection economies more than a year ago and that mechanics have been complaining that the planes are not adequately inspected and therefore "the planes cannot be guaranteed safe."

"Two weeks ago this Friday 44 people were dozing, reading, ordering cocktails in a Pan American Stratocruiser over the Pacific

Ocean, simply waiting to take the next big or little step in their lives when they should land.

"The next step for all of them was fighting with the fear of death and trying, by taking their shoes off and donning life jackets, to stay alive.

"And then death.

"The force of the crash shattered their bodies and disintegrated the plane. The sharks came, but the passengers couldn't have known it.

"The Navy found 19 bodies of the 44 and bits of debris which showed some evidence of fire. The Civil Aeronautics Board is investigating. The board will note the condition of the debris and the bodies. It will note that no distress signal was sent and that there was time, however, for partial preparations for ditching. But it will never recover the engines or likely the propellers. It may discover there was an explosion or fire, but it will doubtless never know why.

"Speculation among those who fly, however, does not stray far from mechanical failure.

"Will the CAA give serious consideration to charges by the Transportation Workers Union 505 that Pan American World Airways is gambling with human lives by curtailing vital inspection services?"

The article claims that while Pan American's San Francisco base has one inspector for every fifty-one maintenance employees, United Airlines and American Airlines have a ratio of one to thirteen. The union had complained to Pan American, the Civil Aeronautics Board, and lawmakers, but its pleas about what it calls "an extremely serious situation" have been futile. The newspaper says Pan Am is not only cutting back on the number of inspectors, but also eliminating some inspections altogether.

Union president Phil Ice had detailed some of his organization's concerns in a copyrighted story a year earlier. Among them:

"Propeller changes are no longer checked by an inspector, although in the past the inspector had to sign that the propeller was secured and airworthy.

"Formerly, an engine which had 'conked out' was pulled apart under the eye of an inspector who also checked re-assembly. Now, the inspector is not permitted to inspect the engine until it is completely re-assembled, when he can only inspect it externally.

"If the fire detection system or fire control system is found to have faulty wiring or if it has been improperly installed, the inspector is not required to see that it is properly repaired. He does not check the fire detection system to see if it functions properly."

Ice also said that Pan Am frequently sends experienced and qualified inspectors home before completing inspections to avoid paying them overtime, and then assigns inspection authority to assistant foremen, people who are not qualified to certify that the plane's mechanical systems are safe and operating properly.

The article also mentions that the crash of *Romance of the Skies* is the third major accident in Pan Am's Pacific-Alaska division in two years and complains that the politically motivated CAB published "discrepancies, omissions and inaccuracies in its whitewashed" report of the ditching of N90944's sister ship, *Sovereign of the Skies*, a year earlier.

The California Labor News Service follows its report with a letter to US Rep. Charles M. Teague, a first-term congressman from Ventura County, and includes copies of its stories.

"For more than a year we have been calling attention to the fact that Pan American Airways, which enjoys a considerable amount of federal assistance, has had faulty inspection services and we are convinced that this may very well be the cause of their accidents," writes executive editor Langdon Post, a Harvard grad and former New York assemblyman with a long and distinguished record in politics and the federal government.

Post encourages the congressman to "call to task" those responsible for a "woeful lack of interest" and says the congressman and his colleagues should be aware of the facts, which the newspaper believes are "being deliberately hidden."

Post laments what he calls a "curious lack of interest" by the CAB and an equal indifference in the daily press. He doesn't point out that Pan Am aggressively cultivates important editors and publishers and routinely takes them on expense-free junkets. (A year earlier, one of the nation's most popular newspaper columnists, Drew Pearson, reported to millions of readers that Pan Am had lied about its air-safety record in response to the 1956 crash of a Boeing Stratocruiser off the coast of

Oregon and that the CAB had found that the Pacific-Alaska Division had been using rusty or corroded propeller blades in more than 13 percent of its planes.)

There is no indication that the congressman ever responds.

As expected, Pan Am blasts the newspaper reports as ridiculous and remains adamant that Stratocruisers are safe, that all inspections are handled by the book, and that the union's complaints are merely public posturing in advance of contract negotiations.

Still, there is concern among Pan Am mechanics and the union that the CAB will once again protect Pan American and whitewash the official investigation report about what happened to *Romance of the Skies.*

Their concerns seem warranted following the issuance of the CAB report on Flight 7 on January 20, 1959, my mother's thirty-fourth birthday.

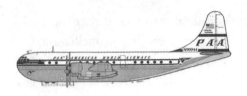

7

GONE TO ETERNAL REST

FBI Director J. Edgar Hoover finishes reading the *Dick Tracy* cartoon in the Wednesday, November 20, morning *Washington Post and Times-Herald* and tosses it onto the seat beside him as his shiny black, bulletproof 1957 Cadillac pulls into the basement garage of the US Justice Department on Pennsylvania Avenue. The cartoon has brought a momentary smile to the director's face this morning, because it features a cute dog confiscated from a crook who has just been arrested.

Hoover is a devoted dog lover, and reading the exploits of the crime-fighting Dick Tracy is a welcome daily diversion from the onslaught of headlines that spotlights a world full of communist subversives who Hoover believes are determined to destroy the America he loves.

Minutes earlier chauffeur Tom James Crawford had arrived at Hoover's upscale colonial home and respectfully listened to the Boss's customary morning grumbling about anything and everything on the short drive to FBI headquarters. Hoover is preoccupied with thoughts of communist subversives even as his agency is being rocked and embarrassed by last week's startling news of the upstate New York arrests of more than fifty Mafia members, arrests made by state troopers and local law enforcement officers, not the all-powerful, all-knowing FBI.

He has built his career on arresting notorious gangsters, but has been consumed in recent years with what he calls the "communist conspiracy" and has publicly discounted reports of a nationwide network of American gangsters operating right under his nose. He has assigned more than 400 agents to keep tabs on and arrest domestic subversives and those he suspects of being commies, but fewer than a dozen to fight organized crime. He sees communists everywhere—hiding behind suits in federal agencies, organizing workers on loading docks, even sowing seeds of disruption in classrooms—all determined to bring the nation to its knees. There is no Mafia, he has claimed, and now he has been proven wrong.

He is more obsessed with what he calls a "burr-headed" young Negro preacher named Martin Luther King Jr., a man Hoover believes is a communist sympathizer and a threat to national security, than he is with the massive criminal enterprise being run by the likes of Vito Genovese, Giuseppe "Joe the Barber" Barbara, and Carlo Gambino.

Hoover has convinced himself and much of the American public that he has the whole world in his hands (or by its cojones), and now he must admit that he has been wrong about organized crime and must take immediate steps to correct his negligence.

Hoover hates it when events spin out of his control and force him to take public action, and he's pissed off this morning by the emerging PR nightmare, which will be hard to manage without the assistance of his capable and loyal assistant director and press liaison, Louis B. Nichols, the number three man in the agency. Nichols has carefully crafted the reputation of both Hoover and the FBI for more than two decades, but he retired three weeks earlier, leaving a big hole in the agency's mammoth PR apparatus and in Hoover's ego-feeding machine.

Nichols had been Hoover's private fix-it man and handled political dirty work that included wiretapping and leaking information to chummy reporters about public officials who were suspected communists. Nichols also was the man who received advance copies of popular conservative radio commentator Paul Harvey's script for Hoover's comments and approval.

"Dammit," Hoover tells himself, "Nichols is going to be a hard man to replace."

The last thing he wants to deal with this morning is a dispute with another federal agency. Nor does he have any desire to be sucked into investigating something like a damn airplane crash that doesn't give him the glowing prime-time/page-one headlines he craves. Hoover does not tolerate criticism of the FBI, and occasionally he will give those who dare a dose of medicine, like investigating the personal lives of reporters who write critical articles or conducting covert smear campaigns against the publications that print their work.

Intimidation is a powerful weapon in Hoover's arsenal, and he doesn't hesitate to use it.

After pulling up to FBI headquarters, chauffeur Crawford dashes around the Cadillac and opens the left rear door as Hoover, impeccably dressed in a black Brooks Brothers custom-tailored suit, picks a tiny, almost invisible, piece of lint from the left vest area and straightens the traditional white handkerchief in his breast pocket. His Vitalis-slicked hair is perfectly in place.

Hoover is a demanding man, a man of precision, and he enters the elevator a few minutes before 9:30 a.m., right on schedule.

Gordon A. Nease has been hard at work for several hours when Hoover arrives. Nease has risen through the ranks from an hourly office clerk and typist in March 1935 to a special FBI agent. By 1957 he has a fifth-floor office right outside the door to Hoover's thirty-five-foot inner-sanctum office suite and is one of Hoover's most trusted confidential assistants. One of his responsibilities is to weed through the stacks of teletypes, letters, and telegraphs each morning before the director arrives and to prioritize, with the assistance of Hoover's long-time personal secretary, Helen Gandy, the director's agenda for the day.

This morning something has caught Nease's eye, and he decides to immediately bring it to the director's attention. He tells the director's secretary that he would like to speak personally with the director as soon as he settles in.

Hoover is seated at his huge, polished, mahogany desk, surrounded by the American and FBI flags, when Nease carefully, but confidently, walks in a few minutes later. Hoover demands respect and adores compliments, but detests sycophantic behavior. Nease knows the drill.

"Good morning, sir."

"Yes, what is it, Mr. Nease?"

Nease places some papers on Hoover's desk and respectfully steps back.

"Sir, I wanted to bring to your attention some information we've received this morning from Texas pertaining to the crash of the Pan Am Stratocruiser."

Hoover immediately interrupts.

"Texas? Pan Am? You know we're not involved in that crash, Mr. Nease, and I'm not about to let the CAB drag us into it. They can't solve it, and we're not going to let them put the blame on us. No way."

"Yes, sir. I understand that, but I think this might be worthy of your attention."

Minutes earlier the FBI in Washington had received a call from Corpus Christi, where a nervous real estate agent named Ray Hostutler claimed he had information that had "direct bearing" on the crash. Hostutler said that he had a letter from a Dow Chemical Company official in Oklahoma City that might help solve the mystery of what had sent the giant airliner to the bottom of the Pacific Ocean. Hostutler had been encouraged to call, collect, to the resident FBI agent in Corpus Christi or the resident agent in Houston and to relay the information, but so far he has refused.

"They might not believe me. Washington should handle this. Some prominent people may be involved," he told an agent who answered Hostutler's call to FBI headquarters..

Hostutler went on to state that on August 23, 1957, he made a phone call to an undisclosed person at Dow Chemical in Oklahoma to set up an appointment the following morning, presumably to discuss a real estate deal.

"The appointment was not kept, but a portion of the Dow Chemical Company blew up the morning of August 24, 1957. He met the official later on other matters," Hoover reads, then places the memo about the Hostutler call aside.

"We're not getting involved in this crash, Mr. Nease, but maybe we should follow up, considering this fellow's claim that some prominent people might be involved."

It is no secret that Hoover has hundreds of top-secret files on the most prominent people in Washington and has kept his job for more than thirty years not only because he has built the FBI into the most respected and formidable law enforcement agency in the world, but also because of the private dossiers he has accumulated on Washington politicians.

Hoover directs that the following teletype be delivered immediately to the special agent in Houston:

11-20-1957

PLAIN TEXT TELETYPE

URGENT

SAC, HOUSTON

Crash of Pan American World Airways, Flight Seven Naught Eight, San Francisco to Honolulu, November Eight, Nineteen Fifty Seven, Destruction of Aircraft or Motor Vehicle

(Several lines deleted) both Corpus Christi, Texas, telephone (deleted) telephoned bureau headquarters this morning requesting that Agent obtain from him a letter he received from Dow Chemical Company, Oklahoma City, Oklahoma, official relative to captioned crash. (deleted) says letter has direct bearing on the cause of the crash. Interview today and SUTEL details bureau.

HOOVER

Former FBI Special Agent Robert A. Collier arrives at Washington National Airport on an early-afternoon flight from San Francisco.

For the past several days he has been working on a contract basis as a crash investigator for Pan Am, and although he has presented what he has learned so far to the FBI office in San Francisco, he feels the need to share that information with someone at FBI headquarters in Washington.

Collier, a Texas-born attorney, joined the FBI immediately after graduation from the University of Texas Law School in 1940 and became an assistant to director Hoover and later one of his top aides. He left the FBI in 1951 to become chief counsel to the US House Judiciary Committee, on Hoover's recommendation, and later worked for the US Senate Subcommittee on Investigations. Over the past few years he has been a lobbyist and an attorney in private practice but has remained in close contact with his former colleagues at the FBI, including the director himself.

Pan Am executive vice president Sam Pryor Jr., had hired Collier a few days after the crash to assist the airline and the Civil Aeronautics Board in determining why the airliner went down.

Perhaps not coincidentally, Pryor has been a key contact for the Central Intelligence Agency and its predecessor organizations, including the Office of Strategic Services, since the 1940s and has provided cover to American spies everywhere Pan Am has a presence across the world. A Republican party luminary and national committeeman, the Greenwich, Connecticut, resident is a close friend of the Rockefeller family and had been a key figure in something called the Airport Development Program, a hush-hush Pan American wartime plan to develop a secret 10,000-mile network for air transport for military cargo and transport planes during World War II.

A call from the wealthy and well-connected Pryor is not something to be ignored. He is known as a man who can make big things happen in business, government, and politics all around the world. Collier left Washington almost immediately after the phone call from Pryor and has been working day and night in California since then in an attempt to unravel the mysterious plane crash.

Shortly after arriving back in Washington, Collier is sitting in the office of assistant FBI director F. C. Holloman and outlines what he knows about the crash and the suspicious circumstances surrounding purser Oliver Eugene Crosthwaite, a man who has not publicly emerged as a suspect. Collier tells Holloman that Crosthwaite had been suspected two or three years earlier "in connection with alleged smuggling," but nothing could be proven, and that Crosthwaite had been suffering some kind of "emotional disturbance" since the death of his wife a few months earlier.

He also passes along claims that Crosthwaite had been having difficulty controlling his teenage stepdaughter, but local police told the investigator that Crosthwaite had been "incoherent when explaining that relationship and what may—or may not—have been going on."

"Medical examiners are conducting a special examination of Crosthwaite's body today," Collier informs Holloman.

"Why would they do that?"

"Well, to determine anything—any significant facts—that might help us understand what brought the plane down. They still don't have a clue, but there is some conjecture that Crosthwaite might have knocked out the crew members who were forward in the plane and that the forward compartment might have actually, up until the crash, been inaccessible to the rest of the crew."

He then explains what they have learned so far about the crash, including the belief that the plane hit the water at full speed and was significantly off course, but had reported everything was A-OK less than thirty minutes before it vanished.

"The plane would have had to be traveling at full cruising speed to have reached the point where we believe it went down," he explains. "This indicates to us that the plane was not slowed down because of any mechanical trouble, but was in full speed up until the time of the crash."

"That does sound strange," Holloman observes.

"In fact, it appears as though the plane hit the water at an angle and at full speed. It probably went directly to the bottom of the ocean, and the bodies and debris floated up from the wreckage."

"Why do you think that?"

"Because the area where the bodies and debris were found had been previously searched without success. There was nothing there one day, and then there was."

Holloman promises to pass along the information to Hoover, but tells Collier what he already knows: the FBI is not going to get involved unless someone provides proof of a criminal act.

By late afternoon it is obvious at FBI headquarters that the Hostutler lead from earlier in the day has turned out to be a dead-end, and the special agent in Houston has sent an urgent teletype to director Hoover informing him of his findings. The agent states that Hostutler had come to the FBI's attention after Jack Gilbert Graham blew up United Airlines flight 629 near Longmont, Colorado, in November 1955 with twenty-five sticks of dynamite he had planted in his mother's luggage. Forty-four people perished in that flight, including Graham's mother, and authorities determined that Graham had manufactured a time bomb in order to collect insurance on his mother's death.

During the investigation of that case, Hostutler contacted local law enforcement officials alleging he had "inside information" about the murderous bombing. The FBI determined very quickly that Hostutler had a "psychopathic condition," and Hostutler was never interviewed. The special agent also told Hoover that he had been advised by a Houston psychiatrist that Hostutler was a paranoid schizophrenic.

"No credence can be put in any statement he might make. No interview being conducted."

The following morning former agent Collier calls Holloman and relays some morbid information he has just learned about autopsies conducted on victims of the Pan Am plane crash.

"Nothing of any interest or significance was really discovered, probably because all of the bodies had been attacked by sharks and were in bad condition. There's also evidence that sharks had apparently attacked other bodies that weren't recovered and completely disposed of them. That might account for the fact that other bodies weren't recovered."

Collier then presses once again for the FBI to investigate purser

Crosthwaite. He tells Holloman that he has just talked with Pan Am vice president Pryor and he is "very anxious for the bureau to conduct an investigation."

"Look, I understand all about jurisdictional limitations, but surely there is some way the director can find a way for the bureau to at least investigate Crosthwaite's background and activities."

"You know the director won't do that."

"Well it seems to me that just a little bit of effort, by someone other than the CAB, might reveal some motive for him to have destroyed the plane in a suicidal act."

"Unless we have jurisdiction to conduct an all-out investigation, it's just not possible for us to conduct a partial investigation," Holloman tells Collier.

Collier reluctantly thanks his former colleague for his time and tells him that he will keep him advised if anything further develops that might be of interest to the agency. He later boards a plane and heads back to California to continue the investigation.

Why are Collier and Pryor so insistent upon the FBI investigating Crosthwaite? Is it because Crosthwaite is the most likely suspect and deserves a thorough, professional background check? Is it because Pan Am simply wants to point the blame away from the airline (and its maintenance practices). Or is something else involved? Could Collier and Pryor be intentionally trying to push the FBI to examine Crosthwaite to divert attention from other passengers and potential suspects?

The remains of twenty-six-year-old stewardess Yvonne Alexander are gently placed into a coffin crate and carried from a basement preparation room into a waiting black Cadillac hearse at the Mottell's and Peek Mortuary on Alamitos Avenue in Long Beach. Recently autopsied and prepared for burial, the body will be driven to Los Angeles International Airport, where it will be loaded onto an airplane and flown to San Francisco International Airport. There, a waiting hearse will carry her remains to the N. Gray and Company Funeral Home at 1545 Divisadero Street, where her grief-stricken mother, Lucille

Heindl, will join family and friends for a funeral service in Chapel B at 10 a.m. tomorrow.

As the hearse bearing her body pulls out of the mortuary, another one backs in. This one will carry what's left of thirty-six-year-old Navy Commander Gordon Richard Cole, whose remains will be flown to Washington National Airport, where a hearse from a local funeral home will carry the body to Arlington National Cemetery for a full military service on Friday. Cole will be buried in Section 30, Grave Number 1847. The left side of the gravesite will be reserved for his widow, Rosemary.

Minutes later the bodies of vacationing pilot Robert Alexander, his wife, Margaret, and their nine-year-old daughter, Judy, are loaded into hearses and driven to Pomona for a private, Saturday-afternoon service. Eleven-year-old David's body was not among those recovered. He will be remembered along with the rest of his family later this month during a memorial service in Los Altos.

The scene will be repeated again and again today as nineteen bodies are removed from Mottell's and Peek and shipped to funeral homes not just in California but in Australia, Indonesia, Japan, Michigan, New York, and all parts in between. The grim task of identifying bodies is over; now it's time to escort them to eternal rest.

THURSDAY, NOVEMBER 21, 1957
WASHINGTON, D.C.

John Edgar Hoover is no man's fool, and he's made it perfectly clear that he isn't about to be dragged into something he can neither control nor win. That is not his style, and he isn't about to change now. Public relations is everything; the FBI gets its man.

In the days following the crash, dozens of Pan American and Civil Aeronautics Board experts have tried desperately to unravel the mystery of the plane's sudden disappearance. With precious little left of the giant Stratocruiser, the investigation has turned to the possibility of sabotage, the sudden and deliberate destruction of the airplane.

An initial background check of passengers and crew has turned up two interesting names and some tantalizing coincidences. But without criminal-investigative training and the resources needed for a full-scale criminal investigation, Pan Am and the CAB are almost at a dead-end. They need professional crime investigators; they need the FBI.

Everyone is screaming for answers—the press, relatives of the deceased, certain influential members of Congress, including US Senator Almer "Mike" Monroney, an Oklahoma Democrat —and they want the answers now. A luxury airliner doesn't just disappear in midair without some warning, some clue of imminent danger, especially just a few minutes after the crew had signaled that everything was fine.

But Hoover is too stubborn to bend his own bureaucratic rules to help solve the tragedy that has cost forty-four lives. He has sent a letter to US Attorney General William P. Rogers explaining his decision to stay out of the investigation, citing a lack of investigative manpower and the fear of setting a precedent in future cases; the FBI requires proof of a crime before getting involved, he explains. Hoover also knows that much of the evidence needed to solve this case is at the bottom of the Pacific Ocean.

* * *

At 9:25 a.m. the phone rings in the Washington office of Civil Aeronautics Board executive James N. Payton. On the other end is W. O. Locke, legal officer for Pan American's Pacific Division. Locke met yesterday with Leon Cuddeback of the CAB office in Oakland and two FBI agents, Tom Sullivan and John Hamicker, both of whom had strict orders from Hoover to ensure that the FBI isn't snagged into the probe.

The CAB is once again planning to formally ask the FBI for its assistance, and Locke wants the CAB in Washington to have the latest information; this new angle is something that must be explored.

"Mr. Payton, at the time of the loss of the airplane we were without any clues whatever as to what happened and we realized that a normal investigation would involve much of the maintenance and routine overhaul matters and things of that kind on the aircraft, so we felt that something further had to be done," Locke explains.

"We started an investigation of every single piece of material, the cargo, the mail, or anything that went on that airplane or had anything to do with it and also every passenger and crewman as far as we could. We advised the local FBI office of our efforts. As an outgrowth of this investigation of ours, we of course looked into the possible planned or intentional destruction of the airplane, which under the circumstances, we felt was of reasonable suspicion. We uncovered several suspicious circumstances which were followed as far as we could but were soon after that dismissed. Then a group of very suspicious facts appeared regarding the purser on the flight. The purser is Oliver Eugene Crosthwaite. And it was this story that we related to Mr. Cuddeback and Mr. MacNamara and which he thought should be related immediately to the CAB in confidence."

"Now what is that suspicion, Mr. Locke?" Payton asks.

"Mr. Crosthwaite is a forty-six-year-old man and has been employed by Pan American for seventeen years. He has been married twice and the first marriage ended in November 1945. That marriage had one daughter, named Billie.

"The second marriage was to Julia C. Crosthwaite. She died August 12, 1957. She had one daughter, named Tania, who was adopted by Mr. Crosthwaite in February of 1949. She is about seventeen years of age. Mr. Crosthwaite was the purser on Flight 7 on November 8, 1957.

"At the beginning of our discussion, Mr. Frank Hull, our service manager, referred to Mr. Crosthwaite on this airplane and mentioned that he had many difficulties with his job and with other people and he seemed to constantly have a chip on his shoulders. He was quite familiar with the man, since he was such a longtime employee," Locke says.

"Mr. Crosthwaite apparently had a feeling that the company was always trying to get his job. His morale was very low, and he had a definite persecution complex. There was some truth in the fact that what he called the company trying to get his job, in that he was considered a marginal employee, and efforts to discharge him were made on several occasions. The union constantly opposed his discharge. In October 1955, Mr. Crosthwaite contracted tuberculosis and went to a TB sanatorium.

He was discharged from there in April of 1956. In August of 1956 this TB was arrested, and he returned to work on August 30, 1956. He still to date, or just prior to his death, was taking various drugs for his TB. Mr. Crosthwaite filed a workman's compensation claim in connection with his TB. This was denied by the company, and once more there was another exchange of dislikes for the company. After that, it developed even further, when the company tried to prevent his return to flight because the company doctor felt that the TB could never be arrested to the point where it would be safe to confine him in an airplane. This was unsuccessful, again through union efforts. On August 12, 1957, as I said, Mr. Crosthwaite's wife died. After this he became even more despondent. Even his most recent physical, on September 13, 1957, had a report from the doctor that the man had not recovered from the death of his wife. After this, trouble developed with his stepdaughter, Tania," Locke reveals.

"How do you spell that?"

"T-A-N-I-A. It was rumored that he couldn't control the daughter, she was out until 3 a.m. every night, and she would not accept any parental discipline. This difficulty, he thinks, was at least partly the cause of the death of his wife. And his job kept him away from home for long periods. A few days after the airplane was gone, we received a call from the Santa Cruz County Sheriff's Office. Mr. Crosthwaite had gone to the sheriff's office to file a complaint concerning the trouble with his daughter. They didn't understand exactly what he wanted and told him to go to the probation officer of that county. The probation officer talked with him and described him as being incoherent, used the words 'psycho' and 'neurotic,' and also stated that he could not understand exactly what he was talking about. They sent him several letters asking that he come back and discuss it further. He never returned. The probation office then contacted the daughter, Tania, to see what the trouble was. The daughter related a sordid tale to the probation officer that the father believed the world was against him and he was against the world. In summary, the probation people were inclined to believe the daughter and doubted the father and tried to get him back in for further discussion. At this time we thought this was reasonably important and we decided on a course to check out this man as best we could, and again notified the FBI," Locke advises.

"On Monday, November 18, while at the wreckage, we received a call at Long Beach, where the wreckage arrived, from attorney Hugh Mullin of 200 Fifth Avenue, San Mateo. He called and inquired into the assets and insurance and various company matters that might exist between Pan American and Crosthwaite and said he held the will of Mr. Crosthwaite. In this discussion it was brought up that Mr. Crosthwaite had written his will within an hour or two hours of the time he boarded this particular aircraft, Flight 7, on November 8. We thought it was quite strange and mentioned that to Mr. Mullin, although he didn't understand that there was any difficulty connected with it. The fact that he wrote a will on his way to the aircraft, in addition to the other suspicious circumstances which we had, made us again go to the FBI and the CAB at the same time. It might be circumstantial evidence. However, we thought it was not something we could ignore. During the course of our handling of this accident we contacted his mother, Marie Crosthwaite. The employment superintendent, Winchester, called Mrs. Crosthwaite and she became very talkative about her son and said that just a couple of days before this particular flight he called and asked her to fly with him on this aircraft and stated that this could very well be the last opportunity for her to fly with him to Honolulu. She said that he seemed to have a premonition that something was going to happen to him and that he wanted to give her his house and to sign documents bringing about this transfer. On October 10 or 20, we cannot read the date, Crosthwaite wrote the company a letter and said his new dependent is Marie Crosthwaite, his mother, and that she will take over his house. Now as to the circumstances of the crash itself, if we were to take these facts and interpret anything from them there is the point that if Mr. Crosthwaite wanted to destroy the airplane he was in a perfect position to do that in that he could bring anything he wanted aboard the airplane in his personal luggage. There is also the interesting fact that the airplane was destroyed in the middle of its journey—just after the point of no return. It also happened just after a radio report. Again, if it was a planned matter, he had almost one week in which to plan it. He was off flight on October 30 and advised on

October 31 that his next flight would be Flight 7 on November 8," Locke concludes.

"I can understand why you would have suspicions along these lines," Payton acknowledges.

"That's true. So many things have led to this man that I think we couldn't do anything but give it a complete checkout, and since you were going to have a discussion with the FBI it was believed that it would be best that you have this information available," Locke offers.

"All right. I sure do thank you. I assure you that we will follow through."

* * *

Later that afternoon, Hoover receives a staff memo outlining the suspicious circumstances involving Crosthwaite. In a separate correspondence, Pan Am asks the FBI to "check for any police record in Hong Kong" on Crosthwaite, an apparent reference to suspicions that he may have been involved in some type of smuggling in the past, among other things.

So far, Crosthwaite name has not been mentioned in the press as a possible suspect, and no one—outside of his immediate family—is aware that he is being investigated by Pan Am and the CAB.

Crosthwaite name will not surface publicly as a suspect for more than forty years, when I first learn about his possible involvement.

Even faced with the strange circumstances surrounding Crosthwaite, Hoover refuses to budge: the FBI will not lift a finger to help the probe until it has some "evidence" the plane has been sabotaged.

FRIDAY, NOVEMBER 22, 1957
WASHINGTON, D.C.

Members of the Overseas Missionary Society are among those gathered today inside the intimate Bethlehem Chapel of the historic Washington National Cathedral, a sacred place where US presidents and the most honored people of the nation have been memorialized. The limestone altar depicts the birth of Jesus, and the arched ceilings and tall columns bring a breath of life to the place, where memorial services are underway for plane-crash victims Philip Beach Sullivan and Bess Lipscomb Sullivan of nearby Arlington, Virginia.

The Reverends George F. Tittman and Lloyd Craighill remember the Sullivans as dedicated Christians whose lifestyles and actions made the world a better place. Their dedication to helping to modernize China and the personal interest they took in students and ordinary citizens of that nation are remembered with fondness and appreciation.

Mrs. Sullivan's body has not been recovered from the ocean, but Mr. Sullivan's remains will be placed in a cathedral crypt a few days from now, a place reserved for people of not only high honor, but also unquestioned patriotism and selfless Christian values.

SATURDAY, NOVEMBER 23, 1957
FELTON, CALIFORNIA

It's a short drive from the Gene Crosthwaite home on Hillside Drive in Felton to the Wessendorf Mortuary on Church Street, where the Crosthwaite family is gathering for the 8:20 a.m. funeral of Oliver Eugene Crosthwaite. Tania and her grandmother and stepgrandfather are accompanied to the mortuary by Tania's godparents, Kenneth and Helen Miller of San Francisco. Mr. Miller, an ordnance engineer at Hunter's Point Naval Shipyard, has been a friend of the Crosthwaites since they were neighbors on Casanova Drive in San Mateo several years ago.

What remains of the purser's shark-ripped body is inside a closed casket.

After the service at the mortuary, the family will travel to a requiem high mass at St. John's Catholic Church in Felton, and then on to the cemetery at Santa Cruz Memorial Park, where Crosthwaite's body will be placed in a mausoleum.

Getting to St. John's Catholic Church is easy enough, but for some strange reason the procession is being delayed. A disagreement of some sort is occurring between Crosthwaite's mother and the funeral directors.

Shortly after 9 a.m., Oliver Eugene Crosthwaite's body is finally placed in a mausoleum at Santa Cruz Memorial Park, and before everyone goes their separate ways something strange occurs between Tania and Crosthwaite's mother, a woman Tania doesn't even know. It will be more than sixty years before Tania explains what happened.

Midland, Michigan, is a company town, and this morning it seems like everyone in town is inside the sanctuary of Memorial Presbyterian Church to remember the Lee Clack Family. Earlier this morning a short burial service for Ann Carter Clack and Scott Clack had been held at Midland Cemetery. The bodies of the rest of the Clacks are still lost somewhere in the Pacific.

"We have gathered here, dear friends, to worship God, to share with one another a common sorrow and to offer a last corporate tribute of affection and esteem to the Lee Clack family, so dearly beloved by relatives and friends," the pastor tells the mournful gathering.

". . . you who numbered Lee and Ann among your friends will always have the cherished memory of a couple who were endowed with life's finest traits—faith, love, honor, kindness, cheerfulness, and generosity. They were sensitive to the beautiful, drinking deeply at the fountains of music and art. They radiated the joy of life that came from living out, in daily life, the great Christian ideals."

A strong wind and cold morning rain beat against the colorful panes of the magnificent church's stained-glass windows as the pastor tells the congregated grievers that the worldly Clacks were "free from crippling prejudices and unhampered by narrow provincialisms."

He says the Clacks were held in high esteem by not only the Dow Chemical family, but also the many people whose lives they had touched in Japan. He reminds everyone that Lee and Ann were devoted and loving parents of four, including the two little girls they had adopted.

"Four little children to the world were given, to bud on earth, to bloom in heaven."

On Friday, November 29, *Time* magazine correspondent and veteran journalist Walter Harrison Lilly Jr. pulls up a chair in the office of Richard Dexter, FBI special agent in charge of the Chicago office and one of director Hoover's most trusted and loyal agents. The forty-six-year-old Dexter is also known to be one of Hoover's commie hunters and is a former member of the Special Intelligence Service, a covert FBI organization created in June 1940 by then-president Franklin Delano Roosevelt to keep an eye on Axis activities in Central and South America.

Lilly wants to know if the FBI is working on the crash of the lost Pan American Clipper, a strange question coming from a Chicago reporter thousands of miles away from where the news is happening.

"No, not to my knowledge. We're not involved in the investigation. Why do you ask?"

"I'm working on a story that the purser on the plane, a man by the name of Crosthwaite, was to have been fired by Pan Am, but the union got involved and pressured Pan Am to keep him on the payroll."

Dexter listens closely but, like everyone else in the FBI, is keenly aware of Hoover's insistence that the agency not be dragged into the investigation.

"What we're hearing is that Crosthwaite had a fight with the captain and somehow that caused the crash," the reporter volunteers.

"Even if that were true, which I haven't heard, we wouldn't get involved, because without actual proof of a crime we have no jurisdiction," Dexter replies.

Offering no more information about Crosthwaite or the crash, and with no help from Dexter in getting his story, reporter Lilly moves on, "confidentially" informing the FBI agent that he is a member of a group at *Time* magazine investigating emerging civil rights activities in the South.

This really gets Dexter's attention because he knows Hoover is concerned about what he believes to be communist influence in civil rights activities. Reporter Lilly leaves the agent's office, and Dexter immediately picks up the phone to pass on to Hoover's right-hand man,

Nease, what the reporter has just told him about Crosthwaite and the civil rights issue.

"Lilly told me that a staff group of *Time, Life,* and *Fortune* magazines are going to Little Rock this weekend as an undercover group to see how things are progressing there, since the National Guard has taken over," he tells Nease.

Two months earlier, violence had erupted in Little Rock over the integration of Central High School and President Dwight D. Eisenhower had placed the state's National Guard under federal control to restore order in the city and to force integration of the school. On September 25, 1957, nine black students enrolled in Central High School under the protection of the United States Army.

"He said they were going to do a big integration series as a result of the Little Rock situation and that they have been riding the Southern trains into Chicago, and specifically mentioned the Illinois Central, to see how they are handling the integration problem."

Like agent Dexter before him, Nease ignores what he is told about Crosthwaite and before he leaves for the afternoon recommends that the FBI's Investigation Division consider the "advisability of notifying the Little Rock office" about the undercover group of journalists.

"Yes!" director Hoover scribbles on the memo as soon as it crosses his desk the next morning, and agents in Little Rock are informed about the impending magazine report.

Once again, Crosthwaite gets no attention from the nation's top criminal investigator.

On Sunday evening, CAB investigator Claude Marvin Schonberger arrives in San Francisco from Washington to begin a more formal investigation of Crosthwaite. The thirty-four-year-old Schonberger, a George Washington University graduate, is not a trained aviation or criminal investigator and until recently had been executive assistant to Sen. William Langer of North Dakota, handling agriculture matters for the lawmaker. Prior to that he had spent eighteen months on the staff of the Kefauver Juvenile Delinquency Committee, investigating pornographic literature and the sale of babies in the black market.

He seems somewhat of a strange choice to be a key player in helping to solve an aviation crash mystery, but Schonberger also has an impressive aviation background.

As a lieutenant in the US Army Air Corps during World War II, he flew dangerous bombing missions over Germany in a B-24 Liberator, and during a final run against the Obertraubling airdome near Regensburg, his bomb-laden aircraft was hit by enemy fire and two engines were crippled. Despite the in-air crisis, Schonberger continued his bombing run and remarkably hit all of his intended targets with amazing accuracy.

That alone demonstrated his courage and flying skills, but less than two weeks later—and more than a dozen bombing missions after the Regensburg incident—his plane was shot down on a bombing mission near the Brenner Pass in Italy, close to the snow-covered alps at the Austrian border. He safely parachuted out of the falling plane, but was captured by the Nazis on February 28, 1945, and held in the notorious Stalag Luft XIII in Nuremberg until the end of the war.

Schonberger may not be a trained investigator, but he knows a thing or two about aviation—and people. He will be the lead man in the early investigation, mentored by fifteen-year veteran CAB air-safety investigator Charles S. Collar, flown in from Miami. The fifty-six-year-old Collar is a legend in aviation—a former Navy airman and test pilot who began his flying career as a teenage barnstormer and rumrunner during Prohibition. He knows aviation inside out, but doing an extensive background check on Crosthwaite without the eyes, ears, experience, and resources of the FBI will be a tough undertaking.

Schonberger and Collar methodically plan who they will interview and how they will pursue the case in the coming days. Separately and together, they will interview Pan Am colleagues, friends, and acquaintances of Crosthwaite, and talk with his doctors at the TB sanatorium in Redwood City. They will develop a forty-one-item checklist that includes everything from Crosthwaite's medical records and work history to where he bought his booze and how active he was in the union. Although they are working under tremendous pressure, they don't want to miss anything, and their time in California is limited; they must make good use of every minute.

At six foot four Schonberger is a towering and impressive figure—some might even say intimidating, if only because of his height. The intimidation factor may assist him in obtaining information in the coming days, and he is fully aware of that. Sometimes all he has to do is look firmly at someone to get them to suddenly remember things.

Born on a family farm, Schonberger learned about not only the land, but also about people, from his father, a past chairman of the North Dakota Federation of Labor and a leader in farming issues. The younger Schonberger is a quick learner and has inherited many of his father's people skills. He is on a career fast track at the CAB and knows that this investigation is critical not only on its face, but also for how it might help him advance in the agency.

Collar and Schonberger make a good combination. Collar is a little rougher around the edges; his approach more direct. Schonberger is more of a smooth talker and a better listener. They are the classic "good cop-bad cop."

It doesn't take the team long to realize that the information Pan Am's legal officer, Locke, recently passed on to their CAB superiors about Crosthwaite is not only accurate, but in some ways making their work a bit easier.

It's clear after their first day on the streets that there are two Gene Crosthwaites.

Crosthwaite number one is a person who is considered by some to be a "regular American," a fine family man, a good purser who likes his job, and a normal guy who mixes well with others.

Crosthwaite number two is a blowhard with a so-so job performance who always blames someone else when something goes wrong. He is insincere, a nutcase, a bully. He's paranoid and on the edge of a total breakdown.

Investigator Schonberger first learns about Crosthwaite number two when he interviews John Huston, a Pan Am purser who lived with Crosthwaite for several months when both were in Hong Kong.

"Tell me about his family, what you know about children, his relationships," Schonberger says to Huston.

"Well, he may have a son, but he only had one daughter."

G O N E   T O   E T E R N A L   R E S T

"A son?"

"Well, I'm not sure. He may not have."

"And only one daughter?"

"The other one is adopted, but he never mentioned her. You wouldn't even know she existed. I read his obituary in the paper the other day and it said he had some brothers. I thought that was weird because he never mentioned them either. Come to mention it, he never even talked about his mother. I also thought it was kinda strange about them having that Catholic service for him. I didn't know he even had any religion."

"You lived with him for what, two, three months?"

"Yeah, when we were in Hong Kong."

"What about his work performance? What do you know about the kind of job he did?"

"Well, he knew how to do his job, I know that. But his service was erratic. I've heard other crew members complain about him. He bragged a lot, and he wasn't liked much by anyone that I know of at Pan Am. I've heard tell that he was involved in something illegal while he was in Hong Kong, but I don't know about that. They say he has some enemies over there and that might be why Pan Am sent him back to California, but I don't know that either."

Schonberger learns even more about Crosthwaite number two when he interviews John Campbell, an insurance broker and former Pan Am employee. Campbell had written the insurance policies on Crosthwaite's house, furniture, and car.

"His wife had a better credit rating than he did. I always thought that was kind of strange. I mean, she never had a full-time job that I know of and didn't make anywhere near as much as he did."

"Tell me about his personality. What was he like?" Schonberger asks.

"Well, the last time I saw him was about two months before the crash. Ever since he was in the hospital for TB, he was a screwball."

"What do you mean?" asks Collar.

"Well, it's hard to say exactly. He just didn't seem to be the same. He wasn't sincere or anything. He was just kind of like a weirdo, a screwball. I don't know."

Crosthwaite number one comes solidly into the picture when the investigators drive up to Palo Alto and speak with Jim Scanlon, a Pan Am pilot who had flown with Crosthwaite numerous times in the past couple of years.

"He was a good purser. Had a strong personality. You know his wife died a few months ago, don't you? He said he was kinda glad to see her go because she was out of pain," Scanlon tells the investigators.

"Did he ever say anything bad about Pan Am?" Collar asks him.

"Not that I know of. I think he had a good attitude towards the company. He seemed like a regular guy."

As Schonberger and Collar continue to interview the people on their checklist, they are puzzled by what they are learning—and not learning. After talking with more than a dozen people they still don't understand who Crosthwaite is. They decide that it's time to visit that cop in Santa Cruz who told the fellow from Pan Am that Crosthwaite was a psycho.

The investigators meet with Sgt. Herbert G. Johnson in the annex of the Santa Cruz Courthouse—the same office where Crosthwaite had been speaking in circles a few weeks earlier.

"He was badly disturbed," Sergeant Johnson tells the investigators. "Twitching all the time. Talking out of his head. Frankly, I couldn't understand what he was trying to say. He just rambled and rambled."

Johnson then tells them essentially the same story the CAB had given to the FBI in the unsuccessful attempt to get Hoover involved: Crosthwaite was paranoid. He was depressed. Pan Am was trying to get rid of him. His daughter was responsible for his wife's death.

Finally, it's time to talk with Crosthwaite's family, starting with his mother, Mary. They drive to Stockton, where she weaves them a story about the good Gene—Crosthwaite number one.

She tells them he had a happy childhood except for that time he fell off a burro and hurt his head.

"He had bad headaches for years after that. They'd come and go. He wasn't bedridden with them or anything, though."

"Was he still having headaches?" Collar asks.

"I'm not really sure. They might have gone away the past few years, but I don't know."

"Did you see him much? Did he come and visit you often?" Schonberger asks.

"Well, he was out of the country a lot, you know. I really haven't heard from him much in the past ten years or so, but I did go to visit him when he was in the TB hospital."

"When was the last time you saw him?" Schonberger asks. "Did you notice anything different about him?'

"It was the twelfth of August. I wrote it on my calendar. No, he didn't seem any different to me."

She goes on to tell the investigators how devoted he was to Julia, his late wife.

"He seemed real happy until Julia died. He called me the Monday before his last flight and said, 'Mother, I've never been able to do anything for you. I'd like to take you on a vacation to Honolulu.' You know, he loved to fly. He was real happy with his job. I don't know. Maybe he had a premonition of some kind that he wasn't going to be flying much more."

They leave her home with more questions in their heads, but they have established two things: Crosthwaite number one was an all-American boy. And Crosthwaite number two? Well, he seemed to be something of a devil.

Collar and Schonberger interview numerous people over the next several days, then head to Felton as their investigation winds down. It's time to talk with Crosthwaite's stepdaughter, Tania, and to then search Crosthwaite's house for any clues that might help them determine if he sabotaged the plane.

Tania is still somewhat in a state of shock when they knock on the door. She's lost her mother and her stepfather in a period of just three months, and the sixteen-year-old is worried about how she is going to cope. No job. No hope of a job. A grandmother who speaks little English, and no stepfather to put a roof over their heads and food on their table.

The investigators identify themselves and are cordial, but professional. Tania is scared stiff and answers their questions, but doesn't offer anything else. A lot of yesses and nos. If asked, she answers directly and succinctly, offering nothing more. It's not that she's trying to deceive the CAB investigators, it's just that she is so afraid of what tomorrow might bring if she says the wrong things.

She tells the investigators some chilling details about her stepfather—Crosthwaite number two—and the information she shares further deepens their suspicions about the purser. She says that Crosthwaite believed that Pan Am was planning to fire him, he was depressed, mean, and downright angry. He kept his bedroom door locked and was gloomy all the time.

The investigators also talk with her stepgrandfather, Peter Stub, and what he tells them further strengthens the mounting case against Crosthwaite as a possible suicidal murderer:

Stub tells them that completely out of the blue a few days before the crash, Crosthwaite showed him some blasting powder. Stub says he thought that was strange because they could have used the powder earlier to blow up some stumps in the yard that had since been removed. Stub says he asked Crosthwaite why didn't he get the powder when they could have used it, but he didn't respond.

A day or so later Schonberger and Collar return to the Crosthwaite house and tear it apart in a futile search for the blasting powder — some evidence that might help them solve the mystery.

The blasting powder is never found.

Collar and Schonberger don't bother to talk with Crosthwaite's Russian mother-in-law or even his sisters or brothers. Maybe the language barrier was too much for the investigators to cross with his mother-in-law, but Tania had often acted as her translator and could have done so for the CAB men if they had asked. Why they don't interview his siblings could be as simple as the fact that they didn't live anywhere near the San Francisco Bay Area and time was running out on their mission.

On Saturday, December 14, 1957, the investigators return to the house in Felton, where Tania and Stub sign statements based upon what they had told the investigators a few days earlier:

SWORN STATEMENT
TANIA CROSTHWAITE

I am the daughter by adoption of Oliver Eugene Crosthwaite. I was born in Shanghai, China, on December 11, 1940. My mother who died on August 12, 1957 was Julia C. Crosthwaite, the second wife of Oliver Eugene Crosthwaite. My real father's name was Korning Fabrena who disappeared during World War II while serving with the Russian Army. After my stepfather married my mother on January 21, 1947 in Shanghai, China, they preceded me to the United States. Because of passport difficulties, I followed them to the United States later and was adopted by my stepfather February 7, 1949, County of San Mateo court action number 47658. All the time I have known my stepfather he has been employed by Pan American World Airways and as a result of this employment, we traveled to China several times. Since returning from China in 1956, we have lived in our present home on Hillside Drive in Felton, California.

My stepfather contracted tuberculosis in 1955 and entered the San Mateo County Sanitorium located at 200 Edmonds Road, Redwood City, California, on October 22, 1955. He was discharged from the sanatorium April 12, 1956 as an arrested case of TB. Prior to entering the TB Sanitorium, my stepfather was normal and only the usual stepfather relationship existed. However, following his release from the TB Sanitorium, he appeared to be an entirely different man, both physically and mentally.

He gained about sixty pounds and became most difficult to live with. The slightest unusual incident on either my mother's or my part would cause him to become most upset and angry. After my mother died of cancer, he became even more unbearable and accused me of causing my mother's death because of worry over my actions. He would keep the bedroom door to his room locked constantly. At one time, he even tried to have me committed to a disciplinary institution. Just prior to his last flight, we used to have many severe arguments and during one of these, he even threatened to disinherit me.

Just four days before leaving on his last flight, he gathered many of the papers in his desk and drawer and burned them. My grandmother, by protesting, prevented him from burning my adoption papers at that time.

My stepfather never was a devout Catholic, but he always wore a cross suspended from a chain around his neck. After his death, we found he had a safety-deposit box in the Bank of America in Santa Cruz. And in this box was this chain and cross wrapped around my mother's and stepfather's wedding rings.

Other items in this box consisted of four insurance policies: one for $1,000 insuring me; one for $3,000 insuring my father; one fire and lightning policy insuring our house; and one policy on our auto. Only three other packages were in the box and they contained my mother's jewelry.

On the day my father left for his last flight, he left the house at 0730 or 0745 in the morning. He carried two suitcases, a gladstone bag, a valet pack, and a briefcase. My grandmother says he always carries these bags on trips.

My stepfather and my grandfather built our home and my stepfather did much of the electrical wiring and the plumbing in the house. My stepfather liked to make things. He had a shop near the house and liked to make gadgets.

At one time I heard my stepfather express the opinion that he thought Pan American World Airways was trying to fire him from his job.

During his off-duty time, my stepfather usually was gone from the house and did not seem to have too many friends.

(Signed)
Tania Crosthwaite
Witness: Claude M. Schonberger

Stub's statement mirrors much of Tania's but goes into detail about the blasting powder that has mysteriously disappeared:

SWORN STATEMENT
PETER STUB

I married Katherine Stub whose daughter was the former wife of Oliver Eugene Crosthwaite. Gene and I did most of the work in building our home on Hillside Avenue, Felton, California.

During the whole week before Gene left on his last flight, he spent all his time here at home working on the plumbing in our home.

About the 1st or 2nd of November, just before Gene left on his last flight, he called me to the house from the yard where I was about to wash my car and said, "Look what I have." Gene had a few small pieces or grains of granular blasting powder consisting of about 20 pieces cupped in his hand. Gene stated this blasting powder was what he had meant when he earlier mentioned an explosive for blasting stumps in our yard. I said it was too late now to use this because our land is already cleared and asked him why he didn't get the blasting powder earlier when we could have used it. Gene didn't answer. Gene returned to some plumbing work he was doing in the basement of our home and then I started to wash my car.

I don't know where Gene got the blasting powder or where it is now. We have looked and searched the basement and Gene's workshop with the two Civil Aeronautics Board men who were here but could find no trace of the blasting powder.

(Signed)
Peter Stub
Witness: Claude M. Schonberger
C.S. Collar

The investigators are on to something big.

The disclosure about the blasting powder and the fact that no trace of it can be found are the best clues yet to strengthen a possible case of sabotage against Crosthwaite. But they need more—much more. A day or so later Schonberger and other officials open the glove compartment of the purser's car, parked near the airport, and discover this:

LAST WILL AND TESTAMENT OF
OLIVER EUGENE CROSTHWAITE

IN THE NAME OF GOD, AMEN:

I, OLIVER EUGENE CROSTHWAITE, a resident of Felton, County of Santa Cruz, State of California, being over the age of twenty-one years and of sound and disposing mind and memory and not acting under duress, menace, fraud or the undue influence of any person whomsoever, do hereby make, publish and declare this to be my Last Will and Testament.

FIRST: I hereby revoke all other and/or former wills and/or codicils to wills by me made.

SECOND: I hereby direct my Executor hereinafter named to pay all my just debts and funeral expenses as soon after my death as can conveniently be done.

THIRD: I hereby declare that I have been twice married; that my first wife was THELMA MAY CROSTHWAITE and that we were divorced by Final Decree of Divorce in that certain action entitled *"In the Superior Court of the State of California, in and for the County of San Mateo; Thelma May Crosthwaite, Plaintiff, vs. Oliver Eugene Crosthwaite, Defendant; No. 36998,"* on November 19, 1945. I further declare that there was one child the issue of this marriage, to-wit, BILLIE JOANN CROSTHWAITE WITHROW, residing in Modesto, California.

I further declare that my second wife was JULIA MIHAILOVNA PAVLICHENKO CROSTHWAITE and that she is dead, having died on August 12, 1957, and that under date of February 7, 1949, I adopted the said TATIANA PAVLICHENKO as my child and that she is now known as TATIANA EUGENE CROSTHWAITE, and that said adoption was made by order of Court. She was adopted in that certain action entitled "In the Superior Court of the State of California, County of San Mateo; In the Matter of the Adoption of TATIANA PAVLICHENKO, a Minor; No. 47658," and that the said TATIANA PAVLICHENKO, now known as TATIANA EUGENE CROSTHWAITE is of the age of sixteen years, having been born on December 11, 1940, in Shanghai, China.

FOURTH: *I hereby give, devise and bequeath all of my estate, whether the same be real, personal or mixed, of whatever kind or character and wheresoever situated, of which I may die seized or possessed or in which I may have any interest or right of testamentary disposition or power at the time of my death, as follows:*

A. *One-half (1/2) thereof to my daughter, BILLIE JOANN CROSTHWAITE WITHROW, or, if in the event she predeceases me, then the interest hereby devised to my said daughter, BILLIE JOANN CROSTHWAITE WITHROW, to her daughter, JACKIE LYNN WITHROW, and to any issue of my said daughter, BILLIE JOANN CROSTHWAITE WITHROW, living at the time of my death, share and share alike; and*

B. *The remaining one-half (1/2) of my estate to my daughter,*

TATIANA EUGENE CROSTHWAITE; subject, however, to the following conditions:

1. That she not be married before attaining the age of twenty-one years; and

2. That if she has married after attaining the age of twenty-one years, that said marriage has been performed in and sanctioned by the Roman Catholic Church.

If either or both of the exceptions 1. and 2. of subparagraph B hereof have not been complied with, then and in that event, I hereby give, devise and bequeath the interest in my estate which I have bequeathed to my daughter, TATIANA EUGENE CROSTHWAITE, to my daughter, BILLIE JOANN CROSTHWAITE WITHROW, in accordance with subparagraph A hereof.

FIFTH: I hereby appoint BANK OF AMERICA NATIONAL TRUST AND SAVINGS ASSOCIATION Executor of this my Last Will and Testament, and in the event of my death prior to the attainment by my daughter, TATIANA EUGENE CROSTHWAITE, of the age of 21, I appoint BANK OF AMERICA NATIONAL TRUST AND SAVINGS ASSOCIATION Guardian of the estate of my daughter, TATIANA EUGENE CROSTHWAITE.

SIXTH: I have purposely made no provision for any other person or persons, whether claiming to be an heir of mine or not, and if any person, whether a beneficiary under this will or not mentioned herein, should contest this will or object to the provisions thereof, I give to such person so contesting or objecting the sum of One Dollar ($1.00), in lieu of the provision which I have made or might have made for the person contesting or objecting.

SEVENTH: I hereby authorize and empower my Executor to sell and dispose of any and all of my property, real or personal, wherever situate and however held, either at public or private sale, without notice or without approval of court, at any such times and upon such terms as it may, in its sole discretion, deem advisable; to execute any and all required instruments and documents; to settle and compromise any claims, either in favor of or against my estate, in accordance with its sole discretion; to distribute in kind or in money, or part in each, even if shares be composed differently; and generally, without notice, authorization or approval of any court, to do anything and everything it shall deem advisable, even though it would not be authorized or appropriate for fiduciaries (except for this specific power) under any statute or rule of law.

IN WITNESS WHEREOF, I have hereunto set my hand this 8th Day of November, 1957.

(Signed)
OLIVER EUGENE CROSTHWAITE

What more could the FBI want from the CAB to open an investigation? Here was a man with motive: depression over his wife's death, depression and despair over his relationship with his daughter, and anger at Pan American for wanting to fire him.

Here was a man with opportunity: he boarded the plane long before passengers, knew he was going on the flight more than a week in advance, and could carry anything in his luggage with no one checking. He had unrestricted access to any location on the plane.

Here was a man with knowledge: He knew when the plane would reach the point of no return, was a gadget maker, knew explosives and electricity, had been in possession of blasting powder, and knew what it would take to knock the airliner from the sky.

Finally, he signed his will the morning the flight left San Francisco to exclude his stepdaughter from his estate unless she did as she was told.

Although Collar and Schonberger learned a great deal about Crosthwaite while in California, they spent only four days on their investigation, and what they learned was not enough to persuade Hoover to put his FBI agents on the case or for them to convince higher-ups at the CAB to devote more time and resources to the purser.

CAB and Pan Am continued to drift.

Fifty-three-year-old Millbrae resident Emil Jacob Sorensen has no clue that his former employer has listed him as a suspect in the possible bombing of Flight 7, but his name has been sent to the FBI for a thorough background check. Pan American and Civil Aeronautics Board officials are now zeroing in on two people of interest: Oliver Eugene Crosthwaite and Sorensen.

Officially and publicly the FBI is still not involved in the investigation of the crash, but behind the scenes field agents in California and some senior officers in Washington, including domestic intelligence chief Alan H. Belmont and the eagle-eyed Hoover himself, are monitoring what they are learning from Pan Am, the CAB, and Hoover's carefully cultivated stooges in the press.

Sorensen, a port steward with Pan Am for about six years, is appealing his August 2 firing for "physical incapacity," and while there is no indication that he has had any involvement in the plane crash, Pan Am wants to alert the FBI of the possibility. The fact that he is Russian born makes him even more suspicious. Pan Am doesn't know it, but the FBI is already aware of Sorensen—not as a sabotage suspect, but as a possible communist sympathizer or worse still, a full-fledged communist.

The FBI had opened a file on him in November 1950 on the authority of the McCarran Internal Security Act, or, as it was more commonly known, the Subversive Activities Control Act. President Harry S. Truman vetoed the bill, calling it "a mockery of the Bill of Rights," but the Red Scare-sensitive politicians in the Congress overrode the veto, and the witch hunt for subversives or suspected communists was well underway. The act gives law enforcement authority for the mass roundup of political dissidents and allows it to detain suspected communists indefinitely without trial.

Sorensen was born in the Kuban River city of Krasnodar in southwestern Russia on April 11, 1904, grew up in Denmark, and has spent nearly all his adult life working on cargo steamships along a northern Europe-US route. He has also temporarily worked as a hotel waiter on some of his long-term visits to the United States. He joined Pan American in 1951 and almost immediately applied to the Immigration and Naturalization Service to become a naturalized citizen. Available records indicate that his request for naturalization was on hold until February 1956, likely because of the FBI's interest in him.

The FBI started its investigation of Sorensen based on information it had obtained from a confidential source who had met him when he was working as a waiter in a Washington, D.C., restaurant.

"He appeared to be extremely interested in cities in the United States where large industrial factories were located, specifically Buffalo, New York and Los Angeles," FBI records sate. "For some strange reason he was also interested in knowing whether Army tanks were made in Buffalo."

The next sentence in an FBI document goes to the heart of the agency's concerns about Sorensen: "Information is in file to the effect that Sorensen said he was a communist."

The FBI file redacted large portions of the next section of its comments on Sorensen, but noted that he had been subpoenaed to appear before a supersecret federal grand jury in the Northern District of California for an undisclosed reason. Sorensen told the grand jurors he went to work for Pan Am because it allowed him to travel at greatly reduced fare, "thereby making it easier for him to return to his home in Denmark on occasion." In fact, Sorensen has made many trips back to northern Europe in the years since joining Pan Am.

The file stated that he was cooperative and furnished "detailed personal information" to the grand jurors, who apparently were trying to determine whether he should be arrested. He denied under oath that he was a communist, and apparently the grand jury believed him; Sorensen was not detained, and never seriously considered as a suspect in sabotaging Flight 7.

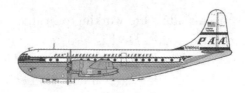

8

DADDY'S NOT COMING HOME

MY MOTHER DISAPPROVINGLY CALLS THEM "bang-bang-shoot-'em-ups," and I have seen enough black-and-white westerns in my young life to know that when the good guys die their bodies are placed inside wooden caskets, lowered into graves, and covered with dirt as sad townspeople stand around with gloomy faces.

This doesn't feel like a "bang-bang-shoot-'em-up" to me.

My mother, my brothers, and I walk slowly down the carpeted center aisle of Shoreview Community Methodist Church on Lindbergh Street in San Mateo shortly after 4 p.m. on Sunday, December 1, the appointed time and date for what I have been told will be something called a memorial service. Mom is unusually strong today, and for the first time in weeks I see no tears rolling down her face.

There is an uneasy, quiet shuffling in the sanctuary, and for some reason people stand and stare blankly as we walk by. A tall, handsome Pan Am pilot dressed in a crisp black uniform with gold stripes on his coat sleeves towers over the others in a right-side pew. He nods and smiles weakly as we make our way to the front of the church. My mother must know him, because she looks his way and nods back.

A hymn is playing on the church's new organ, and I recognize the faces of J. Paul Coleman and Paul Nelson, both of whom are standing solemnly near the pulpit, their arms folded in front of them with that "preacher look" on their faces. Both pastors have been at our house many times during the past several weeks trying to soothe and comfort us during the worst days of our lives. Seeing their familiar faces is somewhat reassuring, but it is still a bleak and depressing scene in a place that I normally associate with interesting stories and good times.

This is where I have heard exciting Sunday-school stories about a white-bearded old man named Noah and his gigantic floating boat filled with animals during a big flood. It is where I learned about Jonah being swallowed by a whale, and about the miraculous birth of the baby Jesus. This is where I have molded clay in my little hands, created scrapbooks from colored construction paper, and have sung "Jesus Loves the Little Children" and "This Little Light of Mine" so many times I know both by heart.

This sanctuary is where I have heard our pastor talk about miracles and something called eternal life, but on this day there are no miracles or eternal life, only the shadow of death. Yet, this is our church. We belong here today, even though the most important member of our family is not here.

An usher leads us to the first pew at the front left of the church, and Jerry and I slide down the polished wood and into our places. My mother gently places two-year-old Craig down beside her and brushes his blonde curls away from his chubby, pink face. Daddy calls him "Little Man," but he has just started walking, has no idea why he is here, and is certainly no Little Man today. It is past Craig's nap time, and he lays his head down on Mom's lap as she turns her face to the left and softly smiles at Jerry and me. We can feel her love even as the tears finally start to fall from her face and turn into tiny black streams of mascara. Her big, brown eyes—usually sparkling like stars over Disneyland and full of life—are sad. She looks worried.

She is surrounded by a roomful of people, but she is alone.

We are all alone.

I glance at a wooden table in front of where the pastors are standing.

It is piled high with pretty flowers—white lilies and red carnations—and is inscribed with the words "This Do in Remembrance of Me." For the first time since we walked into the sanctuary, I realize there is no casket.

This "bang-bang-shoot-'em-up" is real, but the ending is not what I am expecting.

Songs are sung. Prayers are prayed. Words are spoken about the wonderful, loving daddy we will never see again. I look at the mimeographed, Carolina-blue memorial-service program that was handed to us as we entered the church and I slowly read the words to myself, trying to understand what they mean:

"I cannot think of them as dead who walk with me no more
"Along the paths of life I tread, they have but gone before."

Then, it's over.

No casket. No grave. No dirt. No tearful farewells as we walk away from a final resting place high on a western hill. Daddy's casket is the crumpled cockpit of a Boeing Stratocruiser. His watery grave is at the bottom of the Pacific Ocean, and his final resting place is thousands of miles away from us, a place we will never see, a grave we will never visit.

Someone drives us home to a house that is not nearly as full of people as it had been for the past several weeks, and by nightfall reality sets in. The people leave. The house grows quiet. Mom puts Craig to bed, and not long afterward she tells Jerry and me it's time for us to go to bed too. She tucks Jerry in and kisses him good night. He's older and tougher than I am. He keeps his heartbreak inside, but his eyes show his deep pain.

Mom then walks over to my bed and kisses me on the forehead. It feels good, but it's not the scratchy feel of Daddy's whiskers. I feel that lump in my throat—that lump that seems to never go away—and it grows even bigger as she slips out of our bedroom.

It nearly chokes me.

I close my eyes. Tighter. Tighter. Then I see Daddy's face as plain as day. I see that big, wide, toothy smile, and he looks directly at me with his deep-blue eyes. It is a sunny day with a clear sky and a few puffy white clouds. He is wearing flowery colored swim trunks and is on a beautiful island with tall coconut trees behind him. Daddy loves coconuts. He tries to reassure me and tells me that he is OK and that he will be home soon.

I try to believe him, but I just can't.
I cry. And cry. And cry.

WASHINGTON, D.C.

The Civil Aeronautics Board is in a bind and under considerable pressure to determine the cause of the crash of N90944. It is now Tuesday, December 3, and nearly a month has passed since the airliner plummeted to the bottom of the ocean, and the CAB is no closer to solving the case today than it was weeks ago.

Sixty-year-old board chairman James Randall Durfee, a Wisconsin lawyer appointed by President Dwight Eisenhower to the role just a year earlier, has just concluded a meeting of the CAB and has been instructed to contact FBI director Hoover or Attorney General William Rogers in another attempt to persuade the agency to enter the crash investigation. Durfee makes a phone call to Hoover's office and learns that he is out of town, but three senior FBI officials, including J. A. Sizoo of the Domestic Intelligence Division, meet later that day in Durfee's office in the Commerce Department building and listen to his urgent plea.

Durfee briefly reviews the facts of the case and gets right to the point. He tells the FBI agents that the CAB is in an "awkward position" because it cannot determine why the plane went down and is under tremendous pressure from the press and members of Congress for a solution. He acknowledges that no new facts have arisen since the CAB made its last futile attempt, on November 21, to get the FBI involved, but states that the CAB is stumped and desperately needs the FBI's professional investigative assistance.

The FBI agents patiently listen to his request, but they understand what Hoover has directed: do not under any circumstances let the FBI get dragged into this case.

Durfee says that the only suspicious circumstances they have uncovered concern purser Crosthwaite, whom the CAB had asked the FBI to conduct a full background check on several weeks earlier. Durfee points out once again that Crosthwaite's wife had recently died, he had suffered from tuberculosis, was having difficulty controlling his teenage stepdaughter, had recently changed his will, and was having job difficulties with Pan Am. Durfee also notes that a law enforcement officer in Santa Cruz County had described Crosthwaite as a "psycho."

His pleas are falling on deaf ears.

Durfee formally renews his request for the FBI to investigate Crosthwaite, adding that the CAB doesn't have any investigators qualified to handle a case of this magnitude and mystery.

One of the senior FBI men tells Durfee that all the facts have been reviewed and evaluated by the Bureau and that Hoover himself is fully aware of the details.

The FBI will not get involved.

CAB executive director Robert Lowe Kunzig has been listening quietly as Durfee and the FBI men play a game of political chess, and he's had enough. A respected lawyer and former prosecutor of Nazi war criminals at Nuremberg, Kunzig understands politics and knows what it takes to build a case—politically or criminally. He is a former deputy attorney general of Pennsylvania, and he doesn't mince words. He tells the FBI men that it is absolutely critical that the agency enter the probe. He drops names, including that of powerful US Senator Mike Monroney, an Oklahoma Democrat and former crime reporter who, Kunzig says, has been reading in the press about the FBI "doing this and that," but nothing about what the CAB has been doing. Monroney is chairman of the Senate Aviation Subcommittee and is known by his colleagues as Mr. Aviation.

Kunzig says the CAB does not want to be in a position to publicly admit that it cannot solve the case and cannot convince the FBI to assist in the investigation.

He gets nowhere.

Durfee tries again, this time becoming argumentative.

"Gentlemen, the Civil Aeronautics Board has charged me with the responsibility of persuading the FBI to enter the investigation," he implores. "I have been instructed several times to talk with Mr. Hoover personally, but for some reason I have been unable to even get a meeting with him. As you know, the FBI has made an exception to its own rule about plane crash investigations in the past, including the crash of the planes over the Grand Canyon a while back. Your agency's work in that case proved to be very helpful, and we just don't understand why you can't—or won't—help us now."

"Mr. Durfee, our jurisdiction in that case arose from the fact that lawsuits were being threatened against the government because of claims that government radio operators had been negligent," one of the FBI agents responds.

Back and forth. Back and forth. Neither side gives in.

Finally, Kunzig suggests a compromise: Will the FBI "loan" one or more investigators to the CAB to conduct a background check of Crosthwaite?

"We have an extremely heavy investigative burden, Mr. Kunzig. We don't have any surplus personnel to offer."

"Well, will you please—at the very least—pass our request personally on to director Hoover for a decision?" Durfee asks.

Immediately upon his return to FBI headquarters, agent Sizoo dictates a memo about the meeting to his boss, Alan H. Belmont:

"It was very apparent from the outset of the discussion that the CAB is most anxious to drag the FBI into this investigation. They have been unable to solve it. They do not want to admit they are unable to solve it. They want to be able to shift the responsibility to the FBI.

"It is also believed that the FBI should not loan investigative personnel to the CAB to conduct this investigation. This would set a bad precedent," he advises.

Sizoo recommends that the CAB "be advised by liaison that because of heavy investigative commitments, we are unable to loan investigative personnel to CAB."

The following day, his memo is read and approved.

"I concur," J. Edgar Hoover scrawls in the margin of the memo.

Hoover then dictates a letter to Attorney General Rogers, once again explaining his decision, and notes that the CAB is "under much pressure from the radio, press and Congress," but the FBI will not get involved until the agency's jurisdiction is made clear by "evidence" of sabotage.

How that evidence will be secured is anyone's guess. Nearly all of the plane is at the bottom of the ocean, and the FBI won't lift a finger to investigate a primary suspect.

Two days later Hoover dictates a letter to CAB chairman Durfee explaining again why his agency won't get involved in the case, but he promises to reconsider if the FBI obtains information that proves a criminal act.

He follows that letter with a note to the FBI in San Francisco, directing his agents there to stay out of the investigation:

"The CAB has been attempting to draw the FBI into the investigation into this matter. CAB officials have indicated that it now appears that the cause of the crash of this airplane will not be determined."

This is the first acknowledgment by the CAB—more than a year before it holds public hearings—that a cause for the plane crash may never be determined.

"If we are drawn into this investigation, we will undoubtedly be charged along with the CAB for the failure to solve this case. You should be most cautious in your contacts with the CAB in order that we are not drawn into this investigation," Hoover warns.

While the CAB's investigation continues, senior Pan American executives already are taking care of other business, namely the bottom line. They have hired a professional company to assess the value of people's lives—the financial value of those who perished on Flight 7.

In an attempt to determine what the company's potential financial liabilities might be for those who died, the company checks court records, interviews neighbors and coworkers, and examines credit reports. The company then prepares confidential reports that include such things as each deceased's net worth, educational background, physical health, habits, reputation, future income potential, life expectancy, even their social standing.

The report on the Lee Clack family, returning to Tokyo from a vacation in Michigan, is especially detailed, even including separate entries on each of the four children. The report on Lee Clack states that his future with Dow Chemical was "unlimited and his business standing was such that he would have been in line for a much bigger job in managership or presidency of the company entirely. He had the type of imagination and qualities that would have taken him far."

The report states that his reputation was of "very high standards" and even delves into his medical history, noting that while vacationing in Michigan he had a "small operation on his nose for removal of a bump but there was no malignancy there."

Of his wife, Ann, the report states that the Alma College graduate was "highly regarded socially and was in good standing personally and very happy with the foreign climate of her husband's job." It states that she tutored her school-age children for the two months before they returned to school in Tokyo.

The Clacks were known to live on a "high scale," and Dow Chemical provided them with a nice house rent free for their vacation in Midland.

The report on Navy Commander Gordon Cole tells much more about the man than a few paragraphs in the many newspaper accounts about those who died.

"He was a very religious man, a total abstainer, superintendent of his Sunday school at St. Paul's Episcopal Church in Falls Church, Va. His social standing in the community was excellent."

The report describes him as a "model family man, devoted to his wife and son," who "spent much of his leisure time with his family and in church work."

As reports are being developed on the American passengers, Pan Am is eager to ensure that its lucrative Asian market is not jeopardized by the crash and that its important relationships with governmental leaders in Japan don't suffer as a result of how the company responds to requests for financial settlements.

The answer? Pay the surviving families of two Japanese passengers something immediately for their losses. Pan Am authorities order that the Kubota and Tanaka families each receive $1,600 in "mimaikin," or condolence money, and $277 in "koden," or obituary gift money, two weeks after the crash.

Nothing similar is paid to any other passengers or crew members; they ultimately will have to hire lawyers and sue Pan Am for negligence before they get a penny, and even then, what they will receive is minimal.

Passenger William Deck's mother, Lois Deck of Radford, Virginia, is so incensed with Pan Am's pre-lawsuit settlement offer of $5,000 that she writes letters not only to Pan American president Juan Trippe but also to her congressman to complain.

She is seeking only $8,300.

"Certainly this is not too much to ask when the plane itself was insured for several million," she states in a letter to Pan Am.

"No one can ever realize just what that crash, killing my son, did to me. My whole life was wrapped up in him, and we were unusually close. If you will recall, he waited more than a year to go back to marry his Japanese sweetheart because he said he could not go until I approved," she writes.

She tells Pan Am that she doesn't want to sue the airline because a lawsuit would drag on for years and every time she thinks about it "I just go all to pieces."

She ends up settling for $5,164.

St. Elizabeth's Episcopal Church on Orange Avenue in South San Francisco is filled to overflowing on Saturday, November 30, as more than 500 family members, friends, and colleagues gather in the sanctuary where he had often sung in the choir to celebrate the life of John Elvins "Jack" King.

King's wife, Virginia, and their four children—Joan, twenty-one; Jean, nineteen; Richard, sixteen; and Melissa, six—are seated in the front pew as he is remembered as a loving husband and father and a cherished friend who delighted everyone with detail-filled stories about his trips around the world with Pan Am. He was chief steward to many world leaders, including Indonesian president Sukarno, who had requested that King accompany him on a trip around the world several years earlier.

When the trip ended back in Indonesia, King stayed at the president's palace for more than a week and brought home gifts for his family from Sukarno.

Meanwhile, in an orphanage near Tokyo there is also sadness today; the tenderhearted King had supplied the children with clothing for years. His love and generosity will be missed.

The funerals and memorial services have now ended for everyone who perished aboard *Romance of the Skies* except one: William Harrison Payne. Strangely, there has been no obituary, no service, no public remembrance whatsoever for the retired World War II Navy veteran and Northern California businessman. His family has secluded itself and is speaking with no one. It's as if his death never happened.

My recently widowed mother is all business as she gathers her "three little boys," as Daddy used to call us, and helps us board a Sunday evening Pan Am flight from San Francisco to Mexico City. We are served a delicious dinner an hour or so into the flight and then try to fall asleep to the hypnotizing hum of the DC-7's engines. I am not afraid, but my mind is full of thoughts about the flight my father had taken just two months earlier. Is he still alive out there somewhere? Is he on an island awaiting rescue? When will I see him again?

We are seated on the right side near the cockpit, and I occasionally sneak a glance at the calm, professional crew in the dark, gauge-filled command center and imagine Daddy seated there with them. I am comforted and finally drift off to sleep.

In the morning we board another plane, land in San Salvador, and then take another flight, to Brownsville, Texas. It's a long, circuitous, several-day journey because Pan Am has few domestic routes, but eventually we arrive at a little airport in Spartanburg, South Carolina—a place that seems as foreign to me as those places in Latin America we have just passed through.

It is a bitterly cold January morning and I can see my breath, something I have never seen before, but it is just the first of many new things I will learn and see in the coming weeks. I have never been to a place like this, a place where the people speak English but the words sound far different from anything I had ever heard back in California. My Aunt Hazel, whom I had never met, has twinkling eyes and a sweet and a tender smile. She hugs all of us, and her voice sounds like the whisper of an angel. We pile into her Chevrolet with something she proudly calls moon hubcaps, and she drives us to her little, two-bedroom house in rural Boiling Springs, about nine miles away. Along the way I learn that her house is just two doors down from the house my mother and father had lived in when first married. Daddy built it with his own hands, and my mother still owns it, but for some reason we will not live there.

It is a new world. A world with a broken family, but with new family members, including two cousins, Roger and Larry, who will become like brothers to us. I am full of questions. I learn that Jerry and I will stay with Aunt Hazel and Uncle Rich while Mom and Craig fly back to California to wrap things up, list our house for sale, and get ready for a final move somewhere back east, but not anywhere near here.

Jerry and I will rise before dawn the next day, wrap ourselves in warm clothes and goofy-looking earmuffs, board a big yellow school bus, and walk into an old elementary school where our new classmates will look at us if we are from another planet.

Eventually, we will end up in Miami and start yet another chapter in our lives.

FEBRUARY 1958

One of my mother's biggest prayers has been answered. We are now living in our new stucco house in North Miami, and Jerry and I are enrolled at Crestview Elementary, a brand-new school within walking distance. No more buses. No more frosty mornings. No more goofy earmuffs.

We have new friends—Latino friends, Jewish friends, Asian friends. This seems almost like home, back in California.

All our belongings have arrived from Santa Clara—Daddy's oversized, thick-cushioned chair, the handcrafted blond-wood, high-fidelity cabinet speaker he had meticulously created, his carpentry tools, and most of his camping gear. But our car and camping trailer are still in California. In desperation before leaving, my mother had posted a note on a Pan Am bulletin board asking if someone would drive our 1955 Ford and tiny Shasta camper—the one we had camped in from California to Canada—all the way cross-country to Miami. She doesn't expect anyone to take on a challenge of that magnitude, but one day she receives a call from Pan Am purser Fred Sohn, a man she has never met, but who had flown trans-Pacific flights with my father and had worked with stewardesses Alexander and McGrath.

Fred tells her Daddy was a "real gentleman who always treated flight service crew in a friendly manner," and he has some vacation time on his hands and wants to do something to help us. Yes, he would be happy to drive our car and camper to Miami.

He is the answer to Mom's prayers.

Fred gets only as far as Fresno before he is stopped by a California highway patrolman because a taillight on the trailer has gone out. Fred explains his mission to the understanding patrolman, who has read newspaper accounts of the crash. He doesn't issue Fred a citation but tells him he can't drive anymore that first night, so Fred sleeps in the Ford.

He drives like mad the entire next day and by late evening reaches El Paso, Texas, where he pulls into a service station and once again explains his mission. The mechanic installs a new taillight free of charge. Not only that, but he allows Fred to park the car and trailer at the service station for free that night. It is bitterly cold, dropping to sixteen degrees before dawn, but Fred is reluctant to use the trailer's heater, not knowing whether it's safe.

At sunlight he is on the road again, for the three-day trip across the vast Lone Star State. The rear axle of the Ford breaks along US Highway 80 as he nears the Louisiana border, but he manages to nurse the vehicle into the tiny town of Waskom, where he barely makes it into Waskom Motors, a Ford dealership on the west side of town. Again, he explains his mission for the widow Fortenberry, and owner-manager Sam Cooke also remembers hearing and reading about the crash. Cooke instructs his team to unhitch the trailer, tells Fred to get some sleep, then orders his three mechanics to immediately stop what they are doing and get right to work on that axle. Fred rests until midafternoon, wakes up, and while the mechanics are still working on our car, Cooke, the incoming president of the Waskom Chamber of Commerce, proudly takes Fred on a tour of his tiny town and buys him a late lunch. When they return to the dealership our car has been repaired, the trailer rehitched and ready to go.

"How much do I owe you?" Fred asks, expecting a hefty bill.

"Nothing. Not a single penny. It was our pleasure to help," Cooke replies, and Fred is soon on his way again.

"There are some pretty nice people in Texas," he says to himself as he enters Louisiana for what will be an uneventful remainder of the trip to Miami. "Yes, some pretty nice people."

And some pretty nice Pan Am people, too, I might add.

It is nothing but an old push-to-talk airplane microphone with a long cord, but to my brother and me it is much more than that. It's our way to connect with the most important event in our lives and to change the outcome of what happened on November 8, 1957—if only in our dreams and in our playtime.

The bedroom closet that Jerry and I share in our new Miami home is easily transformed from a simple place to hang clothes and store items into the spacious cockpit of a Boeing Stratocruiser. A couple of small cereal boxes creatively marked with crayons become airplane gauges and controls, and the old microphone that Daddy used when flying our "Buddy-Seat" plane crackles to life in our imaginations.

"This is Clipper Nine Four Four. Come in, please. Does anyone read me?"

I pretend to wrestle with the controls of an airplane that is losing altitude over the ocean, and I look down at the fast-approaching shark-filled sea. It is a menacing sight.

Jerry quietly sits on the floor a few feet from the closet-cockpit and listens closely to the urgent plea coming from the airplane. He is planning what he knows he must do next, planning what he will do time and time again over the next couple of months as we reenact the last minutes of Flight 7.

"Mayday! Mayday! This is Clipper Nine Four Four. Come in, please," I shout urgently into the microphone. "We're going down. Middle of the Pacific. Someone help us, please! Mayday! Mayday!"

I scream and make some gurgling, crashing sounds as the plane hits the ocean, and then I tumble out of my closet-cockpit onto the hard terrazzo floor.

That's his signal, and Jerry swings swiftly into action. He rolls over onto his stomach and begins swimming frantically to reach the plane before everyone drowns. He battles waves and bloodthirsty sharks, twisting his head back and forth before he finally reaches me and drags me across the ocean-bedroom to safety.

We both shout with joy. Daddy is alive! Everyone has been saved!

FRANKFURT, GERMANY
WEDNESDAY, DECEMBER 10, 1954

Dear Mom & Boys,

Imagine my surprise today when I came back from a trip of almost a week to find a letter. I had concluded that you had broken both hands and couldn't find anyone to write for you. I still don't know when I'll get home.

One union man said that I could go home when my two months were up. The office here says the end of the year, and I saw a wire from New York saying that they would keep the local people informed. I am ready to come now but they have me scheduled for 95 hours this month. I suppose I can use the $200 overtime that I would make because it seems that there will be another furlough next year about Christmas time.

I still haven't gotten my October overtime, and when it does come, I know it will be wrong. I didn't even get my first officer's pay in the *regular check. They are getting real chicken shit here. They made one captain pay $50 because he took off with the pins in the gear and they called a co-pilot in and reamed him because he had made too many calls from the field. It had cost the company about 36 cents.*

Our chief pilot is on vacation and we have little pricks trying to be big pricks now. Even the German secretary looks way down while she speaks to us, and co-pilots have been forbidden to speak to the dispatcher. If we have anything to say to him, we tell the captain and he can tell the dispatcher. It isn't too bad, though. I have the new camera now and the light meter, and they still give me a check twice a month.

I hope we will have enough money in February to take a vacation down south. You had better not plan on me being there for Christmas. I will be there if I possibly can, but no one will give me much encouragement here.

I like the flying here very much because I get to fly a lot. They had a vacancy here and I bid it. I'm going to bid just about everything that comes up to try to get out of New York. I don't want to be a navigator. Even Columbus could do that in 1492.

I'm glad my boys are well and happy and that they miss me a little bit. I miss them, too, and want to see them very much. Hope they stay well and grow big and strong before I come home soon. I will see you before so very long now. If I came home the 22nd it is just 11 more days and if they keep me until Jan. 1st it is only 20 days. If they should try to keep me beyond Jan. 1st, I'm sure they will send you over. I don't think they will do that because it would cost them even more than 36 cents!

Please don't think I am bitter. I just want to grumble a little. I'll write again tomorrow and then wait until I hear from you before

I write again. I hope it is not a week.

Remember Dad loves all of you ALL DAY. I miss you and love you very much.

Love,

Dad

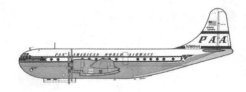

9

MYSTERY CRASH, MYSTERY FIRE

ON FRIDAY, JANUARY 10, 1958, members of the Civil Aeronautics Board executive staff and investigative team in Washington, D.C., make final plans for next week's public hearing in San Francisco. As they work on the agenda, a CAB spokesman puts the finishing touches on an overwritten press release intended for the Sunday newspapers.

The release is unusual for a couple of reasons: First, it promises that the hearing will provide a "dramatic story" about the missing airliner and why it plunged from the sky to the bottom of the ocean. Second, and more importantly, it discloses for the first time that excessive levels of carbon monoxide had been found in fourteen of the nineteen bodies recovered, and that the gas was "possibly disabling" to both crew and passengers.

"Why did a Honolulu-bound airliner fly to destruction last November near the end of a year in which the US commercial airlines chalked up a safety record otherwise never surpassed?" the release asks in its opening paragraph.

"If we find the answer it will be a product of modern technology and an estimated 9,500 man-hours of plain, hard work. If we do not succeed, it will be because the mute evidence of 19 bodies and 72 pieces of wreckage, the largest of which was a 4 x 7 piece of bulkhead, simply did not tell the story."

SUNDAY, JANUARY 12, 1958

Published today in the "Poet's Corner" of the *Oakland Tribune* is this from area resident Warren W. Sullens:

Romance of the Skies

For Hawaii's palm-lined shore
Rose a Clipper plane to soar
High and mighty in her flight
Gliding through the velvet night.

Skimming through the clouds above,
Guided by her pilot's love,
Resting on her perfect luck,
Suddenly disaster struck!

Down she plunged beneath the wave,
Settling to her common grave
Shared by all the ships of yore
Slumbering on the ocean floor.

Far below her native haunt,
Torn asunder, long and gaunt,
Fame shall mark her long demise:
Fallen "Romance of the Skies!"

Sunday-morning newspapers across the country dutifully report the impending CAB hearing at the same time an executive with the

Southwestern Mutual Life Insurance Company in Albuquerque, New Mexico, dictates a telegram to the CAB in Washington:

"This is to inform your agency that Mr. Russell Stiles, chief investigator for our company, has been assigned to look into an insurance claim for a passenger aboard Pan American Flight 7 which crashed last November.

"We look forward to cooperating with you in any way. If you have any questions, please don't hesitate to call."

That unnamed passenger is lodge owner and former Navy frogman William Harrison Payne.

On Thursday morning, January 16, 1958, the Empire Room of the twenty-one-story Sir Francis Drake Hotel in San Francisco's Union Square is filling up with representatives of the media, labor unions, victims' families, Pan American, Boeing, engine maker Pratt & Whitney, and prop manufacturer Hamilton Standard, plus dozens of others, all gathering in anticipation of what the CAB has promised will be the unfolding of a "dramatic story."

Board member Harmar D. Denny gavels the room to order at 9 a.m. and makes an opening statement informing the audience that the hearing is a board of inquiry for the sole purpose of obtaining facts. He outlines the rules and procedures for the hearing and says the board is "not permitted to express any opinion as to the probable cause of the accident." He explains that after the board has examined each witness, certain parties to the investigation, such as Pan Am, union representatives, and others, will be allowed to question that witness "solely for the purpose of developing a factual record of the accident. Cross-examination in the legal sense will not be permitted."

Denny wants to make clear to everyone present that the hearing is an administrative, fact-finding venture, but the admonition against the cross-examination of witnesses will severely limit the scope and findings of the public investigation over the next two days.

"There are no adverse parties and no adverse interests. No one has been made a defendant or respondent."

Not yet anyway.

He says that after the facts have been gathered, the full CAB and its expert staff will make a full report on what they have learned and will issue a report on a probable cause with the intent of preventing any recurrence of similar accidents in the future.

In the coming days there will be testimony that seems to indicate a probable cause for the crash, followed by conflicting testimony that discounts it.

With the official opening out of the way, presiding officer Robert W. Chrisp begins the task of conducting an orderly meeting, examining witnesses and trying to determine why N90944 crashed. This will be a monumental undertaking because many of the witnesses are here to cover their own asses or the corporate asses of their companies and superiors. Pan Am wants to direct blame at anything or anyone other than its own planes and maintenance practices. The pilots want to blame anyone other than the crew; the union wants to blame Pan Am; Boeing and other manufacturers want to blame anything but their equipment.

The families of the victims just want to know the truth.

As the hearing progresses, Chrisp tends to push the testimony away from any blame on Pan Am or its suppliers and manufacturers. Time and time again he redirects questions or rejects them altogether when someone tries to drill down on Pan Am's maintenance practices. Far from being the promised "dramatic story," the hearing is relatively boring, except for a few tense exchanges between mechanics' union representative Phil Ice and Chrisp. Ice, intent on pressing the union's case against Pan Am, zeroes in on maintenance inspection documents that he asserts were not properly signed off on by licensed mechanics or certified inspectors. He also gets a witness to admit that a required inspection of N90944's spar webs (main structures that support the wings) had not been done as mandated after two unexplained hard landings several months before the crash. The inspection protocol required the removal of a surface cover on the wings to allow for inspection of the wing spar webs.

Several times a witness makes a statement that demands a follow-up question or detailed examination. That rarely happens; if Ice doesn't ask it, the question usually goes unasked. A prime example is when CAB Bureau of Safety engineer and investigator Martyn V. Clarke testifies about a strange fluid that was found on some of the floating debris, which included pieces of insulation saturated with what everyone initially thought was hydraulic fluid. That insulation was subsequently tested by the FBI's laboratory in Washington, which concluded that it was some kind of petroleum-based product, though not the kind used by Pan American.

If the fluid was not used by Pan American, why was it in the aircraft? What type of petroleum-based product was it?

Again, no question.

"Are any additional tests planned to determine the nature of this fluid?" Clarke is asked by a hearing officer.

"Not at the present time. The purpose of the test was really more of an academic interest than in trying to determine what it was," Clarke states. He adds that many pieces of insulation were burned on both sides, not just to the waterline. That would indicate a fire after the plane hit the water.

That should lead to another question: If some of the debris was burned on both sides, does that mean there was a fire before the plane hit the water?

That question is never asked. And there is no follow-up.

Clarke testifies that "it didn't seem too pertinent to really try to pin down" what the unknown petroleum product was.

And that is that.

Another evidentiary clue also receives little attention, although it had been the subject of intensive examination by experts before the public hearing: a small section of an engine ring cowl, embedded in a scorched pillow that was floating at the crash site, hinted that a thrown propeller might have ripped through the cabin and disabled the aircraft. A few questions are asked, but little more.

Much of the hearing centers on the unexplained presence of carbon monoxide in fourteen of the nineteen bodies recovered. A much-anticipated witness is Dr. Vernie Stembridge, a pathologist with the Armed Forces Institute of Pathology, who sheds some light on the carbon monoxide poisoning, and provides important information about the victims, including the fact that all were likely knocked unconscious by the crash and thus incapable of attempting to survive. Because the only recovered cockpit crew member's body with carbon monoxide was that of Captain Brown there is the distinct possibility that the three other men in the cockpit also had high levels of carbon monoxide in their systems before the crash. However, their bodies were not recovered so there is no way to establish that.

CAB engineer Isaac Hoover spends a great deal of time discussing his investigators' findings about possible causes of the carbon monoxide poisoning, including a thrown propeller tearing through the fuselage. He testifies that a propeller failure is one of the best possible explanations, because the prop likely would have come through the fuselage, disrupting electrical wires, radio equipment, hydraulic and oil lines, control cables, possibly even heater fuel lines. That would have been followed by engine loss and serious control problems with the airplane.

But Hoover contradicts himself and says that propeller failure was unlikely because the troublesome hollow-steel blades used in the past had been replaced in all Stratocruisers by solid aluminum props with pitch locks to prevent engine speeds in excess of 3100 RPM, and problems like those caused by the hollow-steel blades had not been an issue since that time. All the props on *Romance of the Skies* were well within their lifetime operating ranges. They had been inspected prior to takeoff and were in good condition.

"There is no record of any of the propeller blades having ever been damaged," Hoover states. "Records also indicate that none of the propellers had been involved in overspeeding."

He testifies that each propeller had been inspected visually by mechanics and by flight engineer Albert Pinataro during the predeparture inspection, and a separate sign-off was made for each propeller.

Moving past the prop issue, Hoover suggests other possibilities for carbon monoxide poisoning, including a cabin-heater fire, an engine fire that could have spread quickly into the cabin, and smoldering movie film in the cargo.

The board doesn't question the fact that a CAB investigator took the shipper's word for it that the movie film in the forward cargo area was of the "safety type," and not cellulose-nitrate, which is extremely dangerous—easy to ignite and difficult to extinguish. It can ignite in temperatures as low as 38 degrees Fahrenheit and produces hot, intense flames and poisonous gases.

Hoover's experts have ideas about why the plane went down, but because there is so little physical evidence remaining, they draw no conclusions.

Hoover testifies that passengers in the tourist section near the cockpit had the highest levels of carbon monoxide in their bloodstreams. Strangely, those in the rear, first-class section had little or none. Did that mean that a fire of some sort broke out near the cockpit and the tourist-class area?

"The stewardess who was recovered occupied a first-class seat and had a relatively low carbon monoxide concentration," he says. Hoover states that a smoldering fire in the forward cargo compartment or the cockpit might explain why those in the rear of the plane had lower levels of the deadly poison.

Under questioning from John Miner, a Pan Am pilot and Air Line Pilots Association representative, Hoover also acknowledges that carbon monoxide could have leaked into the cockpit or have been maliciously introduced there. Miner points out that although Captain Brown and three tourist passengers had high levels of carbon monoxide poisoning, none was wearing a life jacket, suggesting they had no indication the plane was going down.

Also unanswered is this critical question: can carbon monoxide be produced by a decomposed body? In other words, could the bodies that were plucked from the sea have become poisoned with carbon monoxide *after* the crash? That question will have conflicting answers in the years to come.

The hearing goes on for two days, and not a single word is uttered about two primary suspects: purser Crosthwaite and passenger Payne. In fact, the possible "human factor" in the crash is never even discussed.

Nothing is mentioned about the huge IBM machine that could have broken loose from its straps, torn into the cabin heater, and caused problems for the crew, despite a statement from lead cargo ramp man Coraino Carvalho, who admitted that "loading in the forward compartment was done a little too fast." The forward cargo compartment is where the IBM computer was placed.

There is no testimony about gobs of tarlike substances that were found on some of the debris. Although the substances were analyzed by labs, the results were inconclusive, just as in the case of the unknown petroleum product found in the insulation debris.

N90944's master-engine logs are entered into evidence, but no one asks any questions specifically about them. That is especially strange because engine number three had had repeated problems in the two months leading up to the flight, involving the loss of oil and fluctuating oil pressures. Also unmentioned is a problem with the engine's sheltered air door, even though pilots had repeatedly complained about it not operating properly—or at all.

Pan Am's Ross Butler, the pilots' representative at the hearing, who by his own description is an "idealistic young man," is disturbed, because he expects the officers and witnesses to be trying to determine the cause of the crash. Instead, he believes, they are "looking out for their own rear ends."

Butler would acknowledge many years later that Pan Am's inspection and maintenance standards "were getting pretty sloppy. Those guys were under a lot of pressure."

The two-day CAB hearing obtains testimony from eighteen witnesses. Nearly 100 pieces of evidence are presented; multiple theories are bantered back and forth about a probable cause for the crash. But when the proceedings end, all that's left are more questions and a statement that further investigations will be conducted.

Investigators remain puzzled by the radio silence from the plane as it dove into the ocean. What could have prevented the four-man crew from using the sophisticated and extensive radio equipment and backups to send a distress signal? Pan American flight engineer F. E. Dysinger testifies that only some kind of unknown "incident" in the crew compartment could have knocked out both the primary and emergency communications systems—an idea that no one can fathom, or seems to have any interest in pursuing. The plane had three separate power systems and backup emergency generators—enough power to operate not only the radios but the aircraft itself.

Again, there was a solid angle to pursue, but no one did. The VHF radio on *Romance of the Skies* had been plagued with problems in the week before the plane's final flight. At least twice the crew had reported to mechanics in their flight discrepancy reports that the radio was not properly working or not working at all. In both cases, ground crewmen checked the radio out, made minor repairs, and reported that it was fixed.

But on a flight from Los Angeles to Honolulu on November 3, just five days before the crash, the captain had reported that the radio transmission was extremely weak, and only eighteen miles after takeoff the VHF transmissions could not be received. Maintenance personnel checked the radio and replaced the antenna after the plane landed.

Testimony is introduced about recorded radio transmissions - strange, very weak and garbled - that may have come from Flight 7, but investigators so far have been unable to determine what the messages said or even if they even came from *Romance of the Skies.*

AIRINC (the radio communication network for airlines) stations in Seattle, Honolulu, Los Angeles and San Francisco routinely recorded all radio transmissions from commercial aircraft.

Another mystery also remains unanswered: How did some passengers (mostly those first-class passengers in the rear of the plane) have time to prepare for a crash before they plunged to their watery graves while others apparently did not? Were people in the front of the plane (and in the cockpit) so incapacitated that they could not don their life jackets?

And finally, why did the crew fly north—away from help, with Ocean Station November only ten minutes off, with a trained lifesaving crew and equipment available to assist? Weather was not a factor.

Perhaps most disturbing is the fact that the "possibly disabling" levels of carbon monoxide exposure are discussed at length during the hearing, but the cause is never determined. Not during the hearing. Not during the promised posthearing investigation. Not during the next sixty years.

Newspaper reporters covering the hearing seem to be as confused as CAB officials when they write their stories. A United Press International report states that the hearing determined that "pilot, crew and passengers may have been suffering from the deadly effects of carbon monoxide gas," which it cites as the "most likely and most plausible theory" to account for the crash. Another newspaper report says a thrown propeller is the likely culprit.

A few days after the hearing ends, CAB Director of Safety Oscar Bakke decides to follow up on an offer that union representative Ice had made before Bakke headed back to Washington, and dispatches investigators Charles S. Collar and A. B. Hallman to San Francisco on a special mission. Ice had told Bakke he would make evidence of Pan American maintenance malpractice at the San Francisco base available to the CAB, and Bakke wants to see that evidence. He instructs the investigators to obtain everything Ice will furnish and "insofar as possible" check the validity of that information with Pan American. He gives them two weeks to complete the assignment.

What they learn validates many of the claims Ice had made at the hearing and in newspaper accounts, plainly suggesting that Pan American maintenance practices were questionable.

In a March 11, 1958, report to his superiors, Bakke outlines what the investigators learned and points out that any possible "company-union contractual controversies are being divorced from the report and its conclusions." Bakke states that some of Ice's allegations were without substance, but that "sufficient factual evidence" was obtained to draw the following conclusions:

1. The maintenance manual had not been followed completely.

2. Qualified mechanics were not always assigned as specified by Pan American's Pacific-Alaska Division standards.

3. Inspection and/or quality control in the engine overhaul was not adequate. Spot inspections revealed repeated rejections of vital parts.

4. Maintenance practices were questionable.

5. There had been a policy at PAA-PAD to dispense

with inspectors in many areas and in doing so transfer responsibility for the airworthiness of the airplanes and components to supervisory personnel.

"Based on our investigation," Bakke stated, "we concluded that in dispensing with inspectors the ability to maintain a consistent satisfactory level of airworthiness has been lost. It is believed that many of the responsibilities of the production supervisor preclude the desired degree of personal supervision, checks, and inspections required to ensure that all airplanes departing meet the required level of airworthiness. Also, in arriving at this conclusion, it is recalled that three airplanes operated by PAA-PAD have been lost in the Pacific."

Bakke recommends the reassessment of Pan American's Pacific-Alaska Division policies, particularly with respect to maintenance and overhaul inspection, responsibility for day-to-day airworthiness, and adherence to the maintenance manual. He blisters Pan Am for fiscal shortcuts in maintenance and inspections and says the airline is putting airplanes in the air that are unsafe to fly.

That report does not sit well with Pan American executives, who immediately begin to lobby the CAB to keep the information from the public.

Harriet Theiler Payne is about to make a very big change in her forty-three-year-old life, and by 9 a.m. on Friday, June 13, 1958, she is seated on a United Airlines DC-6 Mainliner flying from Medford, Oregon, to San Francisco. There, she will board another flight, to Tijuana, Mexico, where she plans to marry Karim Harry "Mugs" Isaac, the much younger man seated beside her.

The lean, dark-skinned Isaac has been her lover and companion since she ditched Ray Parker a few months ago. Parker had been a suitable mate for the widow Payne for a brief period, but like her presumably dead husband, William, he was too jealous when she looked at other men, so she unceremoniously dumped him. Isaac has been of invaluable help in getting Roxbury Lodge in shape, just in case a potential buyer shows up to take it off her hands. It has been a money-losing drag since

All Photos from top to bottom, left to right

1. Pan Am Flight 7 copilot and navigator Bill Fortenberry at the navigator's station in a Pan Am airliner in the mid-1950s **2.** The author's parents, Bill and Ronnie Fortenberry, on their wedding day in 1948 **3.** Author Ken Fortenberry, left, and his brother Jerry get their first peek of their little brother, Craig, after his birth in 1955. Craig would grow up with no memories of his father. **4.** The author (left) and his brother Jerry strum ukuleles in their San Mateo, California, driveway a year before Flight 7 disappeared. Their father bought the ukuleles during one of his many trips to Honolulu.

1. An early 1950s publicity photo of Pan American's *Romance of the Skies*, a Boeing Stratocruiser, the largest, fastest, and most luxurious commercial aircraft of the day [Photo by Bob Whelan]   **2.** Passengers dressed in their finest clothes when they traveled by air in the 1950s, and this photo inside a Stratocruiser shows the luxurious cabin, where passengers are seen quilting, reading, and chatting with each other. [Photo, Pan Am Archives, Otto Richter Library, University of Miami]

1. Captain Gordon Herrick Brown, not long after joining Pan American World Airways **2.** First Officer William Purdy Wygant participated in the bombings of Iwo Jima and Okinawa. [Photo courtesy of Bette Anne Wygant] **3.** Copilot and navigator William Holland Fortenberry **4.** Flight engineer Albert Pinataro celebrated his twenty-seventh birthday a week before the crash. **5.** Stewardesses Marie McGrath, left, and Yvonne Alexander loved their jobs with Pan American. McGrath, a part-time elementary school substitute teacher, dreamed as a youngster of becoming a stewardess. **6.** Purser Oliver Eugene Crosthwaite was one of Pan Am's longest-serving employees. **7.** The front page of the Saturday edition of the *Los Angeles Times* tells the grim news about the airliner that disappeared somewhere over the Pacific.

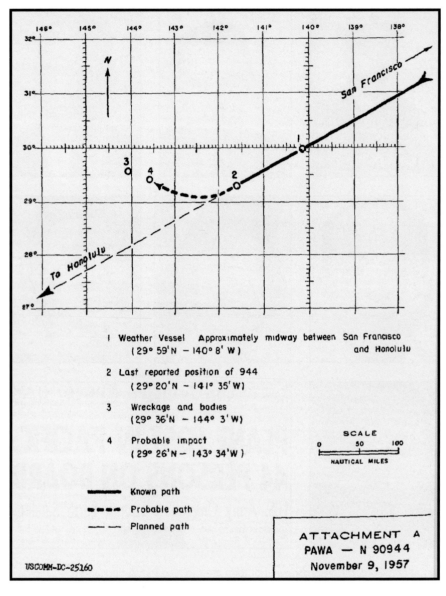

1 Weather Vessel   Approximately midway between San Francisco
   (29° 59'N — 140° 8' W)   and Honolulu

2 Last reported position of 944
   (29° 20'N — 141° 35'W)

3 Wreckage and bodies
   (29° 36'N — 144° 3'W)

4 Probable impact
   (29° 26'N — 143° 34'W)

SCALE

0   50   100

NAUTICAL MILES

━━━━━ Known path
▬ ▬ ▬ Probable path
─── ─── Planned path

ATTACHMENT A
PAWA — N 90944
November 9, 1957

1. A Civil Aeronautics Board sketch of the ill-fated plane's planned and probable flight path. It also shows where bodies and debris were recovered nearly a week after the crash, far northwest of the filed flight path.

1. An unidentified male victim of Pan Am Flight 7 floats in the Pacific as a Navy helicopter hovers above. It took searchers six days to find the first victims and debris from the crash of Flight 7. [Photo by Hal Filan] **2.** A small boat from the aircraft carrier *Philippine Sea* speeds to a floating body (circled) as the search for survivors turns into a search for victims. [Photo by Hal Filan] **3.** A Navy chaplain on the *Philippine Sea* prays over nineteen bodies recovered from the sea nearly a week after Flight 7 perished.

1. Dr. William Hart Hagan, a Louisville, Kentucky, surgeon, and his wife, Norma Jeanne, planned to attend an international surgical conference in Honolulu. **2.** Vacationing Pan Am pilot Robert Alexander and his wife, Margaret, perished with their two children. **3.** Thomas Henry McGrail of New Hampshire was bound for his new assignment at the US Embassy in Rangoon, Burma. **4.** William Homer Deck boarded Flight 7 for his ultimate destination of Tokyo, where he planned to meet his Japanese sweetheart. **5.** Louis Rodriguez was flying to his mother's funeral in Honolulu. It was his first time aboard an airplane. **6.** Businessman Robert Halliday was en route home to New South Wales after a lengthy business trip abroad. **7.** Tomiko Boyd of Maryland was headed to Korea for a brief visit with her US Army husband, who was stationed there. **8.** Robert LaMaison, a Renault auto executive, and his wife, Nicole, were bound for Honolulu on a combination work/vacation visit. **9.** Edward T. Ellis, a senior executive of McCormick & Company, was scheduled to speak at a management association meeting in Honolulu. [Photo courtesy of Fred Ellis]

1. The entire Lee Clack family of Midland, Michigan, perished when Flight 7 went down. They are photographed at Midway Airport in Chicago four days before *Romance of the Skies* disappeared. They were en route to San Francisco and ultimately to Tokyo after visiting family and friends in Michigan. From left: Lee, Mariko, Scott, Ann, Kimi, and Bruce. [Photo courtesy of Norma Clack] **2.** Navy Commander Gordon Cole led an adventure-filled life before heading out to Hong Kong, where he was to take command of a Navy destroyer. **3.** Newspaper reporters and Navy officers inspect debris recovered from *Romance of the Skies*. The wreckage was brought aboard the aircraft carrier *Philippine Sea* and catalogued before it was turned over to investigators. [Photo by Hal Filan]

BLAST PLOT HINTED IN MID-PACIFIC AIR CRASH

San Francisco Examiner

FINAL

MONARCH OF THE DAILIES

AMERICA FIRST

SUTTER 1-2424   TEmplebar 2-7343, East Bay   •CCCC•• •   TUESDAY, SEPTEMBER 18, 1958   46 PAGES — 2 SECTIONS   DAILY 10c, SUNDAY 20c

Sabotage Hint in Pacific Air Crash	Train's Mystery Dive Unsolved	Reds Plan Major War, Chiang Says

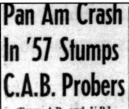

Pan Am Crash In '57 Stumps C.A.B. Probers

(From A.P. and U.P.I. Dispatches)

WASHINGTON, Jan. 20— The Civil Aeronautics Board

1. Nearly a year after the crash, the possibility of sabotage was raised by an insurance company that refused to pay on a policy taken out by a passenger whose body was not among those recovered. **2.** A psychic created this composite sketch of "Western John," a possible sabotage suspect, who looked remarkably like purser Crosthwaite, pictured at right. **3.** Their faces tell a story about their relationship: Purser Eugene Crosthwaite and his stepdaughter, Tania, are photographed in their Hillside, California, home. [Photo courtesy of Tania Crosthwaite Barnes] **4.** Fourteen months after Flight 7 crashed, the Civil Aeronautics Board admitted that the cause of the crash likely would remain a mystery.

she and William bought it, but thanks to the airport vending-machine insurance money, she has paid off the mortgage, and the twice-married widow and mother of three is eager to move on with her life. The handsome, twenty-eight-year-old Isaac suits her just fine, and the thin, good-looking, auburn-haired Harriet has always looked younger than her years.

Whether Harriet is aware that the former Tradeway Chevrolet car salesman and housepainter has a wife and a six-year-old son in Manteca is unknown, and she doesn't likely care anyway. She's always been a take-charge, flirtatious woman, and the seven months since *Romance of the Skies* crashed have seemed like forever as she has worked to get her affairs—all of them—in order. If Isaac is a gold digger, then so be it. Right now, he's just what she wants.

The soon-to-be bride and Isaac have reserved a $12-a-night room at the fancy Hotel Caesar's in Tijuana. They are greeted at the airport by swarms of sweaty child beggars looking for a handout, but pay no attention. Charity is not something in either person's background or character. There are whores along the streets and drunken sailors from nearby San Diego in the alleys, but Tijuana is Tijuana, and it is the perfect place for a quickie wedding and a honeymoon for the newly wealthy widow and her bigamist gigolo.

They check into the hotel on Revolution Avenue, just a few steps from the Mexico-United States border, and look forward to their little getaway.

While Harriet Theiler Payne Isaac and her new husband are enjoying their honeymoon in Tijuana, a small group is gathered in Scott Bar and enjoying a Saturday evening in the atrium bar area of the two-story, metal-roofed Roxbury Lodge. The liquor is flowing, the Everly Brothers are singing "All I Have to Do Is Dream" on the nickel jukebox, and laughter punctuates the air as the guests mix it up. Harriet's friends Steve Sherman and his wife tend the bar and wait on the customers.

US Forestry Service employee William H. Zook Jr., his wife, Dorothy, and her mother, Liduina Sargenti, are among the guests drinking and dancing this evening. Shortly before 1 a.m. they decide to call it a night.

Sargenti leaves the lodge first, walks outside into the warm summer air, and sits in the car while awaiting her daughter and son-in-law. Moments later something catches the corner of her eye: a flickering light in the attic of the lodge. She immediately rushes inside to warn the others that a fire is breaking out.

"Fire! Fire!" she shouts, and then hears a loud, sucking "poof" sound as the lodge goes up in flames. It is now 1:20 a.m., and there had been no warning, no unusual smell, no hint of an imminent fire. Flames burst through the lodge ceiling as everyone inside flees for their lives, including one guest who had been sleeping in a back room and escapes the burning building in only his underwear.

Zook, who lives in nearby Happy Camp and is familiar with the building, races to the back of the lodge to disconnect the gas lines from the butane tank and notices that the French doors leading to the upstairs area are open. Strange, he thinks: no one has exited the building from that area, and no one should have been in the attic anyway.

Someone alerts the US Forestry Service, but by the time rangers from Fort Jones, Seiad Valley, and Oak Knoll arrive, the main structure is engulfed in raging flames so blistering hot that firefighters have to keep their distance. Among the rangers is a high school senior named Kip Payne, the eldest son of the lodge's owner.

By sunrise Sunday, the once luxurious Roxbury Lodge, which doubles as the Payne family residence, is nothing but smoldering ruins, a crumpled mess of fire hose-soaked wood, four chimneys, and tangled metal and wires. The honeymooners in Mexico have been notified of the fire, and their holiday ends abruptly. They make plans to return to California on Mexicana Airlines Flight 590 the following day.

On Monday, June 16, the US Immigration and Naturalization Service in Los Angeles admits Karim H. Isaac and Harriet Isaac back into the United States. The name "Payne" is struck out and written over with "Isaac" on her document. Both list Roxbury Lodge, Scott Bar, California, as their permanent address. Later that day they board a United Airlines flight for Medford, Oregon, a short drive from Scott Bar, and they arrive at the ruins of Roxbury Lodge after dark.

The lodge is insured for less than its worth, but the 200 acres it sits on is prime real estate, for its mining possibilities if nothing else, and Harriet can now reduce the selling price to something more reasonable and more marketable and establish a new life somewhere else.

By early in the week Scott Bar is buzzing with rumors and speculation not only about the fire, but also about that unexplained plane crash seven months earlier. Harriet and her children have kept a low profile and avoided the public glare since the crash, keeping their grief, if indeed there is any, to themselves. Now, in the wake of the fire at the lodge, locals are more interested than ever before in learning what happened to that Pan American plane the previous November, and whether Harriet might have been involved in that—and in the weekend fire. She senses the community's suspicions and decides to move back to Manteca before school starts.

She's had enough of Scott Bar.

Two months later and now freed of her latest husband, Harriet Payne (she's now back to Payne) is loaded with insurance loot and spins around Manteca in her new Austin-Healey sports car. After lover boy Karim Isaac had tried—and failed—to convince Harriet to buy him a used-car lot in Modesto, it finally struck her that he was more interested in her money than in her. She dumped him and moved on. Isaac has returned to his wife and son, and Harriet has recently purchased a new home for her children and her mother. She has taken Kim, Kitti, and one of their friends on a trip to Disneyland, and she is enjoying a new life with no worries and plenty of money—something she has always dreamed about.

Although Harriet has moved from Scott Bar, the mystery about Roxbury Lodge remains, and two months after the fire lingering questions circulate not only in the community but also in the insurance world. It is unusual, after all, for one family to have been involved in two major tragedies in a seven-month period, and many questions remain about Payne, his widow, and those unexplained "accidents."

The US Forestry Service determined within a few days of the fire that faulty wiring had caused the blaze, but insurers are unconvinced. In August 1958 the St. Paul Fire and Marine Insurance Company in San Francisco asks the National Board of Fire Underwriters in New York to review and possibly investigate the case. The board assigns the case to arson investigator and former FBI agent Earl Guisness of San Francisco, who drives to Siskiyou County within days of getting his assignment. Today, he is methodically examining the ruins of the lodge with Deputy Sheriff James Berrian. However, many weeks have passed since the fire, and the remaining evidence has been picked over by the Payne family and curious neighbors. Nevertheless, Guisness works diligently to determine how a 58-by-65-foot building with eight sleeping rooms, a lounge, a dining room, a kitchen, a dance floor, and a bar went up in flames—even though none of the eleven fire alarm bells sounded until everyone was safely outside.

All that is left standing when he arrives at the scene are four chimneys and some flexible copper tubing that had led to a large oil tank, still full, which had fed fuel to heaters in the lodge. After examining the ruins, Guisness turns his attention to Harriet, her newest ex-husband, and anyone he can locate who was at the lodge on the night of the fire or who might have helpful information about the lodge, the Paynes, or Isaac.

It took me more than forty years to obtain a copy of his "privileged and confidential preliminary" report to the FBI, and it is an eye-opener, confirming much of what Guisness later told a colleague.

"Mrs. Isaac advised that she had no idea what caused the fire in the lodge," he reported. "She said that she and her husband were trying to decide whether or not to rebuild the lodge. She stated that the only recent work done to the lodge was from May 30 to June 13 at which time she and Isaac had been making repairs on the rear room of the lodge. Both she and Isaac advised that there were fire alarms around all the chimneys."

Harriet acknowledged that she and her presumably deceased husband, William, had put the lodge up for sale more than a year earlier "and stated that she knew of no one who would have a grudge against her to such an extent as to burn the lodge."

Isaac told the arson investigator that he was self-employed, "but failed to state just what he was self-employed at, and a few minutes later became unresponsive to questioning."

Guisness provided some background information on William Payne, then disclosed details about the Payne family's finances that he learned during a visit to Scott Valley Bank.

"The Paynes' bank account in March 1957 had a high figure of $50. In June of 1957 the high figure was $450. In September 1957 this account was overdrawn on two occasions. Shortly after September 25, $800 was placed in the account and was immediately drawn upon until $5 remained. In October the account went from a high of $631 down to $18.49. On November 4 two checks were drawn, one in the amount of $437.40 and another in the amount of $175.54. The check for $437.40 was to pay the annual premium on the fire insurance covering Roxbury Lodge. At the time of the payment this premium was two months overdue."

Not stated, but presumed, is that the check for $175.54 went to Pan American for Payne's mysterious one-way ticket to Honolulu.

The Paynes were broke.

Guisness noted that the Paynes canceled $5,000 of their fire insurance on the lodge a year before the crash "inasmuch as they could not afford the premium."

The fire insurance investigator wrote about his interview with former lodge owner Charles Brown, who told him that the lodge had been rewired and that all electrical wiring had been brought up to date before he sold it to the Paynes. He added that there was no electrical wiring over the bar and dance-floor area—disputing the Forestry Service's conclusion that "faulty wiring" had caused the fire.

Brown told Guisness that the Paynes had been "very slow and missed many payments" until Payne got a $15,000 loan from his mother and paid off the Brown mortgage.

"Brown stated that he got rid of the lodge as it was no longer suitable for a hunting and fishing lodge due to the increased population in the area. He stated that probably the only worth in this property was in its mining possibilities," Guisness stated.

Brown added further to the mystery about why the Paynes had thought they might be able to turn the lodge into a moneymaker when he himself had been unable to do so.

"He advised that when he owned the lodge their average take was probably $1,000 per month," Guisness wrote.

If Brown had been able to take in only $1,000 a month, how in the world did the inexperienced lodge owners think they could bring in more money? And with a base lodge income averaging only $1,000 a month, there was no way they could possibly have raised their family and paid their personal bills while at the same time stretching that money to maintain the lodge and pay their property taxes, utilities, employees, and mortgage.

What had they been thinking less than two years earlier when they bought the place?

Guisness reported about his interview with a woman he identified only as "Dorothea Moroney" who told him Payne had a jealous streak and that after his death Moroney "gathered the idea that [Mrs. Payne] would probably marry Ray Parker of Seiad as he was always in her company."

He then detailed what he had learned about the lodge building itself, including its electrical wiring, and concluded that although there seemed to be no motive for arson because the building was insured for less than its value, "this fire was not electrical in origin."

"However, no evidence was developed indicating the exact nature of the ignition. The fire was apparently started well away from any alarm system, which area would be above the bar where, according to the former owner, there was no electrical wiring. Entry to the attic area could easily have been gained through the French doors at the rear of the lodge."

Guisness made it clear that in his opinion, someone had intentionally started the fire. Arson, plain but not so simple.

"In spite of this, it is not felt that sufficient corpus delicti could be established to successfully prosecute anyone for arson, nor is there sufficient evidence to attempt recovery of payment on this loss.

"It is evident that William Payne had made every provision possible for having his estate in order upon his death. What this would indicate is not known at this time. This matter will again be discussed with the Federal Bureau of Investigation."

Bottom line: the fire likely was caused by arson, but there was not enough evidence to prove it. That was a strikingly familiar set of words, because no probable cause had been established for the crash of *Romance of the Skies* either, primarily due to a lack of evidence.

This is yet another provocative investigative file passed along to the FBI, and nothing will ever become of it.

Forty-seven-year-old *San Francisco Examiner* investigative reporter Ed Montgomery is already a legend, not only in journalism circles but also among those in the highest levels of law enforcement and the lowest levels of crime.

He has a national reputation for being a patient, determined reporter who has a special ability to get solid information from both good guys and bad guys, and nothing deters him once he digs into a story. Young reporters in the *Examiner* newsroom admire his energy as well as his careful, methodical reporting and strong, detail-filled writing.

He never forgets a name or a face, and he is respected by readers for his honesty. Colleagues say his integrity is unquestioned and his curiosity unequaled. He has sources in both the underworld and the FBI. When he grants confidentiality to a source his word is his bond.

He has worn a hearing aid for most of his life, but his ability to listen closely when a source says something important is part of what makes him extraordinary. Around the newsroom they that say everyone from convicts and con men to doctors and diplomats are among his trusted sources.

In short, Ed Montgomery is a reporter's reporter. He's not only an exemplary investigative reporter, but also a crime solver, and when a story carries Montgomery's byline it leads to even bigger headlines.

For the past couple of weeks Montgomery has been working his sources for information on an attention-grabbing story that is copyrighted on front page of the Tuesday, December 16, 1958, *Examiner*. It will be picked up by the national news services and read coast-to-coast, but more importantly it will be eagerly read by information-hungry family members and friends of those who perished on Flight 7. It also will be read by residents of Scott Bar who have been wondering about their former neighbors, the widow Payne and her children, who had quietly moved away less than two months ago.

The headline shouts:

BLAST PLOT HINTED IN MID-PACIFIC AIR CRASH
Sabotage Hinted In '57 Pacific Air Crash Fatal to 44; Firm Refuses to Pay Off $20,000 Policy

This story is the first time that anyone in the public has a clue that former Navy frogman and miner/lodge owner William Harrison Payne is a suspect in the crash of the Pan Am Stratocruiser.

Montgomery reports that Western Life Insurance Company is refusing to pay Payne's widow on an unsolicited $20,000 policy he purchased just weeks before the crash.

Three days earlier Mrs. Payne had received a copy of the policy along with a letter from Western Life stating that it was taking advantage of a clause in the policy that allowed it not to pay in the absence of a corpse or a legal declaration of the policyholder's death. Payne's body was not among the nineteen recovered.

Montgomery's story quotes a skeptical Western Life president, R.B. Richardson, who defends his company's action:

"There is evidence Payne was on the plane but there is no definite proof. There were many strange circumstances connected with that flight. We have the right to wait seven years before making payment and we intend to do so."

The *Examiner's* story states that Western Life assistant secretary and chief investigator Russell L. Stiles spent months looking into the claim and interviewed more than 165 people before writing a report that company executives want to release publicly but are being strongly encouraged by their legal team not to.

"The whole thing makes you wonder," Richardson says of Payne's "unusual" purchase of the insurance policy.

"He came into an office and applied for a policy shortly before the trip. He did not even know the agent. Agents usually motivate a man to action in buying insurance," Richardson states. "New facts may come up to change our minds but as of now we feel that Mrs. Payne's claim is definitely not proven."

The story says that the widow Payne, who now lives with her three children in Manteca, has hired San Francisco attorney Elliott Seymour to file suit against Western Life sometime this week. She already has been paid $125,000 in benefits for the policies Payne bought at the airport vending machine and has a $300,000 damage suit pending against Pan American. There is no mention of her now-forgotten marriage to Karim. Presumably, the reporter doesn't know about that.

Montgomery reports that Payne had been deeply in debt and that the reason he gave for the purpose of the trip—to collect some money he claimed someone owed him—did not justify the cost of the ticket.

He also states that Payne was an expert in explosives and just three weeks before the flight had been ordered by a Siskiyou County Superior Court judge to pay the county $500 in damages for blowing up and bulldozing a 1.5-mile section of a county road between his lodge and Scott Bar.

In the newspaper story, Payne's widow dismisses all the allegations against her former husband and laughs off the idea that he is still alive.

"Two or three of my real friends let me know that they'd been asked a lot of questions. What does this insurance company think? That my husband swam to some little island in the Pacific? How ridiculous can you get?"

She points out that her husband's mother and stepfather accompanied him to the airport and saw him get on the plane. She also says that Payne bought the large amounts of life insurance out of a deep feeling for his family and wanted enough coverage to clear them from any outstanding debts and to be able to live comfortably if anything happened to him.

The story also states that the Civil Aeronautics Board has received a copy of the Western Life Insurance Company report and is preparing to release its "probable cause" report.

When the public report is released weeks later, the CAB discounts the possibility that the crash was caused by sabotage or an explosion.

Privately, however, an internal CAB memo isn't so clear:

"It is confidentially felt by Pan American officials that the investigation concerning the individual passengers has not been adequate on the part of the Federal Bureau of Investigation and the Civil Aeronautics Board. . . .

The FBI has made a flat statement that they cannot become involved in every aviation accident. . . . They have flatly told the Pan American Airways system that any information which may develop should be turned over to them, but no further investigation is going to be done until something other than circumstantial evidence can be produced. Pan American definitely feels that there has not been sufficient investigation. As the investigation progressed [by insurance company investigator Stiles], it became evident that no one had investigated Mr. Payne as a possible suspect in the loss of the plane."

FBI director J. Edgar Hoover has been alerted about the *Examiner* story and is reading with keen interest the teletype from Webb W. Burke, the agency's special agent in charge in San Francisco, and the blockbuster newspaper story. Burke outlines the circumstances that point to Payne as a saboteur, then gives the director circumstances that suggest he had nothing to do with the crash.

Burke details the last-minute insurance policies, the one-way ticket with no return reservation, and the fact that no valid reason has so far developed for Payne to make a trip to Honolulu. He confirms that Payne was in financial distress and facing foreclosure on the lodge, and that he had been trained in demolitions while in the Navy. Payne also "had been heard to say" that he could build a delayed-action detonator by using two flashlight batteries.

Burke also provides information to Hoover suggesting that Payne had nothing to do with the crash including the fact that his name was on the passenger manifest, "though it should be noted he could have disembarked before the plane left San Francisco." Burke tells Hoover that no evidence has surfaced to indicate an explosion preceding the plane crash, and there is some evidence that the plane was ditched after a warning of an impending crash because fifteen of the nineteen recovered bodies were wearing life vests.

Finally, there are the unexplained circumstances of Harriet Payne's quickie marriage in Mexico, the burning of the Roxbury Lodge while she was on her honeymoon, and two strange phone calls: one allegedly from Payne the morning of the flight asking if it could be delayed because he was running late, and another from an anonymous man asking Pan Am if Payne was on the missing plane. When informed he was, the caller replied, "it couldn't happen to anyone more deserving."

Hoover is especially pleased when he reads the final sentence from San Francisco: "Since there has been no definite allegation of sabotage or willful destruction, it is recommended that no investigation be undertaken at this time."

By this time, every FBI employee from San Francisco to Washington knows that Hoover wants no part in investigating a crash that may never be solved.

Nine months after the hearing in San Francisco, investigators in Washington are still mystified by the cause of the crash, and members of the Civil Aeronautics Board are becoming increasingly frustrated with the agency's failure to determine a probable cause. It's not that investigators have quit working on the case, it's just that the time-consuming research has been inconclusive.

CAB Bureau of Safety Director Bakke is keenly aware of the pressure his superiors are facing, and he prepares a memo for the board explaining the delays and recommending what to do and say next. He says the unusual delay has been caused by the investigation into two crucial questions: 1) Did the aircraft attempt to send a distress signal? and 2) Was the crew incapacitated by carbon monoxide poisoning?

Bakke states in a Friday, October 31, 1958, memo that possible tape recordings from the plane were "subjected to extensive laboratory analyses using the techniques of several different institutions specializing in electronic research." He tells the board that every available technique has been employed in an unsuccessful seven-month attempt to determine if the crew sent a distress signal and, if it did, what the contents of that message were. Investigators conclude that no emergency message was sent from N90944.

He also tells the board that three organizations—the Armed Forces Institute of Pathology, the School of Aviation Medicine, and the Directorate of Flight Safety Research—have conducted considerable research into the unexplained carbon monoxide, but the issue is still unresolved.

He states that in September the Armed Forces Institute of Pathology "advised us that it was firmly of the view that excessive concentrations of carbon monoxide must have been present prior to impact."

This means that the crew and passengers ingested the deadly poison while the plane was still in the air. Something mechanical or man-made had caused the fire and smoke inside the airplane, either accidentally or deliberately.

Bakke says his team had been preparing a report for the CAB with that important finding when, on October 16, the institute advised that a recent Navy accident had "disclosed information that again cast doubt on the validity of the Institute's conclusions."

Back to square one.

Bakke tells his superiors that although the institute is continuing its research, he believes that "further delay cannot be tolerated," due to the "unusually large number of requests for the report from the public, next of kin, and from Members of Congress." He advises the board to adopt the latest revised draft of its probable-cause report—a document that is, to this day, inconclusive and unfinished.

TUESDAY, JANUARY 20, 1959

"WASHINGTON (UPI)—The Civil Aeronautics Board said today that the crash of a Pan American Airways plane in the Pacific Ocean on Nov. 9, 1957, probably will remain a mystery.

The board said it had too little evidence to determine the probable cause of the tragedy which took 44 lives. The most plausible theory, the report said, was that a propeller or propeller blade tore loose and ripped into the fuselage."

Among its conclusions the board found that:

- *The flight was normal and routine until shortly after the last routine report when an emergency of undetermined nature occurred.*

- *The plane descended from 10,000 feet and sent no emergency message.*

- *Some preparation for ditching occurred.*

- *The aircraft broke up on impact and a surface fire then occurred.*

- *Exposure of the crew to carbon monoxide was indicated but incapacitation could not definitely be established.*

- *No evidence of foul play or sabotage was found.*

- *Irregularities of maintenance practices and/or procedures discovered during the investigation could not be linked to the accident.*

The report was carefully crafted to state that the presence of a bomb "within the cabin fuselage" was not evident. That, of course, left open the possibility of a bomb or some type of explosive device having been detonated in a wheel well, for example, or in some other part of the aircraft not recovered.

The board determined that it had "insufficient tangible evidence at this time to determine the cause of the accident," but further research and investigation "is in process concerning the significance of evidence of carbon monoxide in body tissues of the aircraft occupants."

No further investigation is ever conducted by the CAB.

The January 1959 report becomes the incomplete, inconclusive, and last official word on what happened to *Romance of the Skies*. The CAB has decided that it is more important to bow to public and political pressure and to release a report than to finish the investigation.

***

The showplace of the Sonora Pass "Vacationland" sits eleven miles east of Sonora along Highway 108 in the California high country. The luxurious Twain Harte Lodge with its 6,000-square-foot main building and twenty-four poolside apartments is reopening on Saturday, April 30, 1960, under new ownership and management.

Harriet Avah Hunter Theiler Payne Isaac Payne and her business partner, Thomas O. McCarthy, a South Dakota native and most recently a resident of the San Francisco Bay Area, have paid $225,000 for the lodge and are investing in numerous improvements.

Ironically, the lodge had burned to the ground shortly after midnight on Thursday, October 22, 1953, in a spectacular fire that was first noticed by a cook. The fire quickly spread through the kitchen into the restaurant and upstairs into the bedrooms before California Division of Forestry crews extinguished it shortly after dawn. It was a total loss.

The Mother Lode Dining Room will feature a gourmet menu prepared by Russell Barrett, former chef of the Los Gatos Country Club, and beginning tonight there will be dancing, a piano bar, a fancy new cocktail lounge, and a coffee shop for guests.

The widow Mrs. Payne has another new life.

US DISTRICT COURTHOUSE, SAN FRANCISCO

Inside the US District Courthouse in San Francisco, Chief US District Court Judge Louis Earl Goodman peers over his thick black glasses as attorney Robert M. Jones presses Harriet Payne for information about her claim that his client, Western Life Insurance Company, owes her $20,000 for her former husband's death. It is obvious to courtroom observers that the sixty-six-year-old senior judge is not impressed.

Goodman is one of the most high-profile federal jurists in the nation and is an all-business, cut-to-the-chase kind of fellow. Eight years earlier he had made headlines when he restored the citizenship of 2,700 Japanese-Americans who had been interned in Army detention camps after war had been declared against Japan. While this case is certainly not of that magnitude, he pays close attention, but seems to have little patience for what could turn into a long, drawn-out legal proceeding if he doesn't keep both sides focused.

Moments earlier Jones had called the widow Payne to the stand as an adverse witness in an attempt to prove that her husband had either sabotaged *Romance of the Skies* with a time bomb or had snuck off the plane before it departed from San Francisco International Airport.

He questions her about her husband's experience with explosives, but she deflects his attempts to paint him as a saboteur. She admits that he was familiar with explosives and testifies that he used them in his mining operations. She denies the attorney's claim that the Paynes were deeply in debt at the time of the crash and that that may have been a motive for insurance fraud.

"Have you seen your husband since he left for San Francisco?" Jones asks.

"No, I haven't," the widow Payne replies softly.

Jones tells the judge that the insurance company should not be required to pay the claim because Payne's body was not recovered and there is no proof that he died from "wounds and contusions," as the widow claims.

The trial had begun with testimony from William Payne's sobbing mother, who told the court that she and her husband watched her son "march up the ramp" as he entered the Clipper.

"He went up and waved goodbye as he always does," she testified, wiping tears from her eyes.

Minutes later the widow Payne's attorney, George Lieberman, introduced a sworn statement from Pan Am counter agent Walter J. Unck, who said that he had checked a passenger named Payne onto the plane and that a pretakeoff head count showed the proper number of passengers on board.

Judge Goodman has heard enough.

"I cannot see any justification without some kind of proof suitable for a court of law in indulging in innuendos and suspicious contentions . . . even going so far as wanting to investigate the widow's activities which were perfectly normal," he scolds as he stares at insurance company investigator Russell Stiles.

Jones, Stiles, and other insurance company representatives are stunned by the judge's quick decision—even before they have had time to present much of a case.

"I can understand there is perhaps a natural inclination for insurance companies to advantage themselves on what is a technical provision in a contract, but certainly I can see no reason for it in this case," he rules.

He orders Western Life to immediately pay Payne's widow $20,000 and to reimburse her $1,118 for the insurance premiums she has paid since the crash. She walks out of the courtroom on Friday, December 20, 1960, with a wide smile on her face and pauses only briefly to pose for a newspaper photographer, who snaps her picture before she heads home.

Two months later Harriet reaches an out-of-court settlement in her $300,000 wrongful-death suit against Pan Am. The airline agrees to pay the widow $71,156. She has now received over $225,000—the equivalent of more than $2 million in today's money—as a result of the crash.

Across the continent, in Ridgefield, Connecticut, tiny, blonde-haired, blue-eyed Bette Anne Wygant is playing outside her house and trying to remember her pilot-daddy. She's only five years old but remembers holding onto his woolen pants legs and crying when he left for trips because she didn't want him to leave. She remembers the smell of his leather suitcases and the identification and destination tags that hung from them.

Suddenly she hears a plane fly overhead and grabs her toy telephone. She knows that her daddy is in heaven, and to her that means the sky. She dials the phone and talks to her daddy, telling him to please ask God to let him come back home, but her daddy doesn't respond.

PART THREE

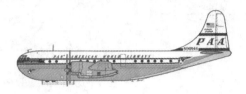

10

THIS MEANS MURDER

It is a chilly evening this Saturday before Easter, and my mother has taken us to Folly Beach, South Carolina, for a weekend getaway and a dose of Charleston history. My brothers and I are kicking along the sand and having a noisy good time when I notice my mother is dragging behind us.

I can tell there is something very wrong.

I turn around and walk back to her, and for the first time in nearly seven years, I see tears rolling down her face. She is so sad.

"What's wrong, Mom?"

"I just miss your daddy so much. So, so much," she says as she breaks down in front of me for the first time since California seven years earlier. "I am so lonely, Kenny. I just can't tell you how much I still love him and miss him."

Her heartbroken confession momentarily stuns me.

"I still love him and miss him too, Mom. We all do," I say as I hug her in a feeble attempt to bring some comfort.

I am only thirteen but feel like I have instantly become much older.

She wipes away her tears and breaks into one of her family-famous fake smiles. For a moment she seems to forget herself and her own misery and focuses once again on the most important thing in her life: my brothers and me.

"I'll be OK, son. You go on with your brothers now and have fun," she says as I hesitatingly walk away, my own heart heavy with a pain I haven't felt since November 1957.

It hurts to see my mother like that. I am heartbroken, angry, and determined. I look out into the ocean as the waves rumble to shore and realize that although they are thousands of miles apart, the Atlantic and the Pacific are the same water—the same water rolling onto the sand here in South Carolina may have once rolled across the Pacific, where my father's body rests somewhere.

I gaze into the horizon and imagine *Romance of the Skies* rapidly falling from the sky, closing in on the ocean, and then crashing in a thunderous, splashing roar into the sea. It disappears as I turn away, but I will see that Stratocruiser again and again every time I walk along a seashore for the rest of my life.

WEDNESDAY, NOVEMBER 20, 1965

I was fourteen years old when I decided that I had waited long enough. I needed to know why my father's plane had crashed eight years earlier, and I wanted to know right now. I had read and reread the 1959 Civil Aeronautics Board's report many times in the previous six years and continued to be bothered by its conclusion:

"The Board has insufficient tangible evidence at this time to determine the cause of the accident. Further research and investigation is in process concerning the significance of evidence of carbon monoxide in body tissue of aircraft occupants."

I wondered what the board's "further research and investigation" had found. Surely after all those years there was something new to report, especially on the carbon monoxide angle, so I wrote a letter to CAB board chairman James R. Durfee and asked for some answers.

The government's response a few weeks later made me feel as though someone had slapped me across the face. Hard.

That slap still burns today.

"You are advised that the CAB file on the aircraft accident that occurred on November 8, 1957, between San Francisco and Honolulu contains no information additional to that contained in the Board's published report, of which you apparently have a copy," it stated.

"We are sorry we are not able to help you in your further search for information pertinent to the death of your father."

"No additional information"? "We are sorry"?

I was stunned. Unsatisfied. Hurt. Angry. Determined. Eight years after my father and forty-three other people lost their lives in an unexplained airline disaster it was clear that the bureaucrats in Washington had done nothing and that the files were simply gathering dust in the archives. No one had lifted a finger to solve the mystery.

As it turns out, that cold letter set into motion a lifetime search for my father's killer. I vowed that day that I would search until the day I died if that's what it took to tell the world what had happened on November 8, 1957, and why forty-four people perished with no explanation.

I went to work immediately, poring through yellowed, well-worn newspaper clippings my mother had saved after the crash, reading every one several times. I not only took notes about what officials claimed may have happened, but also wrote down the many unanswered questions I had in my mind.

How in the name of God could a seventy-ton aircraft—the most sophisticated commercial plane ever built, with forty-four souls aboard—simply fall from the sky and plunge to the bottom of the ocean without an explanation?

I wrote a letter to another government agency. And another. And another.

I am still writing letters today.

In addition to the carbon monoxide angle, one of the many unresolved issues that bothered me was this statement from the 1959 CAB report:

"During the course of the investigation, and in view of the circumstances of the disappearance of the aircraft and the absence of living witnesses or crew members, an extensive investigation of personal activities and backgrounds of crew, passengers, and company ground personnel of the San Francisco base of PAWA was made by CAB and other governmental agency personnel. This investigation included personal interviews with all personnel who might have had access to the aircraft for any reason while the aircraft was on the ground on its last stopover at San Francisco from November 6, 1957, to November 8, 1957, and involved some 98 persons. This phase of the investigation disclosed that the aircraft received normal preparation for the flight and disclosed nothing relative to the character or behavior of any person that might point to sabotage in connection with the loss of the aircraft."

Bureaucrats have always had clever ways with words and special ways to slant them one way or the other to suit their purposes.

The final words in that statement were a lie. A bald-faced lie.

The Civil Aeronautics Board had been keenly aware that two people on the plane that day—purser Oliver Eugene Crosthwaite and passenger William Harrison Payne—had been the subjects of superficial investigations, and that their "character" and "behavior" were more than questionable. At this early stage in the search for my father's killer neither the public nor I had a clue that Crosthwaite had been identified as a suspect, but Pan American had suspected him from the beginning, and Payne had been fingered publicly in newspaper reports in 1958. Why didn't the report at least mention these two men, even with a disclaimer, rather than stating that no passengers or crew members had even raised eyebrows from San Francisco to Washington?

Although my father had been physically present in my life for only six years, the things he did and words he said stayed on my mind as my search continued throughout my teen years. They were as much a part of me as my biological DNA. I knew right from wrong, the difference between good and bad, and had a burning desire to seek out, and stand up for, the truth. Although I drifted occasionally as a teen, my father's goodness and character always took me back to the right place. His letters home were a moral roadmap.

I knew my father had been abandoned as a small child, but had fought the odds and had become an educated, worldly man. I also knew he was a World War II Navy veteran who had a passionate love for the United States. He was a patriot, and not the kind of fellow to question the integrity, decency, or competency of the men and women who directed our government and its many agencies, including those involved in aviation safety—the very people I was now setting my sights on.

We call ourselves The Monarchs. The auditorium at Roebuck Junior High is packed for our school's annual talent show, and we tear into "Wipe Out," my hands dancing across the piano keys to a delighted audience that applauds wildly when we finish. We take our bows and return to the stage minutes later, when we are presented with the first-place award. I am old enough to know better, but look across the audience, especially at the rear of the auditorium, for what I hope will be a glimpse of a late-arriving and surprise, special spectator.

He never shows up. Daddy is still missing.

WEDNESDAY, DECEMBER 3, 1952
FRANKFURT, GERMANY

"Dear Mom and Boys:

"It seems almost certain now that we will be able to leave by the end of the year, and I am pretty sure of leaving on the 20th of December. I hope I can come home for Christmas and get a few days off. If I could, I would be fishing in Florida. Someday, my love, you and I will be able to do just that if you want to and I live long enough. All things come to those who work, wait and plan.

"It still is not cold here. It just stays coat-weather all the time. The trees have almost shed all their leaves now, but the forests are still deep, dark and very beautiful. I'm sure no place else has such beautiful forests. I suppose that is why so many beautiful stories have been written about these forests. Hansel & Gretel came from here as well

as the great tales of Siegfried. This is close to the place where the Pied Piper of Hamelin led all the rats into the river and then when the city wouldn't pay what they had promised, he led all the children away. The children were found many years later—now grown—in a valley far to the east of here. Close by, too, is the beautiful Lorelei who leads so many sailors to their deaths at the bend in the river.

"There are parts of the old wall to the city still here. South and east of here the most beautiful and simple song of Christendom was written—'Silent Night.' These are a great and proud people. They are very industrious, and productive. One can hardly know them without feeling a certain amount of admiration mixed with sorrow for them; also, a little hate. The people who had the guts to defy the Roman Empire and founded Lutheranism were too weak to say no to a mustached Austrian paper-hanger. The people who created the V-2 don't know what a shower-bath is. The people who were able to weave their language into the simple classic beauty of 'Silent Night.' don't even have a word for apple pie. They have so much, and they miss and lack so much. . . .

"It is a city of contrasts. The Sunday morning air brings to your ears the peal of church bells over a thousand years old and, it seems, the stench of the gas chambers of ten years ago. From the rubble of the old city still containing the bodies of many super men rises new modern buildings aided by the US dollar. These people have plenty to do for 20 years more. They had their ass WHIPPED this time and except for the benevolent goodness of the United States and England they would, as a people, be as extinct today as the Phoenicians. I hope we have preserved them for the good of man and the glory of God. Time will tell.

"I love all of you, my precious babies—and am thankful that you are what you are, first, last, and always AMERICANS—and MINE!

"Love, Daddy"

That is where Daddy and I parted, and that unfinished, unsatisfactory CAB report was the catalyst. I love America, too, but I didn't believe that the bureaucrats in Washington had done their jobs, and if it were up to me to do it for them and solve the mystery of Flight 7, that's exactly what I intended to do.

Those were the days before the internet, when a long-distance phone call wasn't cheap, and the cost of a flight across the country to interview someone was out of the question. I spent a considerable amount of time looking through library microfilms of newspaper articles and writing countless letters, most of which received no reply. I also began my career as a newspaperman and started a family of my own. I was determined that my children would learn what happened to the grandfather they would never know.

When I began, I had two primary theories for the crash: mechanical failure, and passenger Payne. (It was more than a decade later before I learned about Crosthwaite.) What I had to do next was to gather enough information to rule each in or out, and explore any other possibilities that might arise during the search for my father's killer.

I had no idea it would take me fifty years.

THURSDAY, DECEMBER 16, 1965
WASHINGTON, D.C.

Eight years have passed since Flight 7 disappeared. The headlines are long gone, yet the mystery remains. Officially, William Harrison Payne and Oliver Eugene Crosthwaite are no longer suspects, but two days earlier the Federal Aviation Agency's chief security officer had called A. K. Bowles of the FBI's Identification Division with an unusual request: would he run a fingerprint check on Payne to see if his prints have shown up in agency's database during the past eight years?

Carl F. Maisch, a former FBI agent who would later head the FAA's first sky marshal program, followed up his phone call with a formal written request to FBI Director Hoover:

"In conjunction with an official inquiry as to the possibility of Payne being alive and continuing to be active in the area of crimes aboard aircraft, and in view of his unconfirmed death in a fatal air crash, we would appreciate your making a comparison of the prints of the subject on file in the Deceased Fingerprint Files with known prints on file in the Identification Division, with a view toward establishing that Payne may be alive under an assumed identity."

The letter and the FAA inquiry were never made public, but my discovery of them years later, through a Freedom of Information request, was a bombshell.

For reasons unknown, the FAA was concerned that Payne might still be alive somewhere hiding under an assumed name.

That would have likely meant he was living off the insurance proceeds that he and his "widow" split after the plane crash.

The FAA's letter also was intriguing because it raised the possibility that he was "continuing to be active in crimes aboard aircraft."

Someone at the FAA must have thought Payne sabotaged N90944, because the words "continuing to be active" indicated that he did something once and might be doing it again.

An FBI note at the bottom of Maisch's letter states this:

"FAA is attempting to determine whether William Harrison Payne is still alive. He was listed as a passenger on the ill-fated Pan American plane crash 11/8/57 and his body was never recovered or identified. . . . Subsequent to the crash it was determined that Payne had taken out substantial insurance for the flight, was in financial difficulty, and allegedly had a knowledge of explosives."

Hoover replied to Maisch on December 22, 1965, informing him that Payne's fingerprints (taken when he enlisted in the Navy) were being maintained in the agency's active file.

"The fingerprint file of Payne is appropriately marked to notify your agency in the event his fingerprints are ever received in the future. His fingerprints have not been received since November 8, 1957," Hoover stated.

Once again, FBI Director Hoover didn't even bother to see if there was anything his agency could do to assist another federal agency as it considered the possibility that Payne was still alive. History will prove that Hoover didn't mind ignoring agency rules or breaking federal laws whenever it suited his purpose, but he remained uninterested in Pan Am Flight 7.

Did Payne actually board the airplane? Did someone conspire with him to fake his death for the insurance proceeds?

DECEMBER 30, 1976

For years my investigation had stalled. It's not that I had lost interest; it was just that there seemed to be no decent leads to chase down.

Maybe it was the holiday blues and remembering that last Christmas in California with my father, but whatever the reason I now dug back into my files and started over. Surely there was something I could sink my teeth into that might get my investigation back on track? I zeroed in for the umpteenth time on the only publicly known human suspect in the crash, former Navy frogman William Harrison Payne. Too many things just did not add up. I was particularly interested in the Western Life Insurance Company investigation and its initial refusal to pay off his widow's claim.

By late afternoon I had tracked down and was talking on the telephone from my living room with a very reluctant Russell Stiles, now sixty-four years old and living in Canon City, Colorado. Stiles was the man who had spent months investigating Payne before his probe had been abruptly shut down by his superiors at Western Life.

Stiles, a devout Presbyterian and former US Army detective, let me know right from the beginning that he was a man of very modest means and nearing retirement. The last thing he wanted in his life right now was to be dragged back into the public spotlight about an investigation that had dominated his life for several months back in 1957 and 1958.

"For three months I was very deeply involved in this," he explained. "It was one of the most moving events of my life."

Stiles apologized at first for not wanting to talk with me about the investigation. He understood my desire to know, he said, but he was afraid to talk. It was a statement he would make several more times over the next twenty years as he repeatedly declined to share the details of his investigation.

"I still wake up nights thinking about it," he confessed. "I was so close to a solution to it."

"What," I begged him, "could possibly be a reason for not talking about the crash nearly two decades after it happened?"

Stiles hesitated again, then explained in a somewhat fretful voice that he was afraid of being sued. He started to say something else, but stopped. I let the moments pass without saying a word. It seemed like an eternity, but I hoped he might break the silence with something significant.

He did.

"If it came to their notice, they'd stop at nothing," he pronounced.

"'They'? Whose notice? What do you mean?"

"I would very much like to talk with you, Mr. Fortenberry, but I was told my life was in grave danger."

"Who told you that, Mr. Stiles?"

Silence. Again. This time I couldn't let the moment pass. I appealed to him in the name of my father and the forty-three others who had lost their lives on the airplane.

Slowly, he began to open up, perhaps to ease his conscience. He was still reluctant, but his voice was less harsh and he seemed a bit more at ease. He said I was the first person to contact him about it since the probe had ended decades earlier.

He told me that the lodge the Paynes had owned in Scott Bar "burned down mysteriously" less than a year after the plane went down. This was the first time I had ever heard about the lodge fire.

"Evidence was destroyed. It's amazing the facts that came from the probe of the fire," he said.

He told me that a woman in a town near the lodge (I learned later that this was the town postmaster) had been helpful to him in his investigation—an investigation that he proudly noted had included interviews with more than 150 people. He refused to reveal the name of that woman; nor would he divulge the name of another source—a "Chicago man who mined chrome with Payne."

Mined chrome? That also was a new angle: mining chrome required explosives.

Stiles then worried aloud about divulging further information. He was not only afraid of being sued or physically hurt by a mysterious someone he refused to identify, but also concerned about breaking any confidentiality agreements he might still have with the now-defunct Western Life.

And then he clammed up.

Although we would communicate again by email, that was the last time Stiles and I ever talked by phone. Frightened more than twenty years after the crash, Stiles said he would never talk on the phone for fear of being recorded by someone with an ulterior motive.

"They would stop at nothing," he reminded me.

It would be three more years before Stiles and I communicated again. I tried several times to break the silence but was rebuffed each time, whether by phone or mail.

But one thing was abundantly clear: Stiles honestly believed that his life would be in danger if he publicly pointed the finger at William Harrison Payne or someone else who might have been involved.

Invigorated by Stiles's enigmatic comments, I pressed on for more information about his investigation. Several months later I was able to track down R. B. Richardson, chairman emeritus of Western Life, who had long since retired and was living in Helena, Montana.

Just as he was with reporter Ed Montgomery of the *San Francisco Chronicle* back in 1958, Richardson was eager to talk about Payne and the company's investigation. The details, he admitted, were vague after so many years, but he reminded me there was no proof Payne had even boarded the plane.

"Pan Am wasn't even sure who or how many people were on the plane," he asserted. "Payne was a troublemaker. Every time he got into some kind of trouble, financial or otherwise, something went wrong."

Richardson claimed that Payne had blown up bridges, roads, and cabins in northern California and Oregon, adding that the former Navy explosives expert was a very troubled man.

He strongly suggested that Payne had perpetrated the crash for insurance purposes and hinted that his "widow," Harriet, was deeply involved.

"We were thoroughly convinced that he was still alive in Mexico," he revealed.

More than two years later, and after repeated prodding, investigator Stiles reentered the picture, this time with two brief but revealing letters about his probe of Payne's possible connection to the crash.

"In the course of my investigation I worked very closely with Pan American World Airways. In fact, they paid for a good part of the cost of the investigation. They wanted very much to have someone discover some proof that this did not just happen as an ordinary accident. My reluctance in furnishing information to you is brought about by the fact that you are going to publish this information and if you knew the circumstances as I do, I am sure that you would understand," he stated.

"I do not believe that I would wish to put anything in writing. nor would I want to discuss it on the telephone since I don't know you and even if I did, I would still be reluctant. The San Francisco Examiner *tried every possible way to obtain the information and even published a telephone interview with me, even though to practically every question my answer was no comment.*

"Believe me I understand your desire to know but I must protect myself and the company I worked for at the time."

So here we went again, just like two years earlier. I begged for help and information; he responded with nothing new. Still, he *had* responded, and once again I saw that as a positive sign— that he was weakening in his resolve. I wrote him yet another letter, and a couple of weeks later he replied:

". . . a vigorous pursuit 20 years ago might have disclosed some facts, but I left the company in 1961 and I might say with considerable regret at not having continued the matter. I have had a guilt complex because it was not done but I did not have the finances myself. Believe me, I am sympathetic with your attitude and the need to know. I would like to help you and I've written to the man who was president of the company at that time. He is no longer active with the company.

"In the past week I have consulted an attorney to determine what my

position would be if I give you all that I know. First, he says that I am bound by the rule of law which prohibits an employee from divulging information such as this without written consent from the Corporation. Second, he feels that I am in a vulnerable position legally by giving information in writing or on the telephone. Person to person might be different if it is not recorded.

"Concerning the sixth paragraph of your letter, am I to understand that the wife of the man is no longer living? You state 'as all possible parties are dead.' I might also state that there is no statute of limitations in the matter at hand.

"I will say again that I know how difficult it is for you to understand why I am being so cautious. You do not know the circumstances and therefore can't understand my reluctance. If you did, I am sure you would.

"I have been somewhat puzzled by the fact that I've never been contacted by any of the other survivors on this matter. After the articles in the San Francisco Examiner *and the* Chronicle *everyone in the state of California knew about this. I received many long-distance calls, some bad and some good."*

Stiles's bold statement that "there is no statute of limitations in the matter at hand" could mean only one thing: he believed that someone had committed murder.

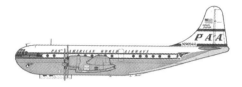

11

A VIOLENT AND
VINDICTIVE MAN

BY 1979 MY CAREER AS A NEWSPAPERMAN was well underway and I already had earned dozens of state and regional journalism awards. I had written investigative stories about unsolved murders in Florida and dirty politicians in the Carolinas. I had crafted feature stories about little old ladies and Little League baseball games, but one story—the one that mattered the most—still eluded me: What had happened to Flight 7 twenty-two years earlier?

Lodge owner William Harrison Payne was still my number one suspect. The name Oliver Eugene Crosthwaite didn't mean much to me at this point. I knew he was the purser aboard the plane, but only that. He seemingly bore no significance to the investigation. Press reports in the aftermath of the crash did not mention him. His name had not surfaced publicly at all during the Civil Aeronautics Board investigation. As far as anyone other than a few officials in Washington and at Pan American were concerned, he was a virtual nobody, just one among forty-four lives lost on that November afternoon.

That all changed on July 5, 1979.

During a remarkable phone call I had that morning with Robert Ashcraft of the National Transportation Safety Board, a new suspect emerged.

During the preceding several years I had had a series of exasperating, back-and-forth interactions with both the National Transportation Safety Board and the FBI and had come up virtually empty-handed every time. I would formally ask for every document in their files about the crash and months later they would formally reply. Their response was usually something like this: There was nothing in the files. Whatever files they may have had many years ago are long since gone. Or, all they have is the official CAB report.

I didn't believe a word of it, and pressed on.

My phone call with the NTSB's Ashcraft that day gave me my first decent lead in years. Somehow, I managed to guilt-trip Ashcraft into looking "just one more time" to see if the agency had anything that might be of help.

It paid off, and Ashcraft read me excerpts from a document pertaining to Crosthwaite. I was stunned beyond words. Crosthwaite? Who would have ever thought that? A crewman as a saboteur? Ashcraft stated that a Santa Cruz County sheriff's deputy had reported that Crosthwaite was "shaky" and "psychotic" and that the CAB and Pan Am had put together a team to investigate him. That was about all Ashcraft would tell me that day, but it was enough for me to once again formally ask both the FBI and the NTSB for all of their files on the crash and for me to zero in specifically on Crosthwaite. I learned that the best way to get what you want from a government agency is to be as specific as possible about the request. In other words, make it easy for them; do their research for them. Above all, be persistent.

Months later some poorly copied documents arrived in the mail, and I immediately tore into them, racing through page after page to get a quick glimpse of my newest suspect. Could Crosthwaite actually have been a suicidal murderer? Could the grieving widower actually have destroyed the plane and murdered forty-three people? After only a few pages into the report it certainly seemed possible, and after interviewing former Pan Am pilot Dick Ogg, the hero who had saved everyone aboard N90943 *Sovereign of the Skies* in 1956, I was even more convinced that Crosthwaite deserved more scrutiny.

Ogg believed that mechanical problems brought down Flight 7, but he also shared with me a chilling description of Crosthwaite, who had been a crewmember on some of Ogg's previous flights.

"He was a violent, vindictive, and unpredictable man who hated Pan American and had said on more than one occasion that he would 'get' Pan Am for what it had done to him," Ogg stated. "Pan American hired private detectives after the crash to follow up on this. Although that work produced considerable confirmation of such suspicions, there was never enough to allow a statement to the effect that the crash was caused by sabotage."

Ogg then added this piece to puzzle: "I think the location of the episode—almost exactly halfway to Honolulu, in midocean—lends some credence to this, since a madman saboteur would pick a spot furthest from land to bring on the disaster."

I began to chase down every scrap of information I could find on Crosthwaite, to develop a rough biography of his life and to learn how his childhood and family background might have affected his adulthood.

It took me years to learn who he was.

Born in Bennington, Kansas, on December 13, 1911, Oliver Eugene Crosthwaite lived a nomadic and unsettled life from the start. About the only thing young Gene could count on during his childhood was packing up and moving to another state whenever the urge struck his father, Herbert O. Crosthwaite. And that urge struck so often that Gene really had no place to call home until his late teens.

His father never seemed to be satisfied, bouncing from one job to another, one town to the next, always chasing an elusive dream. Herbert dropped out of high school before graduation, and as an only son went to work for his father in the family pharmacy before he left home and tried his hand at railroading. That lasted only three weeks before he returned home to Kansas, where he proudly told family and friends that he planned to enlist in the Army. That didn't last long, either: about as soon as he announced his military plans, he changed his mind.

Changing his mind became routine for Herbert Crosthwaite.

Eight months later he changed his mind again, enlisted in the Army, and after boot camp was shipped off to the Philippines for service during the Philippine-American War. After the war ended, he returned to Kansas, where he began to receive a $54.18 monthly government pension, the reason for which is unknown. He soon met and married seventeen-year-old Mary Beeson, a Colorado girl who had been on a summer visit to Kansas with her grandparents.

The newlyweds moved to New Mexico, but four years and two children later packed up and moved back to Kansas, where Herbert opened a bakery and restaurant the same week their son, the future Pan Am purser, entered the world. By all accounts the bakery was a huge success, but Herbert continued to search for that elusive pot of gold at the end of the rainbow, and less than a year after it opened he sold the bakery, packed up his family, and headed to Colorado.

It was near Pueblo that three-year-old Gene was thrown from a burro, struck his head, and was knocked unconscious for five days. The family fretted that he might never be the same mentally and faced the prospect that Gene might never walk again. His back was badly broken, and he struggled to regain consciousness, but miraculously was walking and talking again within weeks with only one chiropractic treatment.

His family was elated, but the concussion may have left him with hidden injuries that plagued him for years to come. His mother later recalled that he suffered from severe headaches for much of the rest of his life.

Pueblo was fine, but there was no pot of gold to be found, so the Crosthwaites packed up a year or so later and headed to California. There was no pot of gold there, either, so they headed back east to Colorado, crossing the Rockies in a covered wagon when tragedy struck again.

On July 24, 1915, near Florence, Colorado—just west of their former home in Pueblo—their covered wagon caught fire and burned to a crisp. The family lost all of its possessions, and in the desert

Southwest, in the middle of nowhere, the Crosthwaites were forced to start all over again.

They finally settled in the tiny farm-and-ranching hamlet of Yellow Jacket, where Gene attended the two-room Yellow Jacket School in a community with a general store that also operated as the local post office. His father homesteaded for seven years in Montezuma County, but just couldn't get the wanderlust—that desire for something more, something better—out of his head.

So, off to California once again.

The Crosthwaites migrated up and down the Golden State for a year or two. Herbert did carpentry work when he could find it and occasionally picked fruit for a paycheck, but these were tough times and the itinerant Crosthwaites were tired of moving and settling, moving and settling. Herbert decided one day that they needed to return to Colorado, so they were on the road once more. They found a farm near Cortez and, now joined by Herbert's financially secure and recently widowed mother, lived there for several years before the siren call of California summoned them once more. They traded their Colorado farm for one near Ripon, California, but lost it not long afterward due to financial hardship.

Then the ultimate blow struck the Crosthwaites: working near Buena Vista, California, one afternoon in May 1927, the forty-five-year-old Herbert was accidentally struck in the head by a piece of lumber while working on a carpentry job. He was in a coma for three weeks.

The sole provider of the Crosthwaite family never saw the light of day again. The Lodi Memorial Cemetery became his next and final home.

Gene was seventeen years old when his father died, and he did what was expected of him: he quit school and got a job, as a bellhop at the Hotel Covell in Modesto, to help support the family. His siblings sold fruits and vegetables, worked as messengers, and graded eggs for a poultry company. His mother became a maid. Without the wanderlust of Herbert Crosthwaite to lead them on another endless search for financial success, the Crosthwaites finally settled down, on Alturas

Avenue in Modesto. They struggled, but managed to get by.

Bellhop Gene was twenty-one years old when he found Thelma Mae Owens, the first love of his life, and they were married on October 20, 1931. They began homemaking on Needham Avenue in Modesto, and five years later he landed a job in transportation, a field he would work in for the rest of his life. Gene went to work for Matson Navigation Company in Frisco and for three years worked as a room steward on the Frisco-to-Australia run, primarily on the luxury ocean liner SS *Mariposa*. Although Gene supported her financially, Thelma Mae was left alone for weeks, sometimes months, at a time, raising their daughter, Billie JoAnn, while Gene sailed the seas.

By 1939, a fledgling American airline company founded by Juan Trippe—Pan American World Airways—caught his eye with its famed "flying boats," the mammoth Boeing 314s. Pan American was hopscotching the Pacific from San Francisco to Hawaii, from Guam to the Philippines and on to Hong Kong, and after years on the high seas, Gene was itching for a change, and flying in the skies in a Pan Am Clipper was just the kind of new adventure he was seeking. He also was deathly afraid that war with Japan was imminent, and the last place he wanted to be was on a sinking ship filled with holes. Pan American hired him on July 8, 1940, as a probationary flight steward on the Pacific route, and his seventeen-year career with Pan Am was underway.

Unfortunately, strained by long separations and Gene's inherited wanderlust, his marriage continued to fall apart, and he and Thelma Mae went their separate ways. Like his migratory father before him, Gene left his life in California behind and transferred to Shanghai, China, where he went to work for the Chinese National Aviation Corporation, a partnership between Pan Am and the Chinese government. Gene was a devoted employee and worked as a ground steward and liaison between CNAC and the US military throughout the war. He immersed himself by learning everything he could about the Chinese people, their customs, their politics, their traditions.

He drank hard. He played cards. He chased the ladies.

With Gene in China and Thelma Mae back in the United States, their marriage continued to deteriorate, and they formally separated on

June 10, 1944. Thelma filed for divorce and accused Gene of extreme cruelty that caused mental suffering. The Crosthwaites signed a divorce agreement a month later. Thelma Mae got custody of Billie JoAnn and the titles to their house and two lots in Belmont. Gene got their 1938 Oldsmobile. He agreed to pay $25 a month in child support and another $25 a month in alimony.

When World War II ended, Gene remained in China and was brought back into the Pan American family as a senior port steward. He mixed it up with the locals. He continued to drink heavily, gambled at cards, and on at least one occasion nearly got into a fight in a bar before a colleague with more common sense intervened.

"He had a tendency to be spring-loaded in a negative position," one pilot recalled.

He also fell behind in his alimony payments, and in December 1946 a San Mateo County judge ordered Pan American to begin deducting more than $100 a month from his paycheck until he caught up, which was fourteen months later.

On October 20, 1948, he was promoted to flight purser, and he was back in the air. It was in Shanghai that he met and married Julia Pavlichenko, a Manchurian-born Russian widow with a child, Tatiana, from a previous marriage. In 1949 Gene formally adopted the nine-year-old, and her new name became Tania Eugene Crosthwaite.

Ultimately Gene was sent back to California and worked the Pacific route for Pan American. Off duty he worked tirelessly and successfully to unravel the immigration bureaucracy so that he could bring Tania and Julia's widowed mother, Katherina, to the United States, and by the midfifties Gene was feeling on top of the world. He had a young and stunningly beautiful Russian-born wife and a well-paying job that allowed him to travel the world, and was building a new house in Felton, known as "the little town in the Redwoods." His home was constructed in large part with assistance from his skilled stepfather-in-law, Peter Stub, and financial help from his mother-in-law, who peeled vegetables at Birds Eye to help the family.

The good life ended on September 22, 1955, when Crosthwaite was diagnosed with tuberculosis, grounded from flying with Pan Am, and hospitalized for what would be six months of treatment.

He would never be the same.

JULY 1992

The bureaucratic negligence and cold indifference of federal authorities in Washington who had put the unfinished CAB report in a file and forgotten about it three decades earlier continued to nag at me, and on June 21, 1992, I wrote a letter to National Transportation Safety Board Vice Chairman Susan Coughlin, seeking her help, particularly on resolving the unanswered questions about the carbon monoxide. The CAB no longer existed by this time, having morphed into the NTSB. Coughlin promptly forwarded my letter to Ronald L. Schleede, chief of major investigations in the agency's Office of Aviation Safety.

Finally, I had someone's attention.

Schleede and I had a conversation a few weeks later, and what he said took my breath away.

He quickly dismissed the decades-old story that elevated levels of carbon monoxide in the plane victims may have been caused by the decomposition of their bodies in the ocean.

"That is baloney," Schleede declared. "Carbon monoxide doesn't do that. . . . It joins the blood through the lungs. The victims have to be breathing."

Learning that the possibility of a link between carbon monoxide and body decomposition had been dismissed years earlier further deepened my frustration and suspicions about how the case had been mishandled.

Schleede, who had previously worked in the agency's Human Factors Division, said he was "appalled" when he had read the CAB report the previous week.

"I couldn't believe [the case] was left hanging," he told me. "It's amazing. I just can't understand why the case was not pursued."

Neither could I.

Schleede assured me that the NTSB would research the circumstances of the crash and get back to me. I was elated and felt that having him on my side to open doors in the federal government was the most positive development in the search for my father's killer in many years.

That positive soon turned into a negative.

On July 31, 1992, he sent me a letter in which he stated that Dr. Merritt Birky, the NTSB's fire scientist and toxicologist, was assisting him in handling my request but "he has been unable to find any toxicology records at the Armed Forces Institute of Pathology and there appear to be no records at the NTSB other than the adopted report."

Schleede said the agency would continue to search for more information about the crash investigation, but told me to "please be patient" because the agency had limited time available due to a heavy accident-investigation workload.

That sounded to me like a bureaucrat who was setting the stage to do nothing, but he concluded his letter with the statement that he "finds this case very interesting and will attempt to get more answers for you."

I *was* patient, for three months, but when he failed to get back to me I sent him a letter asking for an update. He did not respond. I called his office. He did not respond. I sent him emails. He did not respond.

I was patient for another seven years, and on February 18, 1999, I sent a letter to NTSB Chairman Jim Hall briefly outlining the case and expressing my frustration with Schleede. Less than an hour later Schleede sent me an email:

"I think we lost some email during a network problem," he stated. "I have not done anything more about that accident. I am not sure I can be of more assistance.—Ron."

Unsatisfied with that response, I tried him again two months later. This time he was more direct:

"I have retrieved the report of the subject accident and have reviewed it again," he stated in an April 11, 1999, email. "As I mentioned before, I don't see any reasonable means to assist you further. I can't find any practical means to resolve the questions regarding the source of the CO found during post-mortem testing, As the report reflects, the limited wreckage recovered revealed no evidence of an in-flight fire; however, there was a fire on the surface of the water . . . and a possibility exists that the reported CO levels were absorbed during the surface fire. However, it does not seem possible to prove such a theory."

I accepted his answer, but still couldn't accept the fact that the investigation had been stopped stone-cold in 1958.

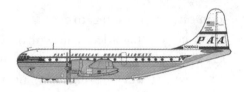

12

THE RIGHT HAND OF GOD

Russell Lawrence Stiles was not a flamboyant fellow, not even close. Like my father, he was one of those conservative, steady, down-to-earth veterans of World War II who returned home from the service, settled down, and raised a family. They didn't make headlines or make waves, but they made a difference.

He was born on February 28, 1913, in Newton, Kansas, to James and Emma Stiles, but the family moved early in his childhood to Colorado, where his father worked as a train conductor. Stiles was an outstanding student and served twice as business manager of *Skyline Flashes*, the Cañon City High School newspaper. He was a studious fellow, who after graduation studied at the University of Colorado and later worked as an insurance inspector for the American Service Bureau in Denver. In 1943 he enlisted in the Army for the duration of the war and was sent with his wife of four years, Maxcy Jane Watson, to Fort Leavenworth, Kansas, where he became a military policeman and detective.

After the war, he and Maxcy moved to Helena, Montana, where he rose through the ranks of Western Life Insurance. Dependable and trusted by senior executives, he was assistant secretary and chief investigator in 1957 when the company president dispatched him to California on a very important mission: investigate the claim of the widow Payne.

That assignment turned out to be a life-changing event for him, and I was disappointed that I had been unable to find out why. In early 1999 I made yet another attempt to persuade him to talk with me and to share what he knew about the crash forty-two years earlier. The search for my father's killer had of late been going nowhere, and I felt the only way forward was through Stiles.

"Dear Mr. Stiles:

"You may recall that we communicated many years ago about the crash of Pan American N90944 as I was researching a book on the project. You had expressed concerns about discussing the matter, and although I certainly respected your judgment, I desperately wanted to learn what you knew.

"I still do, Mr. Stiles. As you know, it has been my life's passion to learn why my father and everyone aboard Romance of the Skies died. Frankly, I have just about hit a dead end with this, and after more than 30 years of pursuing answers, I am writing now in hopes that you might be willing to share the information you learned while investigating the crash.

"Please reconsider your decision of more than 20 years ago and allow me the opportunity to learn what you know about this crash."

I knew that time was running out, given his age, and as it turned out, the letter struck a nerve. He responded on March 9. Although it was his normal courteous but curt response, it did give me hope that after all these years his conscience was finally beginning to overwhelm his fear and concern:

"This will be brief for now, but I will communicate with you later. I have just reached the age of 86 and my family is grown. I retired in

1979. I come close to being an invalid. I still drive an automobile and I can walk only short distances. I tell you this because at my age I feel that anything could happen.

"I make no promises as to what I can do about your request. I wish I could say, sure, here it is, take it, do with it what you will. It's not that easy. I know it is hard for you to understand and I am very sympathetic with your position. I know how I would feel under similar circumstances. Please feel free to communicate if you wish."

That was that. No new revelations. No promises of any new disclosures. Nothing but an opening door, and I could not let it close again. Stiles was getting very old, very feeble, and I did not want him to leave this world without giving me something that might jumpstart my investigation. I sent him a follow-up note the next day, urging him again to share whatever he felt he could. Anything, I pleaded. Anything.

A few days later he responded. Again, not with much information, but I was pleased that something was going on in his head and that he was finally opening up. He shared with me some thoughts about the 1958 lawsuit that Harriet Payne had filed against the insurance company when it refused to pay her, and he lamented the way the case had been handled when it went to trial.

"I am struggling with my psyche to determine just what I can give you without destroying the well-being of my wife and myself. What I must avoid is a lawsuit. Twenty years ago, there would have been more than that.

"In 1957 I was employed by Western Life Insurance Company. It was a very fine insurance firm. I was employed by this firm after leaving the service. In the service I was with a military police group doing mostly investigative work. Before the service I had done investigating for insurance companies, bonding companies and about any kind of business needing information on people. Most

all of my associates with Western are dead now or in rest homes. I was hired by the president of this company and he backed me on nearly everything. He told me he talked to you on one occasion. You then called me; I believe.

"*When the case in question was presented to us, I was sent to work on it and told to report on it only to the president. The legal counsel was unable to accept being bypassed and he sabotaged the case. I was horrified when I began to see the law firm hired by us had not opened the file which we had furnished. They knew nothing about the matter and made no effort to learn any of the details. They were unprepared to try the case, so it was open and shut. The claim was paid as I knew it would be, but we had hoped something would come of it.*

"*The judge sat staring at me, ready to jump for contempt like a sheep dog at his sheep. There was no chance for us to present any kind of defense. It was probably the shortest trial on record.*"

Again, I was pleased we were communicating and grateful to have the information, but his gripes about how the lawsuit had been handled were of no real concern to me. What I wanted, what I needed, was the information in his files and in his head about his investigation into passenger-lodge owner William Harrison Payne. I responded to his letter with information of my own, including tidbits about the autopsies of the nineteen bodies recovered and questions that were troubling me about what the coroner had discovered.

In the back of my mind I was thinking he might find the information interesting, but even more importantly that it might take him mentally back to those days when he drove all over California and Oregon working so diligently to solve the case. More than two decades earlier he had confided that he still had sleepless nights over the case, and I hoped that now, as he neared his final years, the gentleman would want closure just as much as I did.

Something was finally clicking. He responded a few days later:

"Today, I'll respond to your question on the autopsies. We were running out of time. I explained to you before that Western Life was merging with a Minnesota company and our legal counsel was to take over the presidency in Minnesota. Richardson, with whom you have talked, would lose his grip on Western Life and that would be the end for me and the investigation. So, I hastened to do what I could in the time that was left. I felt the autopsy records were no support to our position so did not try to review them. Ordinarily I would have if there had been time.

"I left Western Life in 1961. I had hoped Richardson would finance the continuation of the investigation. I did not have the money needed to go on. I thought once he was going to do it, but he didn't do it. He did not go with the company to Minnesota and he became physically impaired so that he was confined to his home. This man did a great many things for me."

"Come on. Come on, man," I muttered to myself as I read more about Western Life, Richardson, and how wonderful he had been to Stiles. "Give me something decent to work with."

And then the letter took a surprisingly strong turn:

"I was of the opinion that we were so close to a solution and he was inclined to believe it, too, I thought.

"From the postmistress of Scott Bar, I learned that the subject's wife was receiving mail from out of the country which had never happened before. I am sure she was convinced the mail was from the subject. She was terrified that she would lose her job if she told me anymore.

"I begged and pleaded with her, but she was terrified at the possibility of losing her job or prosecution. One day she said if I would take her to the sheriff —a friend of hers—she would ask him if she

should divulge any of the information. I knew this would be bad and it was, for he assured her that she should give me no information. Then he wanted detailed information from me which I would not give him. He could smell a great opportunity for a law enforcement officer in this area."

Bingo! Payne's widow had begun receiving mail from out of the country after the crash? The postmistress was terrified? Finally, something to sink my teeth into. Did Payne and his wife conspire to blow the plane up for insurance purposes?

". . . You may or may not have this information, but you speak of the expertise of the subject. He was a US Navy frogman. This was a very risky branch of the service. The members of this group are highly trained in underwater activity and the use of high explosives. This man had the knowledge of how to detonate an explosive with a delayed device. The details of how he did it, he guarded very closely. The part of it that was known was that he would use flashlight batteries, and no one knew anything about how he did it otherwise. The delay was for 6 hours.

"Subject was engaged in the mining of chrome in the mountains of Northern California. I located his mining partner in Chicago, and I spent considerable time with him. There was another man who lived in a location that, in reaching the area of the mine, it was necessary to drive past his residence.

"Subject was using explosives on a daily basis. He was setting charges in the late afternoon, then getting in his car and driving away. The charges would explode later in the evening. The next day subject and his partner would return to the area and process the ore for shipment.

"The man who lived near the mining site decided to time the length of time from the hour the subject left the area until the charge exploded.

I have not yet been able to find the exact timing, but it was a massive shock to me when he said '6 hours.' You may remember that 90944 departed San Francisco airport at 11:31 AM. It is known that whatever happened to it occurred at 5:27 PM. This is about as close to 6 hours as anyone would be able to compare.

"A Pan Am employee who was part of the boarding party when 944 left San Francisco remembered subject and described his attitude as 'taciturn.' He also remembered him carrying a valise when he boarded the plane.

"In the past 40 years I have talked with a few people including two lawyers, but this story is so vastly incredible no one believes it happened. They just shake their heads at me and say nothing. No one believes it.

"I am a religious-thinking person. I believe there is a God, a hereafter and a person who sits at the right hand of God. I have been driven for years to do something about this. Maybe what I am doing now will suffice."

At the time, I had no idea what a tangled web I was about to try to unweave. The postmistress's name? I learned that she was Jessie Payne.

And her husband? Earle Payne, an explosives expert just like crash suspect William Harrison Payne.

As it turns out there were dozens of Paynes in Siskiyou County— none of them related to the sabotage suspect. It took me more than a year to unravel who was who and what their connections were, and as was too often the case in the search for my father's killer, many of the key people had long since died.

The March 1999 letter was the last I ever heard from Russell Stiles; seven months later, he died.

For years I begged and pleaded with Margaret Stiles Storm, daughter of investigator Stiles, to allow me to see the file he had begun to share with me before he died. Mrs. Storm, her father's caretaker in the final years of his life, was familiar with his communications with me, and I reached out to her again in a March 2007 letter:

"The last letter I have from Mr. Stiles is dated March 21, 1999. After more than twenty years of letters back and forth he was finally beginning to share with me details of his investigation into the crash of Pan American Romance of the Skies which took my father's life.

"His last sentence to me was this: 'I have been driven for years to do something about this. Maybe what I am doing now will suffice.'

"That is the last I ever heard.

"My plea now is that you will finally allow me to look at his notes and records of this investigation to help close that chapter of my life-long investigation into the crash of my father's plane. I have spent many years looking into this crash, and one big hole remains: what did Mr. Stiles discover?

"I would be more than willing to fly to Colorado and review the notes and records in your home, if that is your desire. Please give my request thoughtful consideration."

No reply.

I tried to reach her when I was in Colorado later that year. Again, nothing. Years later she responded to an email and told me that her father's notes were not easily accessible and were somewhere in his personal belongings, which she had not yet had time to go through. I told her I understood how difficult that must be for her and volunteered to fly to Colorado and help her.

Again, no reply.

A few years later, I tried another approach. After learning that she was an amateur historian and active in historical research in Colorado, I tried to convince her of the importance of solving the mystery from a historical perspective.

That may have been what did the trick.

On September 7, 2015—nearly fifteen years after Stiles had begun sharing information with me—an envelope containing an eighteen-page summary of his investigation arrived in the mail. Stiles himself had provided much more than a summary to his superiors at Western Life and ultimately to the FBI, but a summary was better than nothing, and I was delighted to have it.

"This is all I know about the subject; maybe it will be beneficial to you," Mrs. Storm stated in a brief cover note. "God bless."

The summary provided enough evidence, albeit much of it circumstantial and full of unusual coincidences, to point the finger away from purser Crosthwaite—and squarely back at former Navy frogman Payne.

The first pages of the report detailed how Payne had obtained, unsolicited, the life-insurance policy that the company had refused to pay until ordered to do so by a judge. He went into great detail about Payne's insistence that the policy be written as soon as possible, and how he was forced to change his travel plans during his late-October 1957 visit with his mother so that the required insurance company physical could be conducted the following day in Manteca. This was less than two weeks before the final flight of *Romance of the Skies*.

Interesting, but hardly the bombshell I had been hoping for.

Next, the summary provided biographical information about Payne—something I had been desperately seeking for years. It confirmed that he had a brother, David, a mechanic in Fresno, and that his father had died early in his life. That somewhat explained why Payne and his mother had ended up in Sparks, Nevada, where she married Charles Edgar Wilcox, an automobile repairman who later became a card dealer at The Palace casino. Payne grew up in Sparks, joined the Navy shortly after high school, and served without distinction for twenty-one years, until his retirement.

"During the time that he was in the Navy, he was in various classifications which included the following: barber; metals man;

machinist's mate; and during the early part of World War II was a Frogman."

Frogman. That was further confirmation of Payne's claims to friends and family that he had years of experience in the Navy with explosives. Newspaper accounts at the time of the crash repeatedly referred to Payne as a "former Navy frogman and demolitions expert," a statement that his widow had confirmed to reporters.

Early Navy frogmen—the forerunners of today's Navy SEALs—were trained in, among other things, swimming underwater, clearing beach landing areas of enemy mines and obstructions, and planting explosives on enemy ships.

I had determined years earlier that Payne had been assigned to the submarine base at Pearl Harbor in 1940 and had worked on tenders that serviced and supplied subs throughout the war and into the Korean War era. He also had been stationed at the Mare Island Naval Shipyard, north of San Francisco, where numerous submarines and sub tenders had been constructed and repaired during World War II. There was no formal job title of frogman in the early days of World War II, and it is entirely possible that Payne was one of a number of sailors who had become frogmen simply because of their proficiency at swimming and their proximity to submarines.

Stiles outlined Payne's finances and how he had arranged the purchase of the Roxbury Lodge:

"Mr. Payne had a Navy retirement pension of $160 a month. His wife owned a small house in Manteca, California, which was valued at approximately $5,000. The Roxbury Lodge of Scott Bar was purchased with a $5,000 down payment in July of 1955. The $5,000 was partly savings and partly money that belonged to Mrs. Payne. The agreement concerning this lodge was that $10,000 would be paid in six months, and in a year $15,000 would be paid. At the end of the six-month period following the date of purchase it was necessary for Mr. Payne to borrow $10,000 from his mother, which we are advised was approximately her life savings, and at the end of the year it was necessary that Mr. Payne borrow $15,000 to complete payment. The $15,000 was borrowed from Mr. L. R. Zimmerman of Stockton, California. Payments on this loan were to be made at the rate of $250 a month. Mr. Zimmerman was given a Deed of Trust to the Roxbury Lodge of Scott Bar, California."

Stiles's report confirmed what I had learned years earlier about how Payne came up with enough money to buy the lodge, and also that he had not been making enough money to keep it afloat and to make his mortgage payments. The information about Zimmerman, however, was new. I needed to learn more about this man and why he would lend Payne that much money in a risky business venture that clearly was failing.

The fifty-three-year-old Leonard Raymond Zimmerman was a very wealthy man when he bailed Payne out of financial trouble in July 1956. Part owner of a seven-acre shipyard in the Stockton Deepwater Channel on Banner Island and partner in a steel supply and construction company, Zimmerman made a fortune during World War II through lucrative contracts with the Army and the Navy to construct floating crane barges, landing crafts, coastal freighters, sub tenders, and steel tugboats.

It is likely that Payne became acquainted with Zimmerman while serving out his final years in the Navy in the Stockton area or when he worked for a short time as a coremaker at Augustine Brass Casting, less than three miles from Zimmerman's shipbuilding company. Somehow, he was able to convince the businessman to loan him the money when he and Harriet ran into financial difficulty and couldn't make the mortgage payments to the Brown brothers. Zimmerman may have seen this as an opportunity to own a resort lodge at significantly less than value if Payne defaulted on the note—and Payne was in arrears at the time of the disappearance of *Romance of the Skies*.

Zimmerman had told arson investigator Guisnesss that he was ready to foreclose on the note and take over the lodge when the plane went down—another possible reason for Payne to sabotage the plane either by suicide-murder or a straight-out murder-for-insurance fraud.

Again, the summary was interesting, but so far provided no compelling information that might add to the case against Payne.

And that was about to change — dramatically.

Stiles provided insight into not only Payne's personality and character, but also his failing finances, as well as tantalizing clues about Payne's activities in the days and weeks before the plane went down.

Stiles reported that Payne was known to drink "occasionally to excess," but was not a habitual drinker. When the Paynes bought the lodge they also acquired its valuable California state liquor license, which Payne decided to exploit to maximum effect:

"Liquor of all kinds was sold by the drink in this lodge. The area around Scott Bar, California, is largely one of mining operations and lumbering operations. Among this class of people, at least in this area, there appeared to be a great deal of drinking, and this lodge was very accessible to the people who used liquor. Mr. Payne was subjected to some criticism for his lack of control on the use of liquor in this business. His interests seemed to be only in selling liquor and benefiting financially to the fullest extent," Stiles stated.

Payne began to ignore the wealthy fishermen and hunters who had kept the lodge afloat for many years, concentrating instead on his bar business, which tended to drive out the higher-class clients. The bar was easier to manage; it was all cash and didn't require advertising, reservation handling, or the upkeep of accommodations.

Stiles further stated that during his investigation he paid careful attention to Payne's character and personality.

"People who knew Mr. Payne well described him as the youngest in the family and a 'mama's boy.' He was extremely fond of his mother and had a very definite attachment to his mother which seemed to some who were interviewed as being a stronger attachment than to his wife."

That special mother-son bond was important to know about, because later in his investigation Stiles would come to believe that Payne's mother lied to him when questioned about the circumstances leading up to the crash.

"Very close questioning of many people with whom this man was associated in various localities seemed to indicate that he was the type of man who, under pressure, would take on a complete change in personality."

Stiles then introduced the names of three men whose relationships with both Payne and his wife raised intriguing questions: Earle Payne, William Rob, and John D. Sherman, all of whom would emerge as important figures as I continued my investigation in the years ahead.

"Earle Payne, who knew the applicant perhaps better than anyone interviewed, was very close regarding any information which he would give. It was felt that he actually misrepresented and misstated facts on many points, but he did make one very pertinent statement as follows: 'Mic (William Harrison Payne) was the kind of guy that had a complete change of personality when the going got tough.' On numerous occasions it was known that people would call at Roxbury Lodge to see him and he would send his children or his wife to tell them he was not in or not available. There appeared on many occasions to be no specific reason for this action, only that it just happened to be his mood at that particular time not to wish to see anyone. . . . this action did not appear to be concentrated on any one or two individuals. It might be a very close friend one day, on another day it might merely be a salesman or businessman who called to see him, and on a whim, Payne would merely refuse to see them."

OK, so Stiles had established that Payne was moody or may have had some kind of mild personality disorder, but what about the investigator's statement about Earle Payne lying to him? Why would he do that? Who was Earle Payne anyway? Was he a relative, a friend, or business associate? What exactly was his relationship with suspect Payne and why was he so "guarded" in giving answers to the investigator? Could he have been hiding something pertinent to the crash or perhaps even have been involved himself in some way?

Those questions were unanswered in the Stiles report, but I was able to answer the easiest of them with some additional research.

No, Earle Payne was not a relative. Although the Paynes of Siskiyou County (and there are many of them) had lived in the area since before California became a state, I could find no proof of any blood connection between the men. I did find it a strange coincidence, though, to learn that all of the Siskiyou County Paynes had original family ties to Missouri, just like William Harrison Payne.

Although they had no proven family connection, Earle and William Payne were neighbors on Scott River Road and had several other important things in common: both were experts in explosives and shared an interest in mining and a fondness for heavy equipment—and for Harriet Payne.

Stiles made a point of stating that Payne was jealous and short-tempered, so much so in fact that at least once he had used a high-powered rifle to shoot at a man (presumably Earle Payne) because he was jealous of him and for some reason believed Earle had eyes for his wife, Harriet.

On another occasion he took shots at a different man for no apparent reason.

"On one occasion, Mr. Payne became extremely angered without provocation at a man by the name of William Rob, who is a mining promoter in this area. He snatched up a rifle and shot at Mr. Rob three times with the intent to actually hit him," the report stated.

"Mr. Rob was interviewed during the investigation and states that there was absolutely no provocation for an attack of this kind," Stiles noted.

For some reason, neither Rob nor Earle Payne filed police reports. Were they trying to keep something under wraps, so that law enforcement would not find out about it?

Stiles discovered several other strange statements and incidents involving Payne and what seemed to be a penchant for violence rather than discussion when things didn't go his way.

"In discussing his trip to Honolulu, he was known to have made this statement: that if he was unable to collect some money from his debtors there, he would use dynamite and 'blow them up.'"

He actually had used dynamite at least once to make his point.

"On one occasion he was known to have charged logging truckers a trip fee to haul logs over a small corner of his land. The road over which the logging truckers were transporting their logs was known to be a county road. The matter was reported to the county attorney, and Mr. Payne was ordered to cease charging fees for their use of this road. He became so angered that he, by using explosives, blew a large hole in the middle of the road. It was necessary that the county repair this damage so that the road could be used," according to Stiles.

Another time he was known to have used a heavy Caterpillar tractor that damaged some of the county's asphalt roads. He was warned not to do that again, but Payne ignored the warning and not long afterward damaged another road, to the tune of about $1,000. When law enforcement authorities arrived, two Payne accomplices fled the area. They were never identified.

That was enough for the county attorney to act. He filed a complaint against Payne in Siskiyou County Court, and a judge ordered Payne to pay damages and a $450 fine. Payne never appeared in court himself but hired an attorney who filed an appeal that was still pending at the time of the crash.

Payne and violence seemed to go hand in hand.

Years later I discovered that when Payne had shot at William Rob, the mining promoter had been in the company of forty-eight-year-old Dorothea Reddy Moroney, labeled the "Chrome Queen" by *Time* magazine for her huge financial success in mining chrome, which she sold to the US government during World War II. Chrome was extremely scarce during the war and was essential in the manufacture of armored plates, shells, and machine tools, all critical for the US war efforts.

By 1956-1957, when the Paynes were operating Roxbury Lodge, the wealthy and already legendary Moroney was mining chrome and other precious metals all around Scott Bar and was familiar with both Paynes, especially William.

The report then pointed me in the direction of someone whom Stiles had hinted to me about nearly forty years earlier, and raised even more questions that needed to be answered.

"During the time that the applicant [Payne] operated this business [the lodge], he became interested in the mining of chrome and later became involved in a chrome mining venture with a Mr. John D. Sherman, whose address is 21 East Scott Street, Chicago, Illinois. This partnership was dissolved before Mr. Payne's death occurred," Stiles wrote. "Mr. Sherman is reported in some way to be associated with the publication of *Playboy* magazine [a connection I could never verify]. Mr. Sherman was somewhat interested in mining and entered into a partnership with Mr. Payne in the mining of chrome."

Who was this John D. Sherman? How did he meet Payne and get

involved in mining chrome with him? Why would Payne take on a sideline of mining chrome when he had his hands more than full with the lodge? And was Sherman in some way connected with the crash?

I learned that John David "Buddy" Sherman was a wealthy, twenty-nine-year-old adventuresome fellow when he traveled to Roxbury Lodge as a guest in 1956. The gregarious Sherman, whose permanent address was in Chicago, also spent time on California's coast, where his widowed mother, Marjory Kanrich, lived, in Cathedral City. He traveled extensively and was known to enjoy heated political conversations, a good cup of coffee, peasant Greek wine, and brandy.

His father, Harry Wilson Sherman, was a pioneer in the manufacture and sale of wash-and-wear cotton garments, primarily dresses for women, and the creator of the retail chain store concept. His particular chain, The Sherman Shop, included dozens of stores from coast to coast, and all the merchandise was manufactured in his Sherman Wash Wear and Mount Vernon Garment Company factories.

As a child, Buddy Sherman had become accustomed to wealth and its privileges. He lived with his parents in an elegant twelve-room stone home on North State Street in Chicago and graduated from the prestigious Francis W. Parker High School. Two full-time live-in servants—a maid and a cook—took care of the family's needs, and Buddy developed a taste for the finer things in life. By his late teens he was itching to go out on his own and travel the world.

In short, he was bored and rich.

Shortly after high school graduation he enlisted in the US Army Air Corps, but was released early from service because of the untimely death of his father in December 1945. He briefly attended Northwestern University, but with his financial future secure, he left college and became deeply involved in running the family business. As the founder's only son, Buddy took on a major role in the company, and by all accounts he and his mother continued to develop it as a retail giant, adding to its value—and their fortunes. In 1948, he married Jean Marie Fergus in Chicago, but the relationship was rocky from the start, and they separated numerous times.

In October 1955, he and his mother sold the company to the Mode

O'Day Corporation, and both walked away with enviable fortunes.

Still bored and still rich, the twenty-eight-year-old Buddy began a life of travel and adventure—without his wife—that ultimately took him on a fishing trip to Scott Bar and Roxbury Lodge, where he and Payne hit it off and decided to start mining.

For Payne, it was an easy decision. His business was going downhill fast, and he knew that others in the area were making money by mining chrome, so why couldn't he? When Buddy Sherman entered the picture, Payne found a potential partner with both money and a smooth way of talking that convinced "Chrome Queen" Moroney to short-term lease them a portion of the once world-class McGuffy Creek chrome mine near the lodge.

Payne, given his knowledge of explosives, was convinced they would get rich quick. Sherman, on the other hand, didn't need the money; he craved adventure. Sherman rented a trailer from Payne behind the lodge, and Payne walked away from his responsibilities at the lodge, leaving Harriet to mind the store. Neither man had any knowledge of chrome or mining, and had they done some research they might have learned that their specific leased area of the McGuffy Creek deposit was considered by experts to be high cost and low yield in recent years. But Payne, like he had with the lodge two years earlier, thought mining would make him a rich man.

He was wrong again.

"It was felt by some business associates of Mr. Payne that he neglected his lodge operation in order to conduct a mining venture," investigator Stiles reported. "While the lodge was never felt to have been a lucrative business, it probably would have been more so had Mr. Payne devoted his entire time to it."

It's unclear whether Payne and Sherman were actual financial partners or if Payne just rented equipment to Sherman and worked alongside him in the venture. It is known, however, that Payne's stepfather, Lawrence Hansen, drove up from Manteca and worked with them for a short time in the summer of 1956, a period during which, the Chrome Queen told investigator Stiles, a "great deal of chrome" was mined and shipped from the site.

A lot of chrome might have been mined and shipped, but at what cost?

Moroney told Stiles that Sherman never paid her for the lease or her share of the mined chrome. Others in the community told Stiles that Payne and Sherman lost several thousands of dollars in the venture, but the Chrome Queen said that if Payne lost any money it was likely only from equipment he had rented to Sherman that was never paid for.

For whatever reasons, the Payne-Sherman deal fell apart, and within a few months Buddy Sherman was back in Chicago looking for another adventure, this time a little closer to home.

Stiles had a commercial reporting company contact Sherman after the crash of *Romance of the Skies* in an attempt to learn more about Payne, the mining venture, and their relationship, but for some unknown reason Sherman refused to talk.

"The results of that contact is part of our file [that portion has never been made public], and it is obvious that Mr. Sherman was very guarded in any information which he was willing to give. The information obtained from him was practically worthless. He made the flat statement that 'I know what this is all about. I know what you are looking for.' It is felt that the person representing the commercial reporting company probably was not too tactful in the approach and, consequently, was not able to effect cooperation by Mr. Sherman."

Why would Sherman not want to talk about Payne? What did he think the insurance company was looking for? If he knew "what this is all about," what in the world was it?

Sherman later ran unsuccessfully for alderman in Chicago, and he and his first wife, with whom he had five children, went through a nasty and expensive divorce in 1966 after moving to Vermont. He married Anne Ulen about a year later and became an avid collector of rare antiques and vintage cars, trucks, and motorcycles. He traveled the world and owned and operated bars and restaurants in New England, as well as the *Newporter* newspaper in Rhode Island, and became known locally as Lord Budwell of Crudwell.

Sherman died in 2008 in Jamestown, Rhode Island.

"He was mostly attracted to traditional working-class food, drink, art and politics, especially in the company of intelligent, spirited, attractive women of that same ilk," his obituary stated. "He left behind many friends and a few enemies, too.

"His Lordship lived for the open road."

That "open road" had led once to remote Scott Bar, California, but we will never know what really happened there and why he refused to talk about that summer in 1956, when the rich young playboy rolled up his sleeves and became a chrome miner.

I dove back into the insurance company report and finally found what I had been most interested in: Stiles's findings relative to the "explosive" side of Mr. Payne, what the former frogman did in the days prior to the plane crash, and how he might have been involved in bringing it down, killing everyone aboard.

Stiles had shown that financial difficulties might have motivated Payne to sabotage the plane in a suicide-for-insurance plot, but his report so far had not tied circumstances together. Another angle, which he had not yet addressed, was the possibility that Payne and his wife had conspired to blow the plane up and split the proceeds, each going his or her separate way. That was something he had hinted to me about years earlier, when mentioning that the postmistress in Scott Bar told him the widow Payne had begun receiving mail from out of the country shortly after the crash.

"This entire investigation has been conducted with the theory in mind that the applicant for insurance had a definite motive for suicide and the technical knowledge to have sabotaged the Pan American Airways plane N90944."

Stiles then detailed Payne's knowledge of explosives and the ease with which he was able to obtain them.

"It was common knowledge that Mr. Payne had access to explosives in practically any amount that he desired. He is known to have used explosives in his mining venture, since one individual who had occasion to inspect the venture definitely noticed that the rock which was considered as being chrome ore had portions where holes had been drilled for explosive charges."

Stiles stated that he had interviewed a man who sold mining supplies and told him that Payne "on occasion had helped himself to his supply of dynamite."

The man also mentioned that former lodge owner Charles Brown had told him Payne routinely used dynamite in his mining operations, and also to close off mine shafts that might have posed a safety risk for the Payne children and their friends. Brown also told him that Payne had said many times that he had been a frogman while in the Navy.

"The term 'frogman' is a term used by the Navy referring to underwater demolition teams," Stiles stated. "These men, we are advised, are highly trained in the use of explosives of all kinds, also in the use of delayed-action detonating devices. Later, in a direct statement from Mrs. Payne, the fact that Mr. Payne had been a 'frogman' in the Navy was confirmed."

Stiles said many people who knew Payne in the Scott Bar area described him as "man who liked to talk about the use of explosives." Upon further questioning of these sources, Stiles learned that Payne had the "technical knowledge to use explosives of almost any kind and probably had the technical ability and knowledge to build a delayed-action detonating device."

Stiles reported that one man he had interviewed claimed Payne once bragged that he could build a delayed-action explosive detonator by using two flashlight batteries. Others told the investigator that Payne was extremely good at metal work, one of the skills he had learned while in the Navy.

Still, would Payne actually have committed suicide by blowing up the plane while he was on board. Nothing seemed to indicate that, but the fact that he had taken shots at people with a high-powered rifle and was considered by some to be a mean-spirited hothead did raise the possibility that he had blown up the plane without ever having actually boarded, or by placing a "seat occupied" sign in his seat, then exiting before departure?

In November 1957 there was little security provided for airliners parked away from the busy terminal at San Francisco International Airport, and anyone could easily have planted a time bomb in the wheel well of *Romance of the Skies* the night before takeoff. Because passenger and luggage screening were nonexistent in those days, a time bomb also could easily have been placed inside someone's luggage on the day of the flight, even that of a person who may never have boarded the plane that day.

Stiles raised the possibility with Pan American that Payne wasn't on the plane when it left San Francisco. A Pan Am official told him that it was "conceivably possible" that he was not on the plane when it departed, but that a system of precautions had been in place to prevent that. However, the official also told him that the system was not foolproof.

When Stiles asked if the flight crew would notify Pan Am by radio once they noticed that a passenger was not aboard, he was told no, not necessarily, but the passenger's luggage would be returned to San Francisco on the next flight from Honolulu. The Pan Am source told Stiles that getting a plane ready for an overseas flight required a lot of detailed work by both ground and air crews, and that once airborne "radio contact back to San Francisco may not have advised that a passenger was missing."

"He might not have been missed until the plane was well underway, and there is no requirement which would have necessitated their reporting of the absence of a passenger. The plane definitely would not be called back to its home base to unload any baggage," Stiles reported.

"It does appear to be conceivably possible that this man could have boarded the plane and through some pretext left the plane and never returned; or it is possible that his baggage could have been checked and have gone with the plane and he never boarded the plane at all," Stiles stated.

Yes, all of that was "conceivably possible," but it didn't seem likely considering that Payne's mother and stepfather had claimed to authorities that they saw him board. Could they have been lying? Could they have been providing an alibi or cover for Payne? Could they have seen someone else they thought was Payne?

"Mr. and Mrs. Lawrence Hansen were questioned carefully concerning the incidents leading up to the boarding of the plane and its departure," Stiles reported. "The interview with Mrs. Hansen would have to be considered unsatisfactory, since she was in a state of near hysteria even discussing the matter. She constantly wrung her hands and repeated over and over again: 'Why did God have to take my son?' She would answer questions and then when the same questions were put to her a second time, she would contradict the first answer. It was felt that her answers were not dependable."

Their story about the days before the flight and the morning of departure was this: Payne and his ten-month-old daughter, Kitti Ruth, left Roxbury Lodge by car for the Hansen home in Stockton, about 350 miles away. Payne was extremely fond of his daughter and insisted that she accompany him to Stockton while Harriet took care of business at the lodge. The Hansens, Payne, and his baby daughter went straight to the airport on the morning of Friday, November 8, and did not stop anywhere along the way. The Hansens saw him board the plane and did not see him get off at any time. There was nothing unusual about the plane's departure.

Several things about their story didn't add up, which surely crossed the investigator's mind. Why would Payne insist that his infant daughter—still in diapers—accompany him on the daylong drive to Stockton? Why would he leave the baby with his mother while he flew to San Francisco on a one-way ticket with no planned return date? Why didn't the Hansens mention that the flight had been delayed, an engine stopped, and baggage removed? Surely that was unusual and worth mentioning. Perhaps they hadn't actually seen Payne board the plane at all, or watch it depart. Maybe they had walked away before the engines were stopped.

Stiles didn't believe Ruth Hansen's account of the departure, and he remained troubled by lingering questions about the reason Payne was supposedly going to Honolulu. Who was he going to meet there? Who owed him money?

"A great deal of effort was concentrated on this point throughout the investigation, and it is interesting to note that his mother and his stepfather knew nothing regarding his preparations to go to Honolulu, who he intended to see, and the possibility of his collecting money from people in Honolulu," Stiles conceded.

This meant the Hansens wanted Stiles to believe that Payne had left his beloved infant daughter in his mother's care and flown off to Honolulu to see an unknown someone to collect money for an unknown debt, and would return at an unknown date.

Stiles didn't have any more luck in learning about the reason for the trip from Payne's widow, a person he states was "questioned very closely" about it.

"She states that she knew the name of no one in Honolulu that Mr. Payne might have been going to see. Neither the mother, the stepfather nor the wife were able to furnish any information concerning persons in Honolulu who owed Mr. Payne any money. She made a statement to a commercial reporting company indicating that there were IOUs or personal promissory notes, and this investigator attempted to determine from the wife, his mother and his stepfather just where the notes or IOUs are or where they might be. The mother and the stepfather said they knew nothing of any IOUs or notes, and my mention of this point to them was the first they had heard of it."

Payne's widow had a different take on that: she told Stiles it was her understanding that the IOUs were among Payne's personal effects in the possession of his mother. His mother, however, denied that she had any of his personal effects. None.

Someone was lying. Maybe everyone. But why?

"Obviously, in the investigation, it was learned that the feeling between the mother and the wife was not one which was congenial," Stiles stated. Others who knew the Paynes had said the same thing: Harriet and her mother-in-law did not get along.

Stiles also questioned family and acquaintances of Payne about a claim he had made to someone that he owned a ranch in Nevada that "was taken from him by two men now in Honolulu."

Stiles believed that to be another lie, perhaps to provide cover for a scheme of some sort that Payne was concocting—insurance fraud, perhaps?

"After investigation it was felt that this statement was not accurate. At least, if it was, the wife, the mother and the stepfather denied that Mr. Payne ever owned any property in Nevada and [said] that no one to their knowledge had ever taken any property from him," Stiles stated.

Stiles then questioned all of them about a phone call Payne claimed to acquaintances to have made to Honolulu to arrange for the collection of his money. The Hansens "stated indignantly that their son would not make a telephone call from their phone and allow them to pay the bill. They state that no telephone calls to Honolulu ever appeared on their bill."

Harriet also claimed to know nothing about a phone call to Honolulu, and denied that a call had been made from their home or lodge. Others, including Payne's sons, also said they were unaware of any call.

Stiles then concluded with a statement that went to the heart of the case against Payne as a sabotage suspect: "Information concerning the identification or actual existence of persons in Honolulu owing this man money is completely lacking, and it is the opinion of this investigator that no such person exists, and no telephone call was made."

In other words, there was no reason for the financially strapped Payne to scrape together enough money for a one-way ticket to Honolulu unless something secretive, or perhaps sinister, was involved. All of this seemed to add up to just one conclusion: Whether he was on the plane or not, William Harrison Payne blew up *Romance of the Skies* and killed everyone aboard.

Case closed.

So, who was William Harrison Payne?

That is as much a mystery today as it was when I first began looking into his life decades earlier. For the longest time, he simply didn't exist other than in newspaper accounts of the crash and investigation. There are hundreds, if not thousands, of William Harrison Paynes out there, and with no obituary and precious little other biographical information to work with, I had to struggle to piece together a brief biography of his life. During the next few years I was able to develop some raw information about him, but many holes remained—and still remain.

Payne was born December 15, 1915, in Braymer, Missouri, a tiny railroad town of fewer than 500 people, to Ward Payne and his seventeen-year-old wife, the former Ruth Elder. He was their second child; an older brother, David, had been born in California two years earlier. Ruth had moved to California when she was about ten years old and lived with an uncle on his farm near Sanger. In the 1920 census both David and William were listed as residents of the St. Catherine's Orphanage in Orange County, California, having been abandoned by their parents. Presumably, Ward Payne was dead.

By 1930, Ruth had moved to Nevada and was married to a man fourteen years her senior, Charles Edgar Wilcox, an automobile repairman. William was now living once again with mother, but his brother, now sixteen or seventeen years old, remained in California, living on his own. Harrison, as he was called at the time, played baseball for the local American Legion and was a Boy Scout. Ruth was listed as a nurse in the 1930 US census, but that was a bit unusual, because her only other employment had been as a retail salesperson in a department store and as a laundry worker. How she became a nurse, if indeed she was one, is a mystery that remains unanswered.

On November 19, 1934, the eighteen-year-old William enlisted in the Navy as a seaman apprentice, and in 1937 he trained for six months at the submarine school in New London, Connecticut, specializing in radios and signals. He was later transferred to the submarine barracks at Pearl Harbor and served on several ships, primarily sub tenders, across the Pacific during World War II.

He was transferred to Seattle shortly after the war ended, and it was there that he met his future wife, Harriet, a hairdresser recently divorced from Emil Theiler, a former shortstop and second basemen for minor league baseball teams in California and Washington State. Payne and Harriet were married in a private ceremony on October 19, 1945, at the First Methodist Church in Seattle. Payne's mother, Ruth Wilcox, and her soon-to-be third husband, Lawrence Hansen, witnessed the wedding.

Harriet's early life, like that of William's mother, is a bit of a mystery. Harriet Avah Hunter was born October 17, 1915, in Castoria, California, to James and Avah Cox Hunter. She graduated from Manteca High School and married Emil Theiler on April 9, 1934, in Carson City, Nevada. She was nineteen years old. The Theilers had one child, Emil Jr. (Kip), born six years later, on June 25, 1940. The family lived in Castoria, where Emil Sr. worked for the Spreckels Sugar Company. Harriet and Theiler divorced in the midforties, after which she moved to Seattle. For the rest of her life she told people a bald-faced lie—that she had been a widow when she married Payne.

On Aug. 27, 1946, Harriet gave birth to Michael Harrison (Kim) Payne while her husband was stationed at the Mare Island Naval Shipyard northeast of San Francisco, and less than two years later the couple was in Honolulu, where Payne was stationed once again. In 1949 the Paynes were transferred back to California. They lived in Manteca until 1953, when they moved to Stockton, where they lived until he was discharged from the Navy in 1956. Shortly thereafter he and Harriet purchased the Roxbury Lodge in Scott Bar, and their lives began to unravel.

WAKE ISLAND, THE PACIFIC OCEAN
MONDAY, DECEMBER 17, 1956

"Dear Mom:

"It's been so long since I saw you that I almost forgot what you look like. Sure do miss you, although it is not as bad now that I am on a trip. When I was home it was terrible. I missed 'Little Man,' too. I would catch myself sneaking into his room not wanting to awaken him and then realize that he was gone. [When my father wrote this, my mother was in South Carolina with my little brother, Craig, while her mother was dying of cancer.]

"The boys seemed to be doing just fine. They thought of the stay with the neighbors as a big adventure. I forgot to take the African Violets over to Whitneys before I left so I guess they will be dead when I get back. I was busy all day before I left at 10:30 p.m. The house is in pretty good shape except the beds and the kitchen floor.

"I'll be in Japan on Christmas Day. It won't be much of a Christmas again this year. We always hope for next year. I wonder what it will

be next Christmas?

"I'm sorry, Mom, that I can't do anything for you, but we have to look after our family. You stay as long as you like and if you wish, I will try to get an emergency leave when I come home. I don't want to leave the boys farmed out too long. My parents deserted me when I was five and left me to a strange world among strangers. I want to give my boys all the love I can. I miss all of you very much. When I get home, I will probably be home for 10-15 days maybe so you can stop worrying about the boys then.

"Honey, there isn't much I can say about your mother. I know hope is useless, and life protracted in misery is not worth much, so I'll say, 'God bless all of you,' and hope that will suffice. Love you, Mom. Write to me, address on envelope through Dec. 26th, then home.

"Love, Dad"

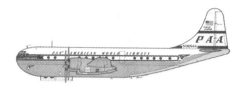

13

PSYCHICS AND A FLYING PRINCESS

DAVID PAWLOWSKI is a self-described conspiracy nut. He also just happens to be one of the most brilliant men I have ever known. He was a Dow Chemical Company engineer when we first met, and his ability to understand complex things, from aircraft engines to chemical compounds, is astounding.

Purely as a background source, David joined the search for my father's killer sometime in the early 2000s, and has provided valuable advice, assistance, and insight ever since. His motive has always been simple: the entire Lee Clack family perished on *Romance of the Skies*, and Clack was a Dow executive who, like Pawlowski, called Midland, Michigan, home.

Pawlowski believed from the very beginning of the search that lodge owner Payne was responsible for the crash, either as a suicidal murderer or as a coconspirator with his wife in a murder-for-insurance plot. Payne's background had been full of mysteries from the outset, and Pawlowski has never hesitated to offer his opinions or to chase leads down in some very unusual ways, always with his own time and money.

One of those unusual ways was something I had never heard of and still don't fully understand, but it turned out to be fascinating. It's called "remote viewing," or RV to those familiar with it. Whatever it is called, I was more than happy when Pawlowski shelled out his hard-earned money to ask the psychics for assistance in solving the mystery of Flight 7.

Remote viewing has been around for decades, and even though it is scoffed at by many mainstream scientific experts, it has been used in the past by no less than the Pentagon and the Central Intelligence Agency to assist in spying and other information-gathering activities. Simply stated, remote viewers are clairvoyants who are "tasked" under controlled conditions to use their abilities to gather information on "targets," which can be persons, places, or things. The targets may be from the past; the targets may be from the future. In all cases the targets are undisclosed, separated, and hidden from the remote viewers by distance, sometimes even by continents.

In most remote viewing sessions, the viewers (usually working from their own homes) are given general "frontloaded information" and some strict rules to follow. For example, in one of the Flight 7 RV sessions, the viewers were given the following information to narrow the focus: "The target is an event. Describe the target with emphasis on causes of the event and persons of interest."

The viewers were given photographs of Crosthwaite and my father (with no identifying information), but nothing else.

Pawlowski funded several remote viewings, the first conducted in 2001 by RV experts Jim and Lori Williams of Amarillo, Texas, who tasked four experienced viewers they described this way:

"Viewer #128 has 15 years' experience as a Controlled Remote Viewer and has an overall accuracy level of 86% in the professional Viewer Association database. This viewer has a great deal of experience working as a professional both nationally and internationally and has worked a broad variety of target types.

"Viewer #418 has 11 years' experience as a Remote Viewer and has an overall accuracy rating in the training database of 84%. This viewer's strength is in describing people and locations.

"Viewer #546 has four years' experience as a remote viewer. This viewer works internationally and has a high level of accuracy.

"Viewer #A32 has worked as an intuitive and a remote viewer for many years and is known internationally for a high degree of accuracy."

Their reports were fascinating, and the Williamses offered these summaries:

Viewer #546 described the event as energy and gave a list of descriptors for that energy with the final perception of a "shutting-down sound."

Viewer #418 described the event with interesting perceptions of motion and sound. The cause of the event was something that caused a very intense impact.

Viewer #A32 described the event in terms of land and motion, where motion meets land. This viewer determined the event was a plane crash very quickly, then gave good descriptors and sketches. The cause of the event was viewed as accident, speed, and broken components.

Viewer #128 provided a description of the airplane, four individuals, and their activities. Using a timeline, the viewer described the time prior to the event, during the event, and a short time after the event. The cause of the event was described as a "failing," with descriptors and detailed sketches of the "failing."

The Williamses concluded this about the viewings:

"When interpreting viewer information, it is important to realize that information comes to the viewer in the form of symbolism, metaphors and allegories. If the viewer has no personal frame of reference for the target, the subconscious mind presents information in a form understandable to the viewer. Therefore, it is necessary to determine what the information represents. It may not be an exact replica of the target."

The most interesting and detailed observations came from Viewer #128, who said the event occurred in a "steel-like metallic man-made object" with a "glassed-in front area where the man-made is controlled."

That sounded strikingly like a Boeing Stratocruiser. He even sketched what was clearly an airplane cockpit, and it was about as close to a Stratocruiser as anyone without professional training could draw.

He said that prior to the event two men were talking and laughing "with no sense of anything being wrong." The weather was nice and the temperature inside the man-made was cool.

Then something happened. Something terrible.

"Fifteen minutes prior to the event, there is something red which is fluttering. Strange smell. Smoky, burning rubber smell. The men in the man-made are concerned, confused, looking around. There is a grinding noise, chortling sounds, sputtering.

"Over the course of the next fifteen minutes before the event, there is a jerking motion up and down. Things are falling as the man-made tips to one side. There is a desperate attempt to right the man-made and a desperate attempt to control the man-made.

"There is yelling: 'I can't maintain altitude! Grab it, Jerry! Hold it! Hold it!' Closer to the moment of the event itself, there is droning sound, huge vibrating, everything angles down.

"Man-made is moving very fast. There is no control. The men inside the man-made are panicked, surprised, caught off guard, not expecting this. At the moment of the event, the man-made is soaring down diagonally, impacting the ground. Loud sound. The man-made is hitting the ground at an angle on the land. . . .

"The impact is hard, noisy, deafening, roaring, fiery-bright momentarily. The event causes crumpling of the man-made, mashing of steel and metal. Sharp impact. The man-made seems to be flaming. The flaming seems to be coming from the rear of the man-made."

My God. Symbolism, metaphors, and allegories aside, Viewer #128 seemed to be describing the final minutes of Flight 7 except for it striking land instead of the ocean. Even the "flaming" after the man-made crashed seemed to dovetail perfectly with the CAB report that a fire had occurred after the plane hit the ocean. But there was more:

"Later (perhaps an hour or less), tearing sounds. Flesh being torn. Lots of blood and guts. Dragging motion. Big carcass. Open, fresh, warm wet, dragging motion. Bony, sinewy being drug away from the site."

That sounded amazingly close to a description of the bloodthirsty sharks that had torn into the nineteen bodies found floating in the Pacific more than a week after the crash.

It was a fascinating report and good reading, but nothing conclusive. Certainly no smoking gun, but a lot of information to absorb and consider.

A few years later, Pawlowski contracted with Dr. Angela Thompson Smith, a psychologist and former research nurse at Manchester University in England, to direct another viewing. Dr. Smith, a founding director and member of the International Remote Viewing Association, is considered one of the world's leading remote-viewing experts, with more than thirty years of experience in psychology, parapsychology, and remote viewing.

She tasked sixteen remote viewers, voluntary members of the Nevada Remote Viewing Group, and they perceived indications of a fire, gave descriptions of the plane, and saw what she called "an anomalous someone watching."

"In addition, they gave descriptions of an individual and connected technology, emotions perceived at the event, and what may have happened prior to the crash," she reported.

So, what was the bottom line? Was it an accident or sabotage? If it was an accident, what caused it? If it was sabotage, who perpetrated the crime and how did they do it?

The viewers were contradictory in what they saw. Some said the crash was the result of sabotage. Others said it was caused by a faulty propeller. Another said the plane was destroyed because someone on board knew secrets and had to be killed.

I really hadn't expected the psychics to solve the case and end the search for my father's killer, but from a layman's perspective the report seemed to be little more than a mishmash of bunk and a waste of Pawlowski's money. Dr. Smith's conclusion left me even more convinced that the remote viewing had been worthless:

"Definitions of the term 'romance' have historically meant a tale based on legend, chivalric love and adventure, or the supernatural: and a prose narrative treating imaginary characters involved in events remote in time or place and usually heroic, adventurous, or mysterious. In other words, was the viewing of the *Romance of the Skies* a result of overriding expectation despite the blind-tasking: telepathic overlay, or actual data? These questions can only be answered when the remains of the *Romance of the Skies* are located and retrieved from the depths of the Pacific."

To me, the report was just psychic mumbo jumbo, albeit creatively written, even almost poetic. Dr. Smith presented her report to the 2016 convention of the International Remote Viewers Association, and I stashed it away in my files. I didn't give it another thought until three years later, when I once again began reading every document I had accumulated in my decades-long research.

I mentally kicked myself in the butt when I read it again in 2017, more closely this time—and learned that an entirely new theory deserved my attention.

As it turns out, a few days before Dr. Smith had made her presentation to the IRVA she had coffee with an RV colleague who had been one of the viewers in the case. She gave him preliminary feedback about what had been seen.

And then he stunned her with a theory of his own:

Viewer LM, a former Pan Am captain who had flown Stratocruisers himself in the 1950s, told her that Stratocruiser cabins were warmed by a gas-fired cabin heater like those used in many homes. He said that the heater was in an area behind the cockpit, close to one of the wings.

"He also mentioned that these often developed cracks in the metal and would leak carbon monoxide into the cabin. If this happened, the pilot, crew, and passengers would have lost consciousness, and this could have crashed the plane. LM was shown the schematics of the plane and this further clarified his theory," Dr. Smith told me.

A cabin heater? That was a new angle, but I was skeptical of his claim that they "often developed cracks" that leaked carbon monoxide into the cabin, because if that had been the case, the issue would have been well established and likely corrected. Still, the plane had flown more than ninety miles off course in less than thirty minutes, no Mayday calls had officially been sent, and carbon monoxide had been found in many of the recovered bodies.

Adding to the mystery was the fact that most, though not all, of the recovered bodies had life preservers on. Could the plane have simply flown on its own into the ocean with an unconscious, incapacitated, or disoriented crew in the cockpit?

I had toyed with that idea for years, wondering if vacationing pilot Robert Alexander, seated in the rear-cabin first-class section, had sensed an emergency in the cockpit and rushed up the cabin aisle, warning those along the way to put on their life preservers. Interestingly, Alexander's body was among those recovered, and an autopsy revealed that he may have been alive, but likely unconscious, for several days after the crash, just bobbing on the ocean.

Could the cockpit crew have become incapacitated in less than thirty minutes? Could a cabin-heater fire or malfunction have sent carbon monoxide into the cockpit and seeping into the front areas of the passenger cabin?

Carbon monoxide poisoning is often referred to as the "silent killer." It can't be smelled. It can't be seen. It can't be tasted. But it *can* kill. Carbon monoxide detectors as we know them today were very much in their infancy in 1957 and were not required in aircraft—although Stratocruisers *were* equipped with them.

I got in touch with Dr. Smith after rereading the report and asked for clarification of LM's theory.

"Even at this late stage, when I met with him [LM] in the coffee shop, we were still in the intuitive/analysis mode, still examining the probabilities," she explained in a written response to my questions. "And very often, even during these later stages, intuitive data can be accessed. It often happens that when a viewer gets some feedback, they may have additional intuitive data emerge that might have relevance to the case. In his case he called it a theory, but it came to him spontaneously as we were discussing the case, a sort of a 'gut hunch.' We looked at the schematics of the plane interior and he pointed out what could have happened. Then, when I went back over the Excel file of data, I remembered that some of the dead had been recovered from the ocean with amounts of carbon monoxide in their bodies. So, of all the possibilities, the cabin-heater malfunction was deemed to be more probable."

She also offered this disclaimer of sorts:

"Because the cabin heater was thought to be a strong possibility, it does not rule out any of the other scenarios. Disasters are rarely due to one cause, but there can be many contributing factors. As a rule, remote viewing is never used as the sole information source but factored into what is already known and what can be found from other investigation sources. It should be used as an adjunct to other streams of investigation. So, we are pleased if anything in the viewing helps the case. Remote viewing is not yet an exact science but, in my experience, has great application to operational work."

No, remote viewing is not an exact science, but that psychic experiment forced me to dig deeper into the mechanics of the Stratocruiser and look more closely into the possibility of mechanical failure, particularly a potentially fatal cabin heater fire. What I learned added credibility to LM's theory, but what was especially surprising was that carbon monoxide poisoning caused by the cabin heater was never seriously considered as a possible cause of the crash, meriting merely a brief statement in a ten-page Civil Aeronautics Board report on the airplane's power plant. Again, it's important to remember that only small bits and pieces of a mammoth seventy-ton aircraft had been recovered, and no parts of either cabin heater were found.

A. B. Hallman, a power-plant specialist with the Civil Aeronautics Board, submitted his report to his superiors on December 16, 1957, a full month before the CAB opened its public hearing on the crash. Hallman had been dispatched from Washington to San Francisco five days after the crash and had been a key member of the combined Pan American-CAB investigative team.

Hallman's report noted that the Stratocruiser had ten combustion heaters throughout the plane, including two Stewart-Warner conventional gas-burning cabin heaters beneath the floor immediately forward of the center section. He noted that the outside air temperature at the time of the crash was about 5 degrees Centigrade (41 degrees Fahrenheit), and that the two cabin heaters automatically turn on at that temperature.

"Consequently, they must be considered as a possible cause of the emergency," he stated. "With the cabin heaters in operation, fuel under pressure is routed into the fuselage rearward of the rear spar, then forward through the center section to the heaters. Thus, there could be leakage of gasoline into the fuselage with the attendant hazards."

Gasoline leakage with "attendant hazards." There it was. Another possible cause for the airliner to plummet to the sea.

He stated that if a leak had begun early in the flight, an "appreciable amount" of gas could have escaped along the line that ran under the floor, from the rear of the plane to the front, where the heaters were in an enclosed cargo area near the cockpit. The overheated, malfunctioning cabin heaters could have churned out undetectable carbon monoxide— the silent killer. The leaking gas also could have caused a below-deck fire.

Hallman pointed out that safety devices should have protected against such an occurrence, but that on rare occasions "the most reliable protective devices fail to perform their functions."

Just two years earlier United Airline Flight 409, a DC-4 en route from Denver to Salt Lake City, had mysteriously crashed, killing all 66 aboard. At the time, it was the deadliest crash in the history of American commercial aviation.

In that case, the routine flight ended when the aircraft plowed into snow-covered Medicine Bow Peak, near Laramie, Wyoming. The cause of the crash was never determined, although there was strong speculation that the crew had become incapacitated because of a faulty cabin heater. The official CAB report, however, stated plainly that no evidence had been found to support crew incapacitation.

Hallman concluded his brief comments on the Stratocruiser's heaters with this:

"Based on conjecture, the cabin heater system could possibly have contributed to the cause of the emergency."

Possible, but still unlikely. In the case of Flight 7 crew incapacitation would have had to occur within a thirty-minute window, between the time of the last radio report, to Ocean Station November, and the estimated time of the crash. It would have required a huge concentration of carbon monoxide—about .40, or 4,000 parts per million—to render the four-man crew unconscious in that short a time period.

In 2013 the Federal Aviation Administration published a safety bulletin entitled Carbon Monoxide: A Deadly Menace, stating that "toxicology samples from fatal US aircraft accidents between 1967 and 1993 showed that at least 360 victims had been exposed to sufficient carbon monoxide before or after the crash to impair their abilities. Non-fatal carbon monoxide poisoning in aviation is likely a more common occurrence than currently believed."

The cabin-heater-fire theory was an interesting combination of psychic and mechanical possibilities, but despite exhaustive research, I could find no verification of pilot-viewer LM's claim of "frequent cracks" in cabin-heater metal resulting in carbon monoxide leaking into a Stratocruiser cabin. In fact, I couldn't find even one incident. Zero. Although I discovered a few cases in which breaks and leaks had occurred in fuel lines leading to the wing heaters in the early 1950s, modifications to the equipment had corrected the problem.

Upon further research I learned that even if the cabin heater had somehow malfunctioned and all of the backup safety devices failed, the carbon monoxide concentration in the cabin would not have been sufficient to produce enough of the poisonous gas to incapacitate the crew or render the passengers unconscious.

Unless an onboard fire had caused carbon monoxide poisoning, ignited perhaps by a thrown prop that instantly tore through the cabin, triggering a chain of uncontrollable events, the malfunctioning-cabin-heater theory could be dismissed.

That brought me back to the remote viewing, and although I still thought it was nonsense, I wondered: What if someone had destroyed the plane with a time bomb and had never gotten on board? What if that person gave someone his airline ticket to Hawaii and that person boarded in his place? What if that someone was lodge owner William Harrison Payne? That would mean he not only got away with murder, but that he likely fled California and started a new life somewhere else, probably with the assistance of his "widow," who split the insurance proceeds with him.

In one of the RV sessions, Dr. Smith's viewers had been given scant information about a character who was given the name Western

John, and who was a composite match for Payne. In March 2016 she tasked thirteen trained viewers with the blind task of providing data on Western John's appearance, character, and possible whereabouts today.

The viewers' perceptions were chilling and indicated that Western John might still be alive and living somewhere in South America.

One viewer, also an accomplished artist, created a sketch of the potential location of Western John. Another, a skilled dowser, came up with a potential location that matched the viewers' perceptions. Finally, a viewer who was a forensic sketch artist provided drawings of Western John.

Dr. Smith summarized Western John like this:

"WJ is described as a male with dark or brown hair and wearing a plaid shirt with dark trousers, sensible shoes and sometimes shorts. He is described as sick and maybe on oxygen or an assisted-breathing device. He is not alone but with others, at least one woman, and children. The local people are described as having dark complexions with straight, dark hair. Obviously, someone is caring for him. WJ is described as an armed and dangerous man. The woman with him is very protective and possibly armed; she warns people that the area is off-limits. The male smokes and may trade with Mexico. The male may have parachuted into the location. He is sick and may have had a heart attack. He is described as anxious about 'being attacked.' It is unclear whether WJ is still alive, but if he is, he is very sick, probably having had a heart attack and with a lung disorder needing oxygen."

Three viewers provided additional information about Western John; one labeled him "a sociopath with a chameleon personality." Another said he was "detached," with a "rigid, no-nonsense personality." A third said he was "controlling, nonaccepting and judgmental. He had a mean streak." Another said he had been in the military but was now dead, the result of an accident or murder.

So where was Western John if he were still alive? Dave Pawlowski again contracted with Dr. Smith, this time to "triangulate on the end point for Western John. Where did he end up?"

"Many of the viewers perceived, wrote about and sketched a very similar location," Dr. Smith concluded in her written report. "It has several levels. At the base level is water, described by some as the ocean, by others as fresh water. The beach area is rocky with rounded boulders. This leads to an area that is habitable with structures. . . . Beyond the habitable area are steep cliffs, leading to an area that is volcanic with at least one active volcano. There are roadways and paths and tunnels in the mountains. The location is hot and green. In the habitable area are trees, plants and green grass. The area is rural and old . . . and there is a waterfall."

The viewers provided other detailed descriptions of the area where Western John might have fled to after the crash. One in particular grabbed my attention:

"In addition to this site being a residential location, it is possible that there is mining in progress. Several viewers mention openings into the hillside that remind them of a mine. However, the mine, if it is that, is not very productive or active. There are indications that some sort of biological, such as tobacco or marijuana, is grown, dried and sold from this location to Mexico."

Mining and Payne: a natural connection.

Using something called Extended Remote Viewing, LM, the so-called expert dowser, zeroed in on Peru, southern Colombia, or Ecuador as the last location of Western John. He determined that Ecuador was a 60 percent probability, then turned his backyard into a giant map and "dowsed for a refined position."

He found that the area around Laguna Pisayambo, Ecuador, was a particularly good match, because it had nearly all the physical features the viewers had described, including rounded rocks, steep cliffs, mining, a waterfall, and a nearby active volcano.

Could William Harrison Payne, aka Western John, have settled in Ecuador after the crash of *Romance of the Skies* and lived happily ever after with his share of the insurance money?

Three months after the viewers initially reported their perceptions, Dr. Smith asked "CB," a person she described as a "skilled intuitive artist who has provided accurate sketches of criminal suspects," to sketch Western John.

Unfortunately, there are no known photographs of Payne, but

remarkably, the sketch CB provided bore an unmistakable resemblance to Crosthwaite, the Pan Am purser aboard Flight 7.

What happened during the process of drawing the sketch was even more stunning.

"As I began to draw his eyes—the first thing I always draw for a suspect's face—I began to see, feel and sense undiagnosed mental and emotional issues," CB stated in his written report. "I came close to writing right on the paper 'mild schizophrenia and borderline personality disorder.' The person of interest is a white male, slightly exotic looking, of British and Scandinavian ancestry. I feel he is in his mid-30s, but I will give him the range of 32-45."

That, too, sounded like Crosthwaite.

Then something even stranger occurred:

"As I drew his left cheek and touched the paper to smudge, add shading, and tapped with my pencil, I felt swelling near his left cheekbone that may have been the result of a fight from several days earlier.

"As I was drawing, my pencil fell out of my hand (this virtually never happens) and it caused a mark on the paper in the upper right that—from a distance—resembles an unidentified object. This may be nothing, but I left it in."

CB planned to send Dr. Smith the sketch as soon as he had completed it, but his instincts told him to wait twenty-four hours and "allow myself the opportunity to sleep and possibly dream."

"Glad I did this, as I had a very vivid dream last night in which I watched a man, not unlike my drawing, walking around a house that I didn't recognize, which had a lot of older furniture, setting fire to pieces of paper and setting several rooms in the house on fire."

Again, that sounded like Crosthwaite on the night he had burned papers from his files in the fireplace.

Still, although I enjoyed reading the psychics' visions, I was unconvinced and closed the door once and for all on remote viewing. I did, however, again ask the international police agency INTERPOL to check and see if Payne's fingerprints had surfaced since 1957, when he presumably died in the crash. There was a chance, although extremely remote, that he was still alive, although he would have been 104 years old.

INTERPOL has not responded.

SPIES AND A FOILED ASSASSINATION

Exploring every possible angle in the search for my father's killer meant that in addition to investigating the more obvious suspects, I needed to look into more obscure possibilities, including this: could the plane have been brought down by agents of a foreign government or, worse still, by our own? Could one of the US government military or civilian employees onboard have been the target of foreign adversaries or have been intentionally silenced by the Central Intelligence Agency or another federal agency because of what he knew or what he might tell someone?

Three people aboard the aircraft deserved more scrutiny: India-bound US State Department employee Philip Sullivan and two men headed to Burma: US Air Force Major Harold Sunderland and US Information Agency attaché Thomas Henry McGrail.

Labor adviser Sullivan, a former missionary and educator in China, had been on government business in San Francisco for a few days prior to the flight and was en route with his wife, Bess, to New Delhi as part of the US delegation to the International Labor Organization's Asian Regional Conference. On the surface that seemed reasonably insignificant, so I concentrated on the other men and what, if any, reasons might have existed for them to be targeted for political assassination, as far-fetched as that might seem.

Fifty-two-year-old Dover, New Hampshire, native McGrail seemed an unlikely target. A former English professor at the University of New Hampshire, he had left academia during World War II and was commissioned in the US Army, serving first in combat in the Pacific, then with Allied occupation forces running the government in Japan. He left the Army as a lieutenant colonel and joined the State Department, where he became a specialist in Middle Eastern and Far Eastern affairs. He served two terms as the cultural attaché at the US Embassy in Tel Aviv, Israel, before returning to the United States, where he was assigned to Washington. He was en route to his new post as cultural attaché in Rangoon, Burma, at the time of the crash. Like Sullivan, McGrail didn't seem to fit the profile of a target for assassination.

Harold Edward Sunderland, however, was another matter. His life, not unlike the reason he boarded *Romance of the Skies* that November day, remains a bit of a mystery. That mystery is compounded by the fact that a devastating July 12, 1973, fire at the National Personnel Records Center in Kansas City destroyed about 18 million military personnel records, including those of Sunderland.

A Sheridan, Wyoming, native, Sunderland grew up on his family's ranch in Powder River County, Montana, and joined the Army in 1940. He apprenticed as a mechanic at the Army Air Depot in Sacramento, California, and by 1943 was in the middle of World War II battle action. He served with the North African Air Force Troop Command, an Army Air Corps organization created to work with Britain's Royal Air Force in support of ground and naval forces battling in North Africa and the Mediterranean.

Tech Sergeant Sunderland was awarded the Air Medal for his efforts during the invasion of Sicily in 1943, and later was awarded an Oak Leaf Cluster (equivalent to a second Air Medal) for other meritorious service.

His postwar history is largely unknown, but sometime after the war he earned a pilot's license, and by 1948 he was stationed at Bolling Field outside Washington, D.C. It was a choice assignment for Sunderland, as it was home to the first headquarters of a new US military branch: the United States Air Force. In March, he married Maria Isotta Analone, a thirty-one-year-old insurance-company secretary, in nearby Arlington, Virginia. He listed his occupation as a pilot, not a military officer, on his marriage-license application.

His job at Bolling Field is unknown, but sometime between 1948 and 1957 he transitioned from being a pilot into what the Air Force describes as an "information gatherer." In short, Sunderland became a military spy, and was assigned to a US Air Force Special Activities Squadron at Fort Myer, Virginia, which also housed the Strategic Intelligence School, where military personnel were taught everything from the duties of a military attaché to specialized spy photography and other intelligence-gathering techniques.

Sunderland's unit at Fort Myer, the 1134th Special Activities Squadron, is nearly nonexistent in public records, but the few records that are available indicate the unit was assigned to the assistant chief of staff, intelligence, for the US Air Force in Washington. The unit was part of a group that later became the 1127th Field Activities Group, whose expertise was worldwide human intelligence gathering—spying—but also was involved in "Project Moon Dust," tasked with locating, recovering, and delivering "descended foreign space vehicles."

Sunderland, who had divorced several years before the crash, had been living in Sacramento for a year or so and had spent the two weeks before the flight visiting his fiancée, C. Jean Speer, who told reporters after the plane went missing that Sunderland had been en route to Burma on a "special mission."

That "special mission" remains unknown to this day, but it is possible he may have been on loan to the CIA at the time, an interagency arrangement that was common during the Cold War. Burma was a hotbed of emerging communist strength and influence in the region during that period, and the United States helped support the government both to stabilize it and so that it would be able to continue using the country as a base for information-gathering in a region that also included Vietnam, which was fast becoming a major concern to communist-wary American leaders.

The CIA was deeply involved in Burma's secret war against the Chinese Communists during the midfifties, and CIA-funded pilots were paid to fly over China and drop leaflets urging the citizens to rise up against the Communists. Other CIA pilots dropped arms, ammunition, and supplies to anti-Communist Chinese nationals who had fled their home country years earlier for northern Burma, waiting and planning for their invasion of the mainland and engaging in massive amounts of opium production on the side, something the US government ignored.

In addition to staging overt flyovers, the CIA and its operatives covertly obtained intelligence about the Communists (inside both China and Burma) in an effort to understand what they were thinking about a possible invasion of Burma and the overthrow of its officially neutral but Western-leaning government. At the same time, the CIA was keenly interested in, and somewhat frustrated by, competing Soviet propaganda and "gifts" to the Burmese government, and deeply concerned about how that might affect the stability and future of the entire region.

I recently discovered a declassified CIA document from April 1956 that notes the agency's own "intelligence deficiencies" and says the CIA lacked critical information on the strength of the insurgency within Burma, as well as what was going on with the Burmese Communist Party and the communist-led Burma Workers and Peasants Party. The memo demands that appropriate US intelligence agencies "continue their efforts to overcome the deficiencies."

Was Sunderland on a secret mission to help overcome those deficiencies?

After researching the histories of McGrail and Sunderland I went back to Sullivan, the US State Department labor expert I had earlier discounted as a potential target, to bring him more clearly into focus.

Sullivan's profile on the world stage was much higher than that of either McGrail or Sunderland. In fact, a biography of his life published in the 2009 International Bulletin of Missionary Research noted that he had a dual career, one as a missionary/educator and another as a government employee. He and his wife had called Shanghai, China, home for more than twenty years, and Sullivan taught economics at St. John's University, an Episcopalian missionary institution in Shanghai. He also closely studied Shanghai's labor scene during a period of unionization and unrest and had just completed research for his doctoral thesis when he was captured by Japanese occupation forces after the attack on Pearl Harbor. They initially placed him under house arrest, but in February 1943 he was locked inside the Pootung Internment Camp, a converted British-American Tobacco Company compound. In September of that year he and other detained Americans were exchanged for Japanese prisoners, and he returned home to Michigan, where he became an instructor with the Army Specialized Training Program at the University of Michigan, where students were trained to become intelligence officers or Japanese or Chinese translators.

In the spring of 1945, he began his second career, as a labor adviser with the State Department, where his experience in East Asia and his knowledge of economics proved invaluable; he testified several times on Capitol Hill and was instrumental in developing United States policy toward Japan following the war.

Yes, Philip Sullivan was a higher-profile target than either Sunderland or McGrail, but there was something else about him that might have attracted the attention of unfriendly foreign governments: his son, Daniel Peyton Sullivan, had recently taken a job at the State Department's Bureau of Intelligence and Research in Washington. He was on a small team assigned to research and write segments of the National Intelligence Survey, a top-secret report used by senior-level government and military leaders in the development of strategic planning and foreign policy.

With brief bios on Sullivan, Sunderland, and McGrail completed, I faced these questions: if any of the three government officials aboard the airplane had been targeted for death, who would have done it and why?

That's when former Dow Chemical Company engineer Pawlowski came back into the picture. Pawlowski suggested that I research the 1955 bombing of Air India's *Kashmir Princess* and consider whether the crash of *Romance of the Skies* might have been "payback" for a foiled assassination plot that nearly took the life of Chinese Premier Zhou Enlai.

Crazy as it may seem, I decided to consider the idea.

On the evening of April 11, 1955, *Kashmir Princess*, a chartered Air India Lockheed L-749 Constellation, was en route from Hong Kong to Jakarta, Indonesia. Its passengers were primarily Chinese and East European delegates bound for the Asia-Afro Bandung Conference, plus journalists planning to cover the event. It was flying at an altitude of about 18,000 feet with all operations normal when a time bomb exploded in a wheel bay and blew a hole in the fuel tank, causing the number three engine to catch fire. Gas quickly filled the cockpit, and the plane was doomed. The pilot fought to control the aircraft and attempted to ditch it but was unsuccessful; sixteen people perished.

The crash was noteworthy in and of itself, but even more interesting was that one intended passenger, the main target of the bombing, had never even boarded the aircraft: China's Premier Zhou Enlai. It was learned that Zhou had canceled at the last minute, citing an emergency medical need—later determined to have been a lie. Investigators discovered that Zhou had canceled his trip after being tipped off about the planned assassination.

A Hong Kong airplane janitor later was identified as the man who had planted the bomb, triggered by an American-made MK-7 device, and he quickly fled the area on a Civil Air Transport flight to Taiwan. Civil Air Transport was a CIA-funded airline, and the Chinese quickly blamed the United States intelligence agency for the assassination attempt, a claim US government officials deny to this day.

Ten years after the crash of *Romance of the Skies*, a self-confessed former CIA employee named John Discoe Smith, a Quincy, Massachusetts, native who said he had defected to the Soviet Union several years earlier, wrote his memoirs in a James Bond-type thriller in the *Literary Gazette of Moscow*. He alleged that the CIA was involved in broad worldwide conspiracies of murder and bribery and stated that four out of five "diplomats" in US embassies actually were intelligence officers. Among his other claims was that he personally had provided a suitcase with the two time bombs that the janitor then planted in the wheel well of *Kashmir Princess*.

Is it possible that Zhou targeted the US government employees on *Romance of the Skies* as payback for the suspected CIA attempt to assassinate him two years earlier? Stranger things happened during the Cold War.

Interestingly, just six weeks before the crash of Flight 7, President Dwight D. Eisenhower secretly ordered the CIA to incite a revolution in Indonesia and to start planning for the assassination of the nation's president, Sukarno—the same man who had welcomed Jack King, flight supervisor on *Romance of the Skies*, to his palace and asked Pan Am to appoint him as steward in charge of Sukarno's trip around the world.

Friends one day. Enemies the next. American foreign policy then, as now, is complex and convoluted.

CHRISTMAS 2014

We didn't have much when I was growing up. Then again, we had everything.

When Christmastime rolled around, my brothers and I knew we weren't going to get everything, or even half of the things, on our lists, but Santa always seemed to know what it would take to bring smiles and laughter to our faces when we raced to the tree on Christmas morning and found what he had left behind.

The first Christmas I can remember was in 1956 when Santa brought me a Davy Crockett coonskin "Indian fighter" cap and a Gene Autry toy gun set. I can still smell the fresh leather of the holster, feel the itch of that hat on my head, and hear the pop of those red pistol caps going off as the smoke settled.

I remember Daddy helping adjust my gun belt so that it would fit a little tighter around my tiny waist, to give this young cowboy just the edge he needed in an imminent gunfight with his older brother, a Roy Rogers man. To this day I remember Daddy leaning close to me, his smiling, unshaved morning face touching mine, and giving my gun belt an extra tug.

Looking back now, I treasure most not what I received from Santa that year, but that closeness, that touch of love from my father.

He would not be with us for another Christmas.

While he never again tugged my gun belt, I felt his love throughout my life, and his love is a Christmas gift that keeps on giving.

It's always the little things that matter the most.

The Christmases of my childhood changed after my father died in 1957. We still got everything we needed (though never everything we wanted), but my mother struggled to raise three boys on Social Security checks, and making ends meet was never easy. It was especially difficult at Christmas. As we grew older, she gave us a "Santa budget" that we'd have to live with that year, and while we didn't especially like it, we learned to live, and wish, within our means.

Her lifetime gifts to us included frugality and responsibility, but her biggest gift was unconditional love. No matter how far we strayed or how far we pushed the boundaries, we could always count on her love.

On Christmas Eve, just as on many other nights, she would shout from her room to make sure we heard her from down the hall:

"I love you boys. My three little boys."

Even as rebellious teens, we were her "three little boys."

On Christmas morning, as other kids in our neighborhood got more "stuff," the latest gizmos and brand-name clothes, my mother somehow managed to save the day and make it a Christmas to remember.

She made the day special with her joyful sense of humor and the way she squinted her eyes, looking closely to see if we really liked what she had scrimped and saved for Santa to bring us. It was the way she scurried about the kitchen to make the Christmas meal, including her famous powdered sugarcoated rum balls. It was the way she acted so pleasantly surprised at what my brothers and I had pooled our money to give her as our Christmas gift. One year we came up with a whopping $3 and bought her a freestanding, cheap, fake-bronze ashtray. She proudly placed it in the living room, right next to the big, stuffed chair Daddy used to sit in. My mother didn't even smoke (nor did my father), but she loved what we gave her.

Things weren't always perfect in our house. Of course not. Three growing boys. One house. One parent. Four separate lives. Despite our hardheaded selves, my brothers and I grew up and flew the nest, and have led reasonably successful lives of our own. Mom died a few years ago from Alzheimer's, and my brothers and I celebrate Christmas separately, in different states and in different ways. But we have a common thread: a mother and a father who loved us, on Christmas and every day of the year.

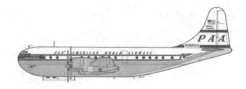

14

MR. X, THE MAN
FROM SATURN

*"I certainly believe in aliens in space, and that they are indeed visiting
our planet. They may not look like us, but I have very strong feelings
that they have advanced beyond our mental capabilities."*
—US Senator Barry Goldwater (1965)

THE EIGHT-COLUMN BANNER HEADLINE in *The San Francisco News* on
November 15, 1957, must have raised a lot of eyebrows as people glanced
at newspaper racks:

DID METEOR HIT PLANE? Experts Checking Pacific Mystery

*"Government investigators said today Pan American's Stratocruiser may
have crashed into the Pacific after being hit by an 'exterior object' such as a
meteor."*
However, there was nothing in the story itself to support the
sensational headline. The article went on to mention several other
prevailing theories about the crash, including sabotage and mechanical

failure, but not another word about a meteor.

Incredulous as it seems, could a meteor have struck the airliner as it flew across the twilight Pacific sky?

That idea was quickly nixed as "mathematically impossible" by George Bunton, manager of San Francisco's Morrison Planetarium, who said that while it was theoretically possible for a meteor to strike a plane, the probability was extremely slim. Bunton said that even predictable meteor showers consist of particles that are too small to survive passage into the earth's atmosphere and that the chance of a larger, sporadic meteor hitting the plane was "improbable."

Improbable, but not impossible.

Just two days earlier something resembling a small meteorite had blazed through the northern California sky and had torn into a field near the W. W. Crocker estate. Hillsborough police officer William Offield checked out the location the following morning and found that the fireball had crashed into the earth under some pine trees and planted a scar in the ground about the size of a six-inch shotput. Scattered molten lead spread all around the small indentation. Another unknown object fell from the sky about the same time in nearby Burlingame.

Could a similar metal fireball falling from the sky have crashed into the Stratocruiser and caused its demise?

This was one of those improbabilities that deserved further study in the search for my father's killer.

I began to look more deeply into what was happening in the skies that week in 1957. Much to my amazement, dozens of sightings of unidentified flying objects and other unusual occurrences had been reported all over the world. Clearly something had been going on.

When the Russians launched Sputnik 1, the world's first artificial satellite, on October 4, 1957—a month before *Romance of the Skies* perished—the Cold War took a frightening new twist, as the space race began in earnest. Would the Russians or the Americans end up controlling the skies above the earth? Who would be the first to put a man on the moon? The launch of Sputnik 1 ushered in a period of exhilarating scientific and technological advancement, but also heightened military and political tensions worldwide.

The man-made satellite circling the earth created excitement, fear, hysteria, and shock among many Americans, who began to believe that Soviet space technology was outpacing American, and that the resultant "missile gap" might lead to Soviet domination of the planet.

Everyone, it seemed, was tense, nervous, and looking skyward.

The first week of November 1957 has come to be known by many UFO enthusiasts as "The Great Sighting Week." Close encounters were reported in every corner of the world, and when the Russians launched a second satellite into orbit, Sputnik 2, on November 2, reports of sightings increased.

An Army patrol at White Sands, New Mexico, reported an "orange, apparently controlled luminous object" near the site of the first atomic bomb test explosion.

Two guards at an Army base on the coast of Brazil observed a similar-looking luminous orange disk racing toward them at fantastic speed. Waves of heat crossed their bodies as they unleashed screams into the night sky. Those screams were alarming enough to send sleeping soldiers in a nearby barracks rushing outside just as the military post's entire electrical system shut down. The UFO streaked away, and the guards were taken to a hospital, where they were treated for first- and second-degree burns.

What had everyone seen? What caused the soldiers' burns? What shut down the post's electrical power? Those events were real. They were documented by perfectly sane people with nothing to gain by exposing themselves to public ridicule or worse.

Were visitors from beyond our planet trying to make contact? Were they trying to learn more about humankind? Or perhaps warn us—all of us—that we were verging on catastrophe if we continued to build nuclear weapons at breakneck speed?

Was the US military conducting supersecret air-and-space experiments to keep America competitive in the space race? Were new supersonic experimental aircraft zooming across our skies, hovering above our houses and somehow shutting our power off?

Whatever the UFOs were, from rural Texas, where the two stunned farmworkers had encountered a UFO that disabled their truck, to

Elmwood Park, Illinois, where two policemen and a fireman reported a "weird, glowing thing" that dimmed their car lights, it was a week of wonder—and worry.

And let's not forget the frightening episodes that same month where two Varig airliners nearly plunged to earth after encountering UFOs over Brazil—UFOs that the pilots claimed knocked out their electrical power and almost sent them to their deaths.

I have spent many hours researching electromagnetic interference and UFO sightings, and the reports are credible and numerous, continuing to this day.

Could the electrical systems of *Romance of the Skies* have been paralyzed by electromagnetic interference from a UFO? Could the crew have lost control of the plane and been unable to radio a distress signal while struggling to keep the powerless plane in the sky? Could something—or someone—have intentionally or accidentally shut down its electrical system? That might explain why it was flying perfectly on course, problem free, at 5:04 p.m. and sinking to the bottom of the ocean less than thirty minutes later, at least ninety miles off course. That might explain why there was no proof of a major in-flight fire or explosion, but there was a blaze after the plane hit the water in what might have been a failed ditching attempt. That might explain why the four-engine plane might have become a huge, powerless, out-of-control missile falling from 10,000 feet in the sky into the waves of the Pacific Ocean.

Interestingly, the first newspaper accounts of the missing airliner had mentioned that a Military Air Transport plane reported "mysterious blinking lights" in the vicinity of the last position report of Flight 7. The Navy Rescue Center at Pearl Harbor had confirmed the report and immediately dispatched Coast Guard and Air Force planes toward the area, about 900 miles northeast of Honolulu. They found nothing, but the report had been made, and it had been made by experienced pilots who were not prone to fantasy.

Honolulu Star-Bulletin managing editor William Ewing, who was among the newspapermen who flew aboard search planes in the days following the disappearance of *Romance of the Skies,* wrote this in a

November 13, 1957, dispatch:

"Interestingly enough, there are men who fly who do not rule out the spaceship theory— that a strange craft able to knock out electrical circuits, as was reported in last week's rash of flying saucer stories— could have been responsible."

During my research I was stunned to discover that on July 11, 1959, less than two years after *Romance of the Skies* disappeared in the mid-Pacific, veteran Pan Am pilot Captain George Wilson of Seattle and officers Richard Lorenzen and Bob Scott of Flight 865 encountered a mysterious object with a cluster of extremely bright lights as they flew a Stratocruiser from Honolulu to San Francisco. Wilson reported to Oakland Air Traffic Control shortly after 6 a.m. PDT that the object had flashed by his airplane "faster than anything I have ever seen. It was something I've never seen before."

Wilson said the lights had no color, but one appeared brighter and larger than the other three or four, which were off to the side and slightly behind the main one.

"It was like looking at a piece of the sun," he stated. "It was extremely hard to judge, but it all could have been part of the same vehicle. It was headed northeast and we were headed southeast. We saw it for about ten seconds. It made an abrupt ninety-degree turn away from us, and when it turned away the lights disappeared."

Wilson, a seventeen-year Pan American veteran, said he had previously disregarded reports of UFOS, but added, "I'm a believer now."

Wilson's report was substantiated by other Pan Am and commercial pilots flying the same route that day. All of them reported seeing an unknown bright object 800 to 900 miles from Honolulu at an altitude of about 21,000 feet.

Their reports were forwarded to officials at the North American Air Defense Command in Colorado Springs, Colorado, where they were predictably and quickly dismissed as "unexplained natural phenomenon" pending investigation.

The strangest twist to the UFO angle in the story of the missing *Romance of the Skies* unfolded two days before the plane disappeared, when a Nebraska grain dealer claimed he had a close encounter with human-like creatures from outer space. Reinhold Schmidt, who became known as "The Man Who Contacted Space People," said he had been inspecting fields of milo and corn near Kearney, Nebraska, on November 5, 1957, when an unusual event occurred:

"I was driving near an old sand bed on the Platte River, and close by was an abandoned farmhouse," he recalled in a self-published 1964 book, *Edge of Tomorrow.*

"It seemed like a good place to turn my car around but, as I started to do so, there was a brilliant flash of light a short distance ahead. I drove on to investigate what I thought might be someone blasting trees, although I had heard no noise. Within a hundred feet of the river bank my car engine suddenly stopped. I turned the ignition off and on several times, thinking that perhaps the battery had gone dead or that maybe the rough road had jiggled some wiring loose. As I started to get out of the car to check the engine, I noticed something ahead that appeared to be a large, half-inflated balloon.

"When I walked toward it, skirting a clump of willow trees and tall grass, it was obvious that it was not a balloon, but a great, silvery craft which seemed to be made of some kind of metal, such as polished steel or aluminum. It was resting on what I later found out to be four hydraulic rams serving as landing gear, but it looked like some sort of balloon more than anything else. As I came within about thirty feet of it, a thin stream of light, about as big around as a pencil, shot out from it and hit me across the chest. It seemed as if I were suddenly paralyzed; I could not move. Maybe I was only scared stiff but, before I could analyze my feelings, a door in the ship slid open and two men came out of it toward me. They asked if I were armed and, although I said no, they frisked me anyway, but they took nothing from me," he claimed.

"After regaining some of my composure and discovering that I could move again, I asked them what they were doing here, what kind of craft they had there, and where they were from. One of the men did the talking. He was evidently the leader and I shall refer to him hereafter as Mr. X. He spoke English with a German accent and said that they couldn't answer those particular questions at that time. However, when I asked to come closer in order to see the ship, Mr. X invited me aboard since, he said, they couldn't leave for a few minutes anyway. He said that I could look around inside but not to touch anything."

Schmidt said that when the flying saucer tour was completed, he was escorted outside, and the aliens told him they would see him again.

The sixty-year-old Schmidt told his story to local authorities, was promptly locked in a mental ward, and then released two weeks later when medical and psychiatric experts could find nothing wrong with him.

That wasn't the end of the story, though. Schmidt claimed that three months to the day after the incident, on February 5, 1958, he was driving along another Nebraska road when he encountered the same spaceship and the same Mr. X, who invited him to climb aboard for a flight.

"You can imagine how intrigued I was with the prospect of a ride in their craft! My mind was whirling with a dozen thoughts. They even knew my name. But how?

"Immediately after that the ship rose straight up in the air. When we were about 150 to 200 feet in the air Mr. X said, 'If any of your friends are watching now, they will not be able to see the ship.' Yet, again, I could see the entire countryside through the walls."

Schmidt says the craft had flown for about a half-mile when Mr. X asked him to obtain the answers to three questions for the space visitors: 1) What would be the reaction of earthlings if a fleet of saucers landed for friendly visit? 2) How would Earth people like it if spacemen were to begin testing H- and A-bombs? 3) What besides passengers was the airplane carrying that crashed over the Pacific?

That, Schmidt believed, was an obvious reference to *Romance of the Skies,* which had crashed just three days after his first "encounter" with the aliens. Flight 7 was publicly known to have been carrying radioactive cargo, something Schmidt thought might have intrigued the spacemen.

Schmidt made headlines all around the world and went on the lecture circuit after his book was adapted into a short film. He maintained that the aliens were from Saturn and routinely took him on trips to the Antarctic and beyond. He once told an amused and skeptical audience in California that his friends from Saturn also monitored his brainwaves.

Monitored brain waves or not, Schmidt was nothing more than a nutcase and a con man. He ended up in prison after being convicted in 1961 of bilking elderly women out of thousands of dollars.

The Reinhold Schmidt case needed no further investigation.

No relation to the Schmidt case: one of the most famous and best-documented UFO sightings in history involved the mysterious encounter of UFOs with a Pan American airliner that my father was copiloting.

On the night of July 14, 1952, pilot William B. Nash and my father were ferrying cargo aboard the DC-4 Clipper *Defiance* at an altitude of 8,000 feet from New York to Miami when they spotted eight flying saucers in the sky over the Chesapeake Bay at an estimated speed of an astonishing 12,000 miles per hour. As soon as the UFOs were out of sight, near Newport News, Virginia, the former Navy aviators began documenting what they had seen.

"How does it feel to see flying saucers? Like most people, we had never consciously expected to face that question, but now we have an answer. When you see 'saucers' from the angle and nearness that we did and watch them go through the astonishing maneuvers that we witnessed, you feel humbled," they wrote in an article for *True* magazine.

"Sitting in the complex cockpit of a fast four-engine airliner, we had the deflated feeling that we and our modern airplane were so far outclassed by somebody and something else that it wasn't at all funny."

The pilots detailed what they saw that night:

"The distant lights of the cities stood out plainly, undimmed by any haze. One of us pointed out to the other the city of Newport News, which lay forward and to our right. Suddenly a red brilliance appeared in the air beyond and somewhat eastward—that is, to our side of Newport News. We saw it together at practically the same moment. The remark of one of us was: 'What the hell is that?' It hadn't grown gradually into view—it seemed simply to have appeared, all of a sudden, in place.

"Almost immediately we perceived that it consisted of six bright objects streaking toward us at tremendous speed, and obviously well below us. They had the fiery aspect of hot coals, but of much greater glow—perhaps twenty times more brilliant than any of the scattered ground lights over which they passed or the city lights to the right. Their shape was clearly outlined and evidently circular; the edges were well defined, not phosphorescent or fuzzy in the least. The red-orange color was uniform over the upper surface of each craft.

"Within the few seconds that it took the six objects to come half the distance from where we had first seen them, we could observe that they were holding a narrow echelon formation—a stepped-up line tilted slightly to our right, with the leader at the lowest point and each following craft slightly higher. At about the halfway point, the leader appeared to attempt a sudden slowing. We received this impression because the second and third wavered slightly and seemed almost to overrun the leader, so that for a brief moment during the remainder of their approach the positions of these three varied. It looked very much as if an element of 'human' or 'intelligence' error had been introduced, in so far as the following two did not react soon enough when the leader began to slow down and almost overran him.

"We judged the objects' diameter to be a little larger than a DC-3 wingspread would appear to be—about 100 feet—at their altitude which we estimated at slightly more than a mile below us, or about 2,000 feet above ground level.

"When the procession was almost directly under and slightly in front of us . . . the objects performed a change of direction which was completely amazing. All together, they flipped on edge, the sides to the left of us going up and the glowing surface facing right. Though the bottom surfaces did not become clearly visible, we had the impression that they were unlighted. The exposed edges, also unlighted, appeared to be about 15 feet thick, and the top surface, at least, seemed flat. In shape and proportion, they were much like coins. While all were in the edgewise position, the last five slid over and past the leader so that the echelon was now tail-foremost, so to speak, the top or last craft now being nearest to our position. Then, without any arc or swerve at all, they all flipped back together to the flat altitude and darted off in a direction that formed a sharp angle with their first course, holding their new formation.

"The change of direction was acute and abrupt. The only descriptive comparison we can offer is a ball ricocheting off a wall. Immediately after these six lined away, two more objects just like them darted out from behind and under our airplane at the same altitude as the others. The two newcomers seemed to be joining the first group on a closing heading.

"Then suddenly the lights of all of the objects blinked out, and a moment later blinked on again with all eight in line speeding westward, north of Newport News, and climbing in a far, graceful arc that carried them above our altitude. There they disappeared, while still in view, by blinking out one by one—not in sequence, but in a scattered manner.

"There seemed to be some connection between the lights and the speed. The original six had dimmed slightly before their angular turn and had brightened considerably after making it. Also, the two others were even brighter, as though applying power to catch up.

"We stared after them, dumbfounded and probably open-mouthed. We looked around at the sky, half expecting something else to appear, though nothing did. There were flying saucers, and we had seen them. What we had witnessed was so stunning and incredible that we could readily believe that if either of us had seen it alone, he would have hesitated to report it. But here we were, face to face. We couldn't both be mistaken about such a striking spectacle."

Upon landing in Miami, both men were interrogated for hours— first separately, then together—by eager Air Force investigators, including Major John H. Sharpe and special agents C. L. Hamilton, Rudolph McCollough, and Louis Johnagin from the Seventh District Office of Special Investigations at MacDill Air Force Base in Tampa. The investigators were impressed by the details the pilots provided about the sighting and the fact that their stories matched perfectly.

One of the investigators confidentially told the pilots during a break in the questioning that seven reports of UFO sightings had been made in the same area the previous night.

After hours of intense questioning, the veteran pilots were finally allowed to go home to their families.

But their lives would forever be changed by what they saw that night.

The lead story on page one in the Wednesday, July 16, edition of the *Miami Herald* highlighted the sighting and gave the pilots' accounts of their bizarre encounter.

"I know enough about natural phenomena and the universe to know that what Nash and I saw must have come from outside our own solar system," stressed my father, a former member of the US Navy's aviation research and development team, during World War II.

"If there were men inside, they weren't earthmen," he observed.

Santes Ceyanes, Pan Am's acting operations manager in Miami, added these words of support, telling the newspaper, "What they saw obviously was not a figment of their imaginations."

Shaken by the sighting but resolute in their stories, both men concluded in their *True* magazine report that the UFOs had been under the control of something beyond our understanding and comprehension.

"Though we don't know what they were, what they were doing or where they came from, we are certain in our minds that they were intelligently-operated craft from somewhere other than this planet.

"We are sure that no pilot, able to view them as we did, could conceive of any earthly aircraft capable of the speed, abrupt change of direction, and acceleration that we witnessed, or imagine any airplane metal that could withstand the heat that ought to have been created by friction in their passage through the dense atmosphere at 2,000 feet. Whether they were controlled from within or remotely, we can't say, but it is impossible to think of human flesh and bone surviving the jolt of their course reversal.

"We have the usual reasons, too, for not believing that they were secret guided missiles. It is not logical that our own armed services would experiment with such devices over large cities and across airways, and another nation would not risk them here. Nor could anybody's science have reached such a stage of development without some of the intermediate steps having become public knowledge.

"One thing we know: mankind has a lot of lessons to learn . . . from somebody."

In his official report to his superiors, Air Force Major Sharpe described the pilots as men of "high integrity and above-average intelligence." He said the observers are "considered reliable and evidently saw what they described."

The detailed report about the sighting and the special agents' investigation was forwarded to senior general Air Force officers at Wright-Patterson Air Force Base in Ohio and Langley Air Force Base in Virginia. Two days later Lt. Col. James Lovenbury of the US Air Force Office of the Inspector General sent an internal memo stating that "no further action is contemplated by the office."

Even though the Nash-Fortenberry event was the first UFO sighting on record in which the witnesses flew *above* UFOs, and was well-documented, the Air Force officially filed it away as just another of the unexplained sightings that occurred that week all across the United States, including in the Washington, D.C. area, where radar operators at Bolling Field and Andrews Field picked UFOs up on radar and the Air Force dispatched two F-94 jets to search for them. In the control tower of nearby Washington National Airport, seven unexplained blips were picked up on radar by four stunned air traffic controllers, one of whom reported the objects were flying at an incredible speed.

The headline in the next day's edition of the *New York Daily News* exclaimed:

JETS CHASE D.C. SKY GHOSTS

The *Washington Post* was a bit more subtle with its banner headline:

Saucer Outran Jets, Pilot Reveals

The *Post* story concluded with these questions:
"Who, or what, is aboard? Where do they come from? Why are they here?

What are the intentions of the beings who control them?"

In private, President Harry S Truman demanded answers from the military about what became known as "The Invasion of Washington."

At the Pentagon, chief UFO analyst Major Dewey J. Fournet, a former skeptic, closely studied the details of the Nash-Fortenberry sighting and proclaimed to colleagues that it was the most detailed UFO sighting he had ever read. Fournet, known by officers and colleagues in the Pentagon as a no-nonsense investigator, later became one of the nation's leading advocates of the notion that we are not alone in the universe.

The Nash-Fortenberry case is considered today to be one of the classic UFO sightings of all time.

Nash retired in 1977 after thirty-six years with Pan American and spent much of the rest of his life tirelessly studying UFO phenomena, with a keen interest in artificial gravity fields and the possibility that unidentified spacecraft are able to flip on a dime, change direction, and fly at incredible speeds because both the craft and their occupants (if any) are not subject to the law of gravity as we know it. He died March 13, 2019, at his home in Florida. He was 101 years old.

In 1964, the respected UFO research group The National Investigations Committee on Aerial Phenomena published a summary of UFO reports from the 1950s through 1963 that included a study of nearly 100 electromagnetic-interference cases. NICAP came up with several possible theories for electromagnetic interference, including Russian and American nuclear testing, as well as the purely speculative notion that nuclear-powered UFOs might have been rendering planes, automobiles, and electrical systems powerless during deliberate and selective tests and experiments.

The report warned against simpleminded explanations of the phenomenon:

"It is false logic for a scientist to deny observations (about electromagnetic effects) on the grounds that we cannot fully explain them. Taken in association with the other accumulated evidence about UFOs, the fact that we have difficulty explaining the electromagnetic effects could also mean that we are dealing with a superior technology about which we know very little."

A March 1977 incident involving a commercial airliner and a UFO lends additional credence to the remote possibility that electromagnetic interference may have caused the unexplained loss of *Romance of the Skies.*

While piloting a United Airlines DC-10 en route from Boston to San Francisco, Captain Neil Daniels was startled by a round, brilliant light off a wingtip. Daniels, who had more than 30,000 flying hours and a US Air Force Distinguished Flying Cross for his combat experience in World War II, was not alone. His copilot and his flight engineer saw the same unidentified flying object about 1,000 yards away from the jet, which was flying on autopilot.

Suddenly, the plane was forced into a sharp left turn, and all three compasses showed different readings. The plane's unusual shift prompted Boston air controllers to ask:

"United 94, where are you going?"

"Well, let me figure this out. I'll let you know," Daniels replied.

The crew turned off the autopilot, and the saucer light followed alongside the jet for several minutes before rapidly disappearing. The plane's instruments returned to normal after the UFO vanished.

Fearful of ridicule or blowback from United Airlines, the crew did not report the incident.

Daniels later said the UFO raced away so swiftly that it could not have been a man-made, or human-occupied, machine. Whatever it was, "it did cause a disruption in the magnetic field around the aircraft to the point where it pulled the aircraft off course."

Today, airline passengers are routinely ordered to turn off all portable electronic devices before departure or landing. Why? Airline safety officials have determined that electromagnetic interference from the devices can have a critical effect on an aircraft's systems and put everyone on board in peril.

While technology has advanced by leaps and bounds in the sixty-three years since Flight 7 went missing, the notion that electromagnetic interference from a UFO back in 1957 might have somehow caused the crash should not be written off as impossible. After all, there once was a time—not so long ago—that the very idea of creating artificial gravity or putting a man on the moon was scoffed at by the most renowned scientists. Today, we routinely produce artificial gravity, and even our concept of life itself is being transformed daily.

Someone once said that unbelief grows out of ignorance and that skepticism is born of intelligence.

Consider this: We used to think that the world was flat.

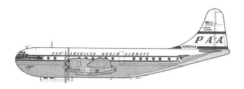

15

MILES TO GO BEFORE
I SLEEP

BOEING'S 377 STRATOCRUISERS may have been the largest, most luxurious, and most sophisticated commercial aircraft of the time, but they had troubling safety issues, particularly with engines and propellers. While I continued to focus on suspects Payne and Crosthwaite, I had no clue that another person was also deeply involved in trying to solve the mysterious crash, and this sleuth was focusing on mechanical failure.

Rarely during the search for my father's killer did something good just happen, but on August 21, 1998, it did. I had been posting messages on various internet boards for many years asking if anyone had any knowledge or interest in the crash, but had had very little success. That changed one morning when I received an email from a fellow I had never heard of: Dr. Gregg Herken, an accomplished nonfiction author and history professor and then-curator at the Smithsonian's Air and Space Museum in Washington. We ended up developing a friendship and a researching-and-writing relationship that has continued for more than twenty years.

Gregg told me he had lived in San Mateo as a youngster, that Marie McGrath, one of the stewardesses on Flight 7, had been one of his favorite substitute fourth-grade teachers, and that their families had known each other. Gregg said he had deeply felt her loss as a child and was stunned when his class was told that the plane had simply vanished. We formed an instant bond, and over the next few months shared everything we had learned about the loss of the airliner. Both of us had a burning desire to solve the case, and when Gregg visited my office in North Carolina sometime later we were both amazed to learn the wealth of information we had between us.

Luckily for both of us, what I had learned through the years, Gregg hadn't. What Gregg had learned, I hadn't. Gregg, who understands technical and mechanical things far better than I do, concentrated on that end of our probe while I continued to work on the human factors. Our informal researching partnership ultimately resulted in two coauthored stories, the first of which, "The Mystery of the Lost Clipper," was published in the October-November 2004 issue of *Air and Space* magazine.

Our story concentrated on the prop-and-engine angle as the possible cause of the crash, and we reported some new findings that strengthened that argument, primarily our discovery that the CAB report had completely ignored an incident a few months before N90944 crashed in which a runaway prop had nearly brought the plane down.

"A runaway, or 'over-speeding,' propeller was a nightmare for any flight crew," we reported. "If the variable-pitch propeller could not be feathered—its blade pitch changed to point the leading edges in the direction of flight—centrifugal force wrenched the blades to the lowest pitch stop. The resulting drag was equivalent to that produced by a solid disk the diameter of the propeller in front of the wing. At that pitch, even if the prop simply wind-milled, there was a danger that it would fly apart and pieces could tear into the cabin."

We also determined that a runaway prop could occur virtually without warning and leave pilots only seconds to react. A sudden change in propeller noise, from the normal dull throbbing to a rapidly ascending, blood-curdling whine, was sometimes the only warning, and by then the problem was a full-blown emergency.

We pointed out that just a year before N90944 crashed, an overspeeding prop and engine failure had forced down its sister ship, N90943, *Sovereign of the Skies,* on its flight from Hawaii to San Francisco at nearly the same spot *Romance of the Skies* had disappeared. *Sovereign* ditched next to a Coast Guard weather station, the *USS Pontchartrain,* and all thirty-one passengers and crew safely evacuated the airplane before it sank to the bottom of the ocean.

The final CAB report on Flight 7 paid no attention to earlier Stratocruiser overspeeds and claimed that N90944 had never experienced an overspeeding incident. That was another bald-faced CAB lie, and a telephone call from one of our sources proved it.

A former Pan Am Stratocruiser pilot named Clancy Mead told Gregg that he had been piloting N90944 in June 1957 when the plane experienced a runaway propeller on a flight to Hawaii. That was only about five months before *Romance of the Skies* disappeared. Mead said that he was unable to feather the prop on the number three engine and was losing altitude at a rate of 100 feet per minute, even with the remaining engines at full power. Captain Mead turned N90944 around and headed back to San Francisco. He said that he miraculously cleared the mountains along the California coast by only about 500 feet before safely landing the plane at the airport.

Nothing of that was mentioned in the CAB report, and I have subsequently determined that for whatever reason, investigators went back only about three months when asking flight crews about any incidents with the aircraft. Whether that was standard operating procedure or not I don't know, but it is interesting when you consider that Pan Am had successfully lobbied the CAB to essentially bury information about mechanical and maintenance issues in its final report.

We also reported that veteran Pan Am pilot Frank Garcia Jr., the flight engineer on *Sovereign of the Skies* when it successfully ditched, had said he suspected the cause of his plane's runaway prop was a small part in the engine-nose case that moves oil to the prop dome.

"A failure of the oil transfer tube or the bearing connecting it to the dome would make it impossible to feather the blades on that propeller," we reported, but noted that conclusive proof of Garcia's theory remained inaccessible, on the ocean floor with the wreckage of *Sovereign of the Skies.*

We also disclosed that Tony Vasko, retired director of overhaul at Eastern Air Lines and an expert on aircraft engines and propellers, found evidence that Pan Am, the manufacturers, and the Federal Aviation Administration had recognized by the time of N90944's accident that the transfer tube, which had been brazed rather than bolted in place, represented a potentially fatal flaw on Stratocruisers.

An emergency airworthiness directive, issued by the FAA in early 1957, warned: "As a result of propeller shaft oil transfer bearing failures, several cases of loss of propeller control occurred which make it impossible to feather the affected propellers." The directive ordered that the brazed joint be inspected on every engine and either replaced or repaired "not later than May 31, 1957."

That date was particularly noteworthy because Captain Mead's prop runaway incident had occurred on June 18, 1957—more than two weeks after the compliance date had passed. Did this confirm claims by some that maintenance standards had slipped at Pan Am? More importantly, we wondered if the joint had been repaired or replaced before *Romance of the Skies* took off on its final flight five months later. Surely Pan Am had fixed that simple, inexpensive issue after Mead's midair incident?

We'll never know for certain.

Our magazine report concluded with questions about garbled tape recordings of possible radio transmissions from *Romance of the Skies* in its final minutes in the air. To this day, despite dozens of inquiries to every conceivable source of information, we have been unable to find a copy of the recordings. We believe that if a copy can be found, today's technology might be able to decipher what the experts couldn't in 1958 and provide us with some important information about the last minutes of Flight 7.

NOVEMBER 2007

A favorite childhood poem of mine, "Stopping by Woods on a Snowy Evening" by Robert Frost, is always in the back of my mind. The last words have been both an inspiration and a haunting burden throughout my life and frequently remind me of the promise I made back in 1965 to find out what had happened to *Romance of the Skies.*

". . . but I have promises to keep,
And miles to go before I sleep.
And miles to go before I sleep."

I had that poem on my mind as November 8, 2007, approached. I still had promises to keep.

It had been fifty years. Fifty years since I had heard my father's voice, held his hand, and watched him carry his luggage and confidently walk away from our Ford into the Pan Am terminal at San Francisco International Airport.

Always searching for new information and new sources, I contacted the *San Francisco Chronicle* as the anniversary date neared and pitched a story about the crash and my investigation, hoping the paper would publish what I call a "fetch 'em story" so that someone might surface with new information.

Reporter Kevin Fagan embraced the idea, and on Sunday, November 4, 2007, the front page of the *Chronicle* recounted the crash and the investigation Dr. Herken and I had been conducting:

Romance of the Skies Plane Crash Haunts Pair 50 Years Later

"Somewhere below the ocean waves, probably about 2,000 miles west of the Golden Gate Bridge and 15,000 feet deep, lies a pile of cold metal that may yield answers to a mystery that has agonized two men for most of their lives.

"That pile is the wreckage of the Romance of the Skies, *a Pan Am luxury airliner that left San Francisco International Airport 50 years ago this week en route to Hawaii—and vanished.*

"Investigators eventually found a handful of bodies and a few bits of wreckage floating a hundred miles north of the flight path—but nobody has ever figured out why the plane crashed, exactly where it crashed, or even whether all 44 people who were booked for the flight were actually on board that day.

"What the disappearance left behind is a whodunit worthy of Agatha Christie, only real.

"It involves two suspected onboard bombers, the possibility that the propeller assembly was so bad it shattered, and a missing flight tape recording—which, if found, could be processed through modern machinery to finally reveal what manner of chaos was going on in those final moments before death.

"Did fire bring down the Romance? *Mechanical malfunction? Sabotage by bomb or poison gas? All are possibilities.*

"The questions haunt Ken Fortenberry, 56, and Gregg Herken, 60. They are determined to never rest until they get answers."

The coverage was more than I could ever have hoped for, and within days my brothers and I were winging our way to San Francisco to memorialize our father and remember the others who had perished. We arrived on different flights and met late one evening at a motel near Santa Clara. We didn't talk much about the crash or our mission. It was more like a brotherly reunion, but in the back of minds was the curiosity of what we might see, what emotions might surface, and whether it was worth a costly trip all the way across the country.

In the morning we drove by our old house in San Mateo, parked the rental car along Sharon Place, where we had once lived, got out, and looked around. It was still very much as we remembered it, and memories flowed. A few minutes after we parked the car a gentleman walked out of our old house and came over to greet us with a welcoming smile.

"We've been expecting you," he said, catching us all by surprise. Ronald Hall explained that he had lived in the house since we moved out back in 1956 and had read in the newspaper about our impending visit to the Bay Area. Without our asking, he invited us to walk inside the house and take a look around. Jerry silently took it all in, and I wondered what was going on inside his head. Craig, who had been a baby when we lived there, was curious and a good sport, and I had a strange but comfortable feeling as I walked inside and stepped back into yesterday.

Our next stop was a few blocks away at Shoreview Methodist Church, where I slowly walked down the aisle and sat in the same pew as I had on the day of my father's memorial service in December 1957. It seemed like only yesterday. We asked a church volunteer if something called the *Book of Remembrances* still existed. A pastor had told Mom after Daddy's death that a book had been bought in his name and he would be the first person memorialized in it. We were pleasantly surprised when we were ushered to the back of the sanctuary, where the huge, dusty old book sat on a glass table. I opened it, and just as we had been told fifty years earlier, the name of William Holland Fortenberry was the first entry.

I thought I would die right there.

Later we drove north again, this time a short distance to San Francisco International Airport, where museum director John Hill had graciously arranged our visit. After guiding us on our tour, John led us up into the old control tower and then onto an observation deck, where my brothers and I stood in silence at 11:51 a.m.—exactly the moment fifty years earlier that *Romance of the Skies* had lifted off the runway heading west on its fatal flight to Honolulu. I whispered, "Goodbye, Daddy," and fought back tears as an airliner roared down the runway and sailed into the misty California sky, headed for parts unknown.

A few minutes later John persuaded officials in the ground control tower to allow my brothers and me to take a short but unforgettable journey down the same runway. Our driver turned left off the tarmac, slowed the vehicle, lined it up on Runway 28R, and then gunned the engine. He raced down the runway, faster and faster, and for a moment it seemed as if I were in the cockpit of Daddy's plane on that fateful November morning.

It was a morning I will cherish until my last breath.

Afterward we drove south to Santa Clara, where George Heeg allowed us to visit our old house on Loyola Drive. As I walked into the kitchen, I could almost see the nameless, worried faces that I remembered from that sad Saturday morning after Daddy's plane had disappeared.

Then we headed to Millikin Elementary, where I had attended kindergarten and, for a short time before we moved to Miami, first grade. I got out of the car and walked the last few blocks along the same route I had walked as a child. I remembered that Jerry and I always brought our lunch from home in little brown paper sacks, and we were often surprised to open them at lunchtime and read an encouraging note from Daddy, usually on a day he would be departing for one of his long trips before we got home from school.

Later that afternoon, my brothers and I traveled to Yosemite National Park, where Jerry and I had so many fond memories of family camping trips. I can still see Daddy tying a shiny gold-and-orange lure onto his fishing line and gently tossing it into a rushing creek, hoping a trout would strike.

We soaked in the natural beauty of that magnificent area, and Craig, who was just two years old when our father died, listened patiently as Jerry and I talked about old times. The only thing Craig knows about his father is what he has learned from us or by looking through family pictures.

We tried to find some of the campsites where Daddy had pitched our tent. We walked along several creekside trails where we played as kids, and after dinner we talked for hours about our father, our family, the crash, and how our lives might have been different had he not been taken from us while we were still children.

It was one of the few times that the three of us had bonded as adults, and it felt good. Very good.

When I went to bed that night in a Yosemite cabin, for the first time since I had been a crying six-year-old in my Santa Clara bedroom I felt a sense of relief and closure. Something came over me and said that everything was going to be OK, that it would be all right to let go of yesterday and get on with my life.

And that's exactly what I intended to do.

But I couldn't.

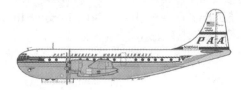

16

CONFUSED OR LYING?

WITHIN A WEEK I was back in the search for my father's killer. Nagging at me now were the troubling comments purser Crosthwaite's stepdaughter, Tania, had made to the *San Francisco Chronicle* reporter who wrote the front-page story about the anniversary of the crash.

"It's hard to believe that my stepdad did this," she said. "He was so good to me, so kind. All those police reports, I think they got something confused."

Confused? So good? So kind?

The only person confused was Tania, and I had her sworn statement to a federal investigator back in 1957 to prove it.

She told the newspaper that she hoped I would find peace and noted that we shared "a terrible thing that happened . . . we lost loved ones."

How could I ever find peace until I solved this mystery? Why was she lying to the newspaper? Had she forgotten that she had once stated that her stepfather had treated her like dirt? Why would she intentionally try to paint Crosthwaite as a loving, caring father? Was she trying to send me off in another direction and divert attention from her stepfather, or had her memory failed her after all these years? What could possibly be her motivation for lying to the reporter?

I reached out to Tania several times in the following years, but she would not respond. It would take me more than a decade to get the answers to those questions.

Simply on a hunch a few years later I persuaded a researcher at the Otto Richter Library in Miami to look into a specific file in the Pan Am archives and see if she could locate any records about the weak and garbled radio transmissions that may—or may not—have come from the plane. By this time archivists at the library were making significant headway in categorizing and archiving the now-bankrupt Pan Am's historical records.

What she found in that file folder was nothing short of a bombshell.

Dr. Herken and I knew that on January 17, 1958—the day after the formal CAB hearing had concluded—audio engineers from the Dictaphone Corporation volunteered to study the recordings once again. Two weeks later, using advanced equipment on loan from the Voice of America, Dictaphone claimed to have deciphered a weak transmission from *Romance of the Skies*, beginning approximately seven minutes and thirty seconds after Flight 7's last position report. This information was sent to the CAB before its final report was issued in 1959, but the CAB for some reason ultimately decided that no emergency transmission had ever come from the airplane.

That didn't make sense, because the Dictaphone transcript report in the archive's files included what appeared to be an urgent emergency call and an unusual exchange among crew members over open microphone:

"SO 292 Special Number and Flyer. (Also understood as '. . . number on fire.')

"Attention All Stations Pan American Air.

"Verification Channel Bearing 11.

"Still have one tank full. Am ditching flight.

"CQ, CQ, Syracuse, New York.

"J arm is missing, tail.

Then, in a voice different from the one who gave a position report:

"Did you chart me? [Inaudible]... Special position.

And then the same voice who made the position report:

"Fuel control—3, 4, 5, 6,

"Zero 2 fuel flow! Zero 2 fuel flow! Coordinate."

Then, two voices speaking excitedly, and these final words:

"What about 3 engine?"

Dr. Herken and I concluded that Flight 7 did indeed send some kind of distress message. However, even after speaking with numerous Stratocruiser pilots and aircraft experts and sharing the transcript, we could not locate anyone who was able to understand what the crew was trying to say, other than the plane was in distress.

In 2013, Dr. Herken and I received the Dave Abrams and Gene Banning Research Grant from the Pan Am Historical Foundation and headed back to the Richter Library at the University of Miami. We spent days poring over hundreds of documents and in January 2017 wrote a follow-up article for *Air and Space* magazine titled: "What Happened to Pan Am Flight 7? Sabotage? Negligence? Fraud? New clues surface in 60-year-old aviation mystery."

We reported that statistically, the B-377 was half as safe, per passenger-mile flown, as other aircraft used on the same routes by Pan Am's rival airlines at the time: United's Douglas DC-6s and TWA's Lockheed

Constellations. Of the 56 B-377s built, ten were lost in accidents, and in five of those cases the crash occurred after a propeller failed, causing that engine to be torn from the wing.

We also reported another troubling tale: In the weeks before the crash, N90944's engines had experienced a "constant fluctuation" in oil pressure, leaks from the turbochargers, and persistent cooling problems—problems Pan Am didn't want the public to know.

"In May 1958, J.J. Cantwell, an attorney representing Pan Am, wrote to CAB official Robert Chrisp to protest Chrisp's plan to cite Pan Am's lax maintenance in the government's report. In a separate letter to the airline's legal department, Cantwell frankly admitted that he hoped to persuade Chrisp 'to withhold the maintenance report from the public record.'

"Although the CAB report acknowledged the board had found a 'number of irregularities in maintenance procedures and/or practices' at the airline, the absence of a clear distress call and the dearth of physical evidence from the crash made it 'obviously impossible to associate (those irregularities) with, or disassociate them from the accident.' The report makes no mention of union rep Phil Ice's allegations of poor maintenance," we reported.

We disclosed that the report's conclusions had been hotly debated within the CAB and that documents we discovered showed that three weeks before the report's public release, CAB chairman James Durfee dissented from the conclusions reached at the Bureau of Safety meeting at which the final report was approved.

"I am not satisfied with the language, the discussion, or the findings with respect to Pan Am's maintenance practices," he wrote. Durfee also noted that the CAB's parent organization, the Civil Aeronautics Authority, had yet to reprimand Pan Am for its maintenance deficiencies or to ensure that the deficiencies had been corrected.

There may have been a reason for that: The CAA had a built-in conflict of interest. Even though it was the agency responsible for investigating commercial aviation accidents, it was also charged with promoting flying to the public.

"CAA and CAB officials, including members of the Bureau of Safety, were routinely given free tickets by the major carriers, and were wined and dined by the companies they were supposed to be overseeing. One mechanic at the 944 hearings testified that he'd overheard a CAB investigator and a Pan Am executive discussing where to go to dinner that night, and what time to play golf the next morning. The CAA was subsequently abolished and replaced by the Federal Aviation Agency (later the Federal Aviation Administration), which had responsibility for investigating aircraft accidents, not for promoting air travel," we reported in the *Air and Space* article.

"The government never fully investigated the role that shoddy maintenance may have played in the loss of PAA-944. Nor did the CAB conclude that the cause was catastrophic mechanical failure, despite the evidence of the Dictaphone transcript."

Our conclusion was this:

"Ultimately, what brought down *Romance of the Skies* was human fallibility. A propulsion technology had reached its limits. A government agency had become cozy with the companies it was meant to police. And an airline, in its rush to enter the Jet Age, had decided to cut corners, ignoring the risk to passengers and crew."

Years after Herken and I wrote this story I learned that CAB chairman Durfee frequently had been the recipient of unusual hospitality by airline companies regulated by his agency. In September 1957, for example, Eastern Airlines treated him to a four-day trip to Mexico, and a month later Trans World Airlines gave Durfee and his wife a four-day free trip to Rome. A year earlier, he was the guest of Flying Tiger Airlines on a three-day golfing party trip to Pinehurst, North Carolina.

Although we concluded in the *Air and Space* article that mechanical failure was the most likely cause of the crash, I still had nagging questions—questions that we had never been able to answer. Dr. Herken was convinced that mechanical failure, probably a thrown propeller, was the culprit, but I remained skeptical even though I had coauthored and signed off on the article with him.

Clearly, the Stratocruiser had been a troubled aircraft, and the arguments in favor of mechanical failure were compelling. Maybe a propeller did tear away from an engine, rip through the fuselage, and bring the airliner down. Maybe an engine did catch fire, and it could not be extinguished before flames spread and entered the fuselage, crippling the plane.

Maybe.

Was mechanical failure possible? Of course. Was it probable? I wasn't so sure, and neither was the Civil Aeronautics Board when it had issued its tentative and inconclusive report in 1959. I still can't fathom the possibility that Pan Am failed to make a quick, simple, inexpensive repair to an oil transfer tube.

I continued to believe that there was as much evidence or more, if only circumstantial and coincidental, that the plane had been sabotaged by passenger Payne or purser Crosthwaite. I kept reminding myself that investigators had only bits and pieces of the giant airliner to work with when they had issued their report, and even after thousands of hours of study they had been unable to agree on a probable cause, leaving the mystery unsolved.

As a journalist I had been trained to check everything out, and then check it out again. An editor once told me: "If your mother says she loves you, check it out." So even after the *Air and Space* article I continued to check things out.

Lodge owner Payne remained my prime suspect, and I hadn't yet fully written off purser Crosthwaite. Payne's son, Michael (Kim), and his stepson, Kip, clammed up and declined to talk with me once they realized I was writing a book. I have been unable to reach their estranged sister, Kitti Ruth, a former high school rodeo star who briefly surfaced in the news several years ago when she unsuccessfully sued Publisher's Clearing House. She had no established address or working phone number. The owner of a California trailer park she had used as an address for several years told me she had never heard of her, and even the homeless women's shelters in the area had no knowledge of her existence, even though she had given their addresses as her own. I have left numerous messages on her Facebook page, but she had refused to answer them.

Although the Paynes weren't talking, which seemed suspicious to me, I was able to find a man in California who had gone to school with

Kip and Kim Payne when they lived in Scott Bar, and his recollections of the days after the plane crash were revealing.

"I think people wondered why they moved up there in the first place. It was like they were hiding from something," recalled William Nowdesha. "Anyway, it was a very strange thing when he disappeared. Everybody had their eyebrows up. There's only about fifty people around there, and everyone was wondering.

"The community was talking about [the crash], and they were feeling sorry for [the widow Payne]. All of a sudden, the FBI [likely the CAB] shows up, and that became the talk of the town. It was quite a big event for the year. We always figured somebody did it for the insurance money."

Nowdesha, who used to wait for the school bus at Roxbury Lodge with the Payne boys, then said some things that raised my eyebrows:

"Not long [after the crash], what we would call a gigolo moved in with her [Payne's widow]. He wasn't involved in anything, but we did see her carry him around the town. He was a tall, good-looking man. He was dark-complected. People notice that sort of thing in a small town. When that fellow moved in so soon after the crash it was a big red flag.

"And not too long later the place burned down. FBI agents were around to try to prove that she had done something to it. I believe the kids were with relatives in Manteca when it burned."

Nowdesha said he and others in the tiny community visited the ruins of the lodge a week or so later.

"There wasn't much left. Just a fireplace and a few things, like a metal walk-in freezer."

I wondered how the widow Payne and her children had handled the news of the plane crash and their missing husband and father.

"They didn't seem concerned," he said. "They just faded into the background. They never talked about it. They were very quiet. They more or less withdrew into the house and never had much to do with anyone after the crash. They retreated into themselves."

Nowdesha's observations seemed to add fuel to the fire that Payne and perhaps his widow were involved in some sinister plot to blow up the plane. Then again, the Paynes may have been so consumed by grief that they simply did not want to interact with nosy neighbors.

Nevertheless, having covered my bases as best I could with the Payne family, I turned once again to Crosthwaite's stepdaughter, Tania. I continued to be puzzled by her comments to the San Francisco newspaper years earlier, when she had claimed that her stepfather was a wonderful man who would never, ever do something as awful as sabotaging an airplane and killing innocent people.

Why would she lie like that? My gut told me something just didn't add up.

Still dissatisfied with the CAB's 1958 report and getting nowhere with either the Paynes or with Crosthwaite's stepdaughter, on Monday, August 14, 2017, I formally asked the National Transportation Safety Board to reopen the investigation or to at least finish what its predecessor agency, the Civil Aeronautics Board, had left undone. I also asked Congressman Rick Larsen of Washington, a member of the House Transportation and Infrastructure Committee and ranking member of the Aviation Subcommittee, for his assistance. Not surprisingly, Larsen, whose major contributors include The Boeing Company, did not even offer me the courtesy of a response.

The NTSB, however, did respond, with an email on September 13, 2017: "Regarding the loss of Pan Am Flight 7, the NTSB is not planning any further investigative action because this type of aircraft and major systems onboard are not in commercial service within the United States and the air carrier no longer operates," Dr. Elias Kontansis stated. "In essence, commercial aviation operations have moved well beyond the state of the industry in 1957 . . . and reopening the investigation would not contribute significantly to improving the safety of current or future commercial aviation operations."

Dr. Kontansis advised me to contact the FBI if I believed the crash may have resulted from an intentional act, and that's exactly what I did. Not surprisingly, the FBI turned me down again. I was disappointed, but not surprised.

With no help from the FBI or the NTSB, I turned to another federal agency, the National Oceanic and Atmospheric Administration, and pleaded for its assistance in searching the ocean bottom for the wreckage of *Romance of the Skies*. NOAA has been involved in undersea exploration for many years and I thought that because several active-duty servicemen and other government employees had perished in the crash that the agency might consider a search of the area, perhaps when it was working on an unrelated project nearby.

On Thursday, July 20, 2017, I received a courteous rejection from the agency.

"I appreciate your interest in this specific wreck and the meaning its discovery would have for you and your family. Unfortunately, at this time we do not have any planned deepwater operations for the area and will be heading to the Atlantic Ocean this fall to begin several years of operations in that ocean basin," Alan Leonardi stated in an email.

"As such, we will not have any near-term opportunity to support your request. I hope you may have luck in your quest in the coming years and can find partners who can meet your expedition needs," he stated.

I wasn't ready to give up on a deep-sea exploration so I asked Leonardi to suggest one of those "partners" to me and he recommended two organizations that had the kind of assets needed for such a monumental undertaking—the Ocean Exploration Trust and the Schmidt Ocean Institute.

I immediately contacted both.

Dr. Carlie S. Wiener, director of marine communications for the Schmidt Ocean Institute, told me that her organization's schedule was very tight for the next several years, but encouraged me to send coordinates of the search-and-recovery area in the remote chance that a team might be in the area in the future. She also said that the Ocean Exploration Trust might be better suited to handle a search for *Romance of the Skies*.

Ocean Exploration Trust is perhaps best known for its discovery of the *RMS Titanic* and the German battleship *Bismarck*. Its founder, Dr. Robert Ballard, is considered by many to be the preeminent ocean explorer of our time.

I reached out to Dr. Ballard's team, and although they also turned me down, there was some slight encouragement in the response, and we remain in communication.

"Our day rate for chartering the ship for expeditions we are not specifically funded by NOAA to support is $55-$60K (depending on the assets required). Is that feasible within the realm of the budget?" chief operating officer Allison Fundis asked.

That, of course, was impossible, and I thanked Fundis for her reply.

"Understandable," she responded. "I will plan to keep in touch if we have an opportunity arise in the near future that will potentially allow us to help with this search involving other funding partners."

Like Schmidt Ocean Institute, she asked me to send coordinates of the search-and-recovery area, which I promptly did, and Fundis has kept the door open to the possibility that one day Dr. Ballard's team may search for what remains of *Romance of the Skies.*

With the federal government refusing once again to help, and having been rejected by the deep-sea exploration organizations, I had two choices: either admit defeat and give up or continue the search for my father's killer.

The search continued.

PANAMA CITY, PANAMA
MONDAY, MAY 26, 1952

"Dear Mother and Boys,

"Daddy Bo is in Panama after a nice flight last night on the 'El Inter-Americana.' Most of the passengers had dinner and went to bed soon after we left Miami, so I suppose they were going on south of the Equator. Today has been uneventful. I've been eating and looking the 'El Panama' over most of the time. Soon, I'm going to take a nap.

"My little Jerry Boy was sweet yesterday. I could hear him very well and he knew who was on the other end of that wire. He seemed to be quite interested in telling me 'I wove you!' I love that little Bee Bo, too, and all of you. Kenneth, I could see looking for his daddy. He is too young to fully understand the miracles of science and therefore

couldn't comprehend fully what was going on.

"I don't know why you wanted me to write. If I write now, I was there less than a day ago, and if I wait longer, I'll probably beat the letter to you. I guess you must still love me a little bit. I still love you, Mother Dear. When I quarrel and fuss with you, I don't mean any harm by it. When I say something about you not being able to swim, I'm only trying to make you resolve to learn. I don't suppose you will ever learn, though. You are too afraid of water. It is not your fault. You didn't have the chances of other girls when you were young. That only makes me want to give you more of the nice things now that you are older. I hope you will be happy with me. I'll try to give you the things you need.

"You should be glad I'm gone for a few days because I don't help you when I am there anyway. I only grumble because I haven't eaten in the last hour, etc.

"Hope to see you before the 1st of June. In the meantime, take care of all three of my babies and remember this old mean, grouchy, nearly bald-headed old cuss loves all of you sincerely. Love my Babies,

Daddy."

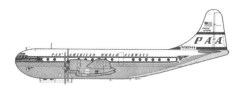

17

GRIEVING GENE GOES CRAZY

I WAS FRUSTRATED AND DISCOURAGED, but I was accustomed to those emotions after searching for my father's killer for more than fifty years. Determined to never give up until I had the answers I had been seeking nearly all my life, I had reached out once again in late September 2018 to purser Gene Crosthwaite's stepdaughter, Tania, this time on her Facebook page. Tania had been living in Texas for more than twenty years, but for reasons unknown had been unwilling to talk.

Midmorning on Tuesday, October 2, my Facebook alert sounded. Someone was sending me a message. And that someone was Tania.

We exchanged a few get-to-know-you pleasantries before I asked her again to please sit down with me and talk about 1957. After all these years, something seemed to be tugging at the seventy-eight-year-old widow's conscience. Why else would she have responded to my message? Maybe she had finally decided to get some things off her chest? In the Facebook chat it became clear she was about ready to talk, although she still hadn't convinced herself that she should.

Tania: *I feel guilty I didn't share what I knew before. I was really scared.*

Me: *Scared?*

Tania: *Yes.*

Me: *About what?*

Tania: *Well, it's something that affects more than u and me. My pastors felt I should leave it alone but maybe I shouldn't.*

For whatever reasons, she was still reluctant to talk, so I decided that for the moment I would not press her. The mere fact that we were communicating was positive, and I didn't want to risk that. We chatted occasionally throughout the day about nothing significant, and in the meantime she checked out my Facebook page and learned that we had something in common other than the loss of our fathers on the airplane: we were both cancer survivors. It was enough of a hook to keep the doors of communication open to the possibility of a sit-down interview. Fearful that she might change her mind about talking after all these years, I told her that evening that I could book an airline flight and be in Texas the following afternoon.

Tania: *My goodness. You would do that after all these years?*

I told her a little bit about all the work I had done trying to solve the airline crash mystery, and used a reporter's technique to pique the retired secretary's curiosity about what I knew. I let her know that I was aware that her stepfather had been out-of-his mind nuts in the weeks before the crash and that I had some notes taken by one of the federal investigators who had questioned her after the crash.

Tania: *Wow! Would you share?*

Me: *I will gladly share everything I know—if we can talk openly and honestly.*

While I was still Facebook-chatting with her I opened another screen and booked a morning flight to Houston. I told her I would meet her at her apartment the following day at 3 p.m. if that would suit her.

Tania: *OK. I have a feeling this is long overdue.*

The deal was done. Tania Crosthwaite was finally going to sit down for an interview that could shed new light on the lifelong search for my father's killer.

I was running purely on adrenalin as I boarded the early morning flight from Charlotte to Houston, where I planned to rent a car and drive about an hour to League City for what I considered to be the most important interview of my life. What little sleep I had the night before had been repeatedly interrupted by a thousand questions buzzing around in my head.

Was I being led on a wild-goose chase? What had prompted her to agree to an interview after all these years of refusing to give me the time of day? Was Tania going to be open or was she going to be deceitful? How was I going to break the ice, win her trust, and get her to go back in her mind to those troubling days sixty-one years earlier, when she was just a sixteen-year-old with a bully stepfather? Does she really have anything new to offer or is she just trying to clear her conscience of something I already know? Will she be angry? Will she be hostile, thinking I am trying to finger her stepfather as a suicidal murderer? Would I have to struggle to get her to open up and share not only her remembrances of those days back in November 1957, but also her emotions at the time?

As it turns out there was no ice to be broken; Tania was ready to talk, and I was more than ready to listen.

Precisely at 3 p.m. I took a deep breath and rang the doorbell to her first-floor apartment. It was an awkward moment for both of us, perhaps more out of nervousness and curiosity than anything else, but we had both been waiting for this moment for many years, and the desire to share outweighed everything else. Why it had escaped me I don't know, but as I sat down in her small living room filled with beautiful Chinese antiques that had belonged to her parents, I realized that this was the first time I had ever met face-to-face with anyone whose family member had died on *Romance of the Skies*. Her stepfather may have been a suicidal murderer, but I felt a kinship with her from the beginning of the interview and held no ill feelings toward her in any way. She, too, had been a victim of whatever had happened on November 8, 1957.

I asked her for permission, then tapped "record" on my iPhone. Tania talked freely for nearly thirty minutes about anything and everything except her stepfather and the crash. I let her do so without interruption. It seemed to me that she was trying to convince herself that talking with me was the right thing to do. I learned that she was still grieving from the loss of her husband of twenty-two years, Steve Barnes, who had died after a long battle with cancer and Alzheimer's less than a year earlier. His death had left her not only in an unexpectedly bad financial situation but also with a deep hole in her broken heart.

As she talked about Steve, I learned why she had told the San Francisco newspaper reporter those lies about what a wonderful stepfather Gene had been to her and why she had stated that Dr. Herken and I must have been wrong to suggest otherwise. I had the distinct impression that Tania hadn't told Steve the details of her troubled teen years and didn't want to bother him with the heavy burden she had borne all her life. His medical problems were overwhelming both of them at the time, and the last thing they needed was a ghost from yesterday haunting their lives.

She wasn't clear about this, and I didn't press her. It really was none of my business, although she had told me in the Facebook chat that her pastors had encouraged her not to talk with anyone about what happened. That meant that she had told them something—something so secret and so important that they worried about how it might impact her emotionally if it got out to the public.

I also learned that she was recovering from breast cancer and had just recently moved from San Antonio to the apartment in League City, wanting to be closer to her grandchildren now that she was a widow in her late seventies and in questionable health.

She spoke several times about her faith, a faith she said had helped pull her through many tough times in her life, and it was obvious that she had faced a great deal of heartache and trouble since her childhood in California. She didn't blame anyone for anything that had happened to her. In fact, several times she pointed the finger squarely at herself for mistakes and bad decisions she made after the plane crash. She reminded me that she had lost her mother and her stepfather in a period of only three months and suddenly felt alone in the world, with only her Russian-speaking grandmother, whose old-world customs and expectations of a teenage girl was tough on them both.

She admitted that after the crash, but not before, she had turned into the wild teen that Gene had often accused her of being. She said she was ashamed of some of the things she did back then but had spent much of her life trying to forgive herself.

"I never really started acting up until after his death," she disclosed. "Before that I was just an innocent kid. I don't know what his complaints were. I never did anything. I never knew him to hug me. I never knew him to take me anywhere. He never like mistreated me, but it was like I wasn't there."

When the plane crashed, she was finally free from her overbearing stepfather, and she began to hang out with the wrong crowd. She became pregnant when she was barely eighteen, only sixteen months after the plane went down. She and the child's father, a twenty-four-year-old ne'er-do-well hell-raiser named George Freeman Tolbert, married seven months later in Oregon, and had three more children in quick succession before they divorced. The marriage was in trouble from the beginning, and George had numerous run-ins with the law in California and Oregon. He had a thing for fast cars, booze, weapons, and beating women.

Tania never benefited from her father's estate; she had married before the age of 21 and not in a Catholic church, in defiance of the last-minute changes to his will.

Tania didn't share the details of her troubled life after her parents died, but I had pieced some of them together through my own research and didn't let on during the interview that I knew about those dark days. They were important to know, to be able to understand what went on in her mind back then and to be able to write a factual story not only on the crash itself but also on how it had impacted her life and the lives of others.

Nearly two hours after the interview began, I started to steer her in the direction of why I had come halfway across the country in the first place, but I didn't want her to feel like I was pressuring her. She seemed at once both fragile and resolute, but slowly began to return to her childhood and wove an interesting and heartbreaking story of a girl who felt unloved and unwanted by her intimidating stepfather, rejected and ignored by her stepfather's family, and puzzled to this very day about why he seemed to hate her so much and why he had told the Santa Cruz juvenile officer that she was uncontrollable.

"I remember he never had anything positive to say to me. He was always negative."

It was painfully slow, but the interview I had been seeking for decades was finally getting somewhere, and before I left that evening I would have the closest thing to a "smoking gun" I would ever have in the search for my father's killer.

We talked first about her stepfather's funeral.

"I was just in a state of shock, you know. Mama died in August, and he died three months later, in November. Grandma and I thought it would be nice if, well, my mom had a huge picture of Gene in his Pan American uniform, and it was real beautiful picture. And as a surprise he had bought Marie [Crosthwaite's mother] a trip to Hawaii, and she didn't know about it. I could have torn it [the ticket] up, but that was not in my thoughts. And so we thought, well at the funeral when we met her, 'cuz we didn't know how to contact her, I'd give her the picture of Dad and her ticket to Hawaii."

"Was he close to his mother? Did he see her often?" I asked.

"He never mentioned her. It was strange."

"So, we're standing outside and I'm holding this and all the people are in their cars and there's some kind of hold-up. So, Helen [her godmother] was very bored and she says, 'I'm going to find out what the hold-up is.' She got a hold of the men from the funeral parlor and they came over, and she wanted to know why we weren't going to the cemetery. And they said, 'Well, there's a fuss over there.'

"They [Crosthwaite's mother and brothers] felt they should be in the first car instead of me, and then, you know, Helen goes, 'I don't believe this. That's what they're fussing about?'

"And I just didn't even know what they're talking about other than somebody's upset about which car they were in. I didn't know it dealt with me, you know, and I said, 'I'll be right back,' and I went over there, and I've got [the picture] in my hand and I didn't really get to say anything.

"I said, 'This is for you,' and that's as far as I got. She [Crosthwaite's mother] grabbed it out of my hand and just turned her back to me. I didn't even know why, and so I go back there and then Helen is fussing with the funeral people, and then I heard this thing about me being in that car.

"I told that funeral director, I said, 'I don't care what car I'm in,' and Helen says, 'Let's go. If they want to come, they can follow us,' and that's all I know.

"And we went to the cemetery and then I never saw them or ever heard from them again or nothing. I told Grandma what happened. I said, 'Grandma, she was really rude,' and that's all I know. I don't know why they didn't like me. We suspicioned that it was 'cuz we were Russian and at that time, not long after the Second World War, the fifties, some American people were very touchy about it.

"I think they were unhappy that he married a Russian, but other than that I don't know, 'cuz we did not personally offend them in any way. We never heard from them again."

"You never saw your dad's mother or his family again?"

"I never heard from them again."

"Where is your dad buried?"

"It was closed casket. He wasn't in there. I don't know what they put in there. They said the sharks ate him, and they said they identified him by his arm."

"Do you know the name of the cemetery?"

"It's the Santa Cruz Mausoleum. He's there and so is my grandpa Peter. In fact, they had a vault for me, and I don't know why, but Grandma managed to get the $600 back and it was my vault and I didn't even know till years later. I'll tell you, there's a lot of people who stole from me."

She paused to take a phone call from her granddaughter, who was calling to check if everything was going OK with the interview. She assured her that it was, and then I tried to steer her back to the final years of Gene's life.

"Going back to when Gene had TB: what do you recall about him before and after he was in the hospital?"

"For sure he wasn't the same person when he got out. Something happened and he was very cranky, and he was mean even. I'll never forget that first breakfast [after his TB hospital discharge] we were having in Felton at our home. Mama fixed the breakfast. We were sitting there, and he wanted the syrup, I believe. And I don't know why but he took his fist and slammed it hard on the table like this and said, 'I said I need the syrup!' and Mom's eyes got this big and I froze in my place and she got him the syrup.

"We wondered what happened to the man that we all loved and that did all that work to bring me to America and a horrible lot of work to bring Grandma to America. What happened to him? What did I do that he didn't like me? After he had TB, we didn't know him at all. He was just not the same person.

"He had these outbursts of anger, so much that he had her in tears for a whole month, and she finally called the doctor, whoever that was who was treating him. Later she was telling Grandma, and I was listening, and the doctor said, 'Oh, Mrs. Crosthwaite, I wish you had called me sooner.' He said, 'We've got him on medicine, and we can adjust it. If you had told me earlier, I could have spared you a lot of misery.' I guess it was adjusted. I don't know. He stayed mean.

"I always stayed out of the way when he was home, because Mama would tell me, 'Daddy's home. It's our time, so why don't you just stay in your room,' or whatever, and that's what I did."

We talked about her days as a Russian-speaking Pan Am child in Hong Kong before the Crosthwaites returned to California.

"I learned how to speak real good English while I was going to the British school in Hong Kong, and I had their accent, their way of speaking. I remember one night we were eating dinner together, which was rare, and after dinner I said, 'OK, I'm going to go next door to see somebody.' I said, 'Cheerio,' and I could hear him saying, 'Why is she talking like that? She sounds just like a Brit,' and a bomb goes off! He gets real mad and my mama says, 'What do you expect? She's going to a British school and she's learned to speak their way.' It was always something with him. It was like there was always something wrong with me, so I never really felt loved. Really. I always felt there was something wrong with me, and I believed it."

The Crosthwaites returned to California in September 1955 and the fifteen-year-old Tania enrolled as a junior at Holy Cross High School.

"You know, I never had parents come to any school events. I was always so alone, and I felt so alone, and all he did was reprimand me for something."

Her mother worked at various locations as a waitress and saleslady at a department store and, for a time, cut vegetables at Birds Eye with Tania's grandmother, Katherina.

Tania mentioned several times that in spite of her stepfather's meanness, she was extremely appreciative of the fact that he had worked so hard to bring her mother, Julia, and her to their new lives in the United States, and for convincing authorities on two continents to allow grandmother Katherina, a Chinese concentration camp survivor, to emigrate from China and ultimately become a US citizen.

"We were very grateful to him, because our entire lives depended on that man. All I know is that I was a little girl and there were bombs going off, roofs being blown down. Dead people. Grandma running and me getting hurt with blood all over me.

"And then to have this man bring us from China, from all that terror and horror, to America. We were grateful and we felt we owed him everything. Everything."

Tania's next statements about her childhood and her relationship with her stepfather were somewhat contradictory.

"I would hear stories about stepfathers doing the 'dad thing' and maybe sexually hurting girls and stuff like that, and I always thought I had a great stepfather. I mean after all, we had it pretty good. A nice house, you know, pretty things. We traveled. So I felt I had a very happy childhood. But as I grew older and began to be around families and see fathers hugging on children and girls running to their fathers I would just stare because it was so unusual for me, and even in my senior year there was no relationship. There was nothing kind from him to me."

What she said is that her stepfather provided the necessities of life and plenty of material things, but no love.

She admitted that she wasn't perfect.

"In my senior year we kids decided that every time we would go to a hamburger place we would start saving the salt or pepper shaker with the name of the place, and I would take them home and put them in a drawer. We never talked about what we did or anything, 'cuz nobody was interested, nobody cared. Anyway, one day he went through my drawers and I guess he found the salt and pepper shakers. I had a big reprimand from Dad on the Ten Commandments and I shalt not steal and everything. I just felt miserable, but for some reason something snapped in me and I called him an old goat.

"I said, 'You're just an old goat,' because I felt like he just didn't understand kids. My friends did the same things and they never got in trouble and I always did. I called him an old goat and that was the only time he hit me, and he hit me in the face. He just hauled off and hit me right here, real hard. It shocked me and I shut up.

"You know what? I knew I deserved it because I called him an old goat, and then after that, boy, let me tell you, there was quietness when he was home, and it got worse. I mean, I was in my room and he was in his room and it was that way until graduation.

"You know, Mom was already sick then. We didn't know she had cancer, but she was really sick, and she got out of bed and actually came to my graduation. They were both coming to my graduation."

And then Gene stabbed her in the heart on graduation day.

"My dad called me and said very sternly: 'We need to have a conversation' and I said, 'Oh, no! What have I done now?' So, we go into my bedroom and he closes the door and I'm sitting on the bed and he says real sternly,

'I'm not your father. I want you to know that. I adopted you and I'm your stepfather, but you're not my blood child.' I just went 'OK,' and he just stared at me. I didn't know what else to say. I was afraid if I did."

"Did you not know that you were adopted?" I asked.

"I remember seeing Mom and him at the church where they had their wedding, but you know, I thought in my mind that maybe he wasn't my dad, but when he said that to me it hit me in the heart and it shocked me. I mean, did he have to do that now, on my graduation day?

"And 'cuz I was always told, 'If anybody asks you, he is your American father, so you are half-American and half-Russian,' that's what my parents and Grandma said and so that's what I did.

"Anyway, it took the excitement of my graduation away, because his attitude was like he was finally glad to get rid of me. That was what I felt, 'cuz it was like very harsh: 'I'm not your dad!' And so we went on to the graduation and I was like, things were kind of like a blur to me, 'cuz it left me emotionally drained.

"And I was afraid to ask him any questions, because I grew up as a little girl in war and I was in situations that we don't need to go into. There were so many secrets. I even got spanked harshly for one time speaking out saying something true, and I learned really fast that you had to keep your mouth shut during the war because your life depended on it. My whole family was always fearful for their lives, and so when he said that, plus his attitude to me and everything, I was just afraid."

Getting rid of Tania may have been exactly what he had in mind when Gene ruined her graduation day. She didn't know it, but on the day of her mother's funeral he told two friends that he was planning to sell his house in Felton, give the in-laws some of the proceeds, and move closer to San Francisco.

Tania would not be in the purser's plans for his new life; she would have to find a place of her own and fend for herself.

The graduation-day slap in the face wasn't the first or the last time Crosthwaite would break the girl's heart.

"A week or two after that Mama was throwing up and losing weight. She went to the doctor, who said she had ulcers."

Tania was in Los Angeles at the time, having been sent there to live with one of her mother's friends after she had no luck finding a job in the San Francisco Bay Area.

"She wanted me to find a job, maybe to get on with my career as a ballet dancer. I was looking for a job, maybe five or six weeks, and there were a few things that were happening with my ballet dancing, but then I got a call that Mom was terribly sick. That panicked me, and I came back. I walked into a home that I didn't even know. My mother was just staring at me. My dad was not happy I came home. I remember my dad saying, 'What are you doing home?' I said, 'Well, Mom was sick, and I came home.' It scared me that things were so bad. It was the spirit of the thing. I just went into my bedroom and cried. I was so stressed."

As it turns out, the thirty-two-year-old Julia Crosthwaite didn't have ulcers; she had terminal cancer, and a few days later was lying in a hospital bed.

"They were going to do an exploratory and we all went. Grandma, her husband, Peter at the time, and me and my dad. And we were all waiting 'cuz they said that once they got in there, they could tell us more, and they'll probably be an hour. So four hours later, you know, I was a nervous wreck. My grandma was in a panic and my dad was pacing. And then they tell us that she has thirty days to live and that she was ate up with cancer!

"And I mean all I know is my dad's face was white. I just stared at him and Grandma said, 'She's dying, Tania! She's only going to live thirty days,' and we were just so broke up. I think all of us needed some special care at that moment in time."

Gene virtually disappeared from Tania's life after Julia's fatal diagnosis.

"I don't know where he was staying, where he went. I didn't know nothing, and all I knew is that my mom's going to be dead in thirty days and I want to see my mom."

A few days later, completely out of the blue, the absent Gene called home.

"I said, 'Daddy, I want to see Mama. I want to see Mama,' and he goes, 'Well, she don't want to see you. So you stay away. She don't want to see you! You tell your grandma that.' And he hung up.

"So I had, you know, I had some friends and this kid Jack, which is kind of my first boyfriend sort of, and he wanted to know, 'How is your mama doing?' 'cuz everybody in Felton by then had heard that she had cancer, and so they asked me, 'When you going to see your mom?' and I say that I can't see my mom and they go why and I go, 'Daddy won't let me go.'

"And they said, 'What do you want to do? Go see her?' And I go yeah, and she [Jack's mother] says, 'I'll tell you what, honey. I'll buy you a round-trip Greyhound bus ticket for you to go to where you mom is if you promise you won't tell your dad where you got the money.' And they bought me the ticket. And so they gave me the ticket and I got ready to go. I didn't even tell my grandma. I just went on that bus to the hospital and found out what room Mama was in.

"I went up there and opened the door and my mom is sitting up in bed and she's looking at me and she goes, 'Who's there?' I covered my face and she goes, 'Is somebody there?' and I just froze on the spot. And then I started backing up real slow and went out and I realized Mama couldn't see. She couldn't see! So apparently that cancer got all up all over her and she couldn't even see. I got a hold of myself and I went back in. This time, I knocked on the door, made some noise, and went in and I go, 'Mama?' and she goes, 'Oh, baby!' I said, 'How are you, Mom?' and she hugged me. 'Oh, I'm so glad to see you,' I said, and 'How are you doing?' And she said, 'Honey, well, I'm doing good. I probably look bad and I need my makeup and everything,' but she says, 'I'm feeling good,' and then my dad walks in.

"It was like the Devil showed up. I literally froze, and he looked at me. He goes 'Tania! Come out here!' in that terrible voice of his, and I said 'OK.' Then I told mom, 'I'll see you later,' and she says, 'OK, honey."

So I walk out of there and he takes me to the hall and says, 'What are you doing here?' I said, 'I came to see Mama,' and he says, 'How did you get here?' I said, 'I took the Greyhound bus and he says, 'Where did you get the money?' I said, 'I just did.' He said, 'Who bought you the ticket?' and I never told him. I figured with his attitude he'd go find them and tell them off. He says, 'You go home! Get out of here! Get on that bus and you go home!'

"Well, I was scared, so I got on the bus, and that's the last time I ever saw my mom.

"Eight days later I'm upstairs and I hear a scream. I mean a bloodcurdling scream from downstairs and I knew. Then Grandma says, 'She died, Tania. She died.'"

Things went from bad to worse after Julia's death. Gene became even angrier and more hateful toward Tania.

"You know he blamed you for your mama's death," I told her. "He said that you worried her to death."

Instantly, I realized that I shouldn't have said that, but I wanted to learn what was going on in Crosthwaite's mind in the months before the plane crash, and I remembered that the Santa Cruz deputy had told authorities that Crosthwaite was "psycho" when he had tried to have Tania detained.

Tania bent her head down, and I could tell the interview was wearing on her. It was wearing on me, too, but I knew that this was likely to be my one and only chance of getting her to talk.

I wasn't about to walk away now and call it a night; she might never talk to me again.

And after that evening, she never really did.

The afternoon was getting late, and although I was learning some interesting things, she still hadn't given me what I was really looking for: the secrets she had been hiding for six decades. Was she going to take those secrets to her grave?

I continued to listen as Tania rambled on. She shared lots of interesting tidbits but nothing earthshaking. I decided to take her to dinner at a seafood restaurant nearby, and we talked about nothing in particular before returning to her apartment for round two of the interview.

She told me that Gene had been deeply in love with Julia and that Tania had adored her mother as well. She and Julia both loved ballet, liked the same clothing styles, and enjoyed occasional girl talk—they even looked alike—but Gene was king of the house, and when he was home her mother's attention was solely on him.

I decided that it was time to steer the conversation back to the days before Julia became ill, thinking that maybe Tania would work herself to the place I really wanted to be.

"Did you ever hear him say anything bad about Pan Am?"

"OK, before the incident [TB], he loved his job, but he, he, griped about everybody. I don't know why, but he didn't seem to get along with anybody."

"Did you ever hear your mama and him talking about Pan Am and them not wanting him to fly again?"

"Yeah, right after he got home from the hospital and stuff like that, and I know Mama always tried to coax him into feeling better and saying, 'Well, you know, they're just worried about your health' and, you know, 'You will be alright,' you know. I remember her coaxing him, trying to mellow him out, but it didn't work. He just kept us all in a dither."

Tania recalled that when she was a child in Hong Kong the Crosthwaites rarely intermingled with other Pan Am employees and their families, although the other families seemed to enjoy one another's company. She said she once asked her mother why that was.

"She said, 'I don't know. Your dad is so fussy. He doesn't, he doesn't like most of the people in Pan Am.'"

"Did Gene drink a lot?"

"Him and Mama had a lot of arguments about his drinking. She would get after him. He drank at home. I don't know about what he did anywhere else, but he drank a lot of whiskey."

"Did he ever get drunk?"

"I never saw them both drunk, but I don't know, 'cuz I would go to my room, and who knows? He might have kept on drinking, though, but I know there's times Mother tells me, 'You go downstairs and spend the night with Grandma.' I never ask why, but they would fight, and Grandma would say, 'Don't worry. Your dad's drinking too much and your mom is just saying he can't do that.'"

"Did he ever hit your mom?"

"I don't know if he ever hit her, but I know that one time she hit him.

I don't know if it was in retaliation or what. But they were fighting very bad because of his drinking. She just couldn't stop him from drinking."

Tania said she and her grandmother "could hear them fussing up there. They had to take him to the doctor for stitches 'cause she picked up a vase and she hit him over the head. I think he got two or three stitches. It must have had an effect, because after that he wasn't drinking as much."

"Did Gene gamble or anything like that? It seems to me that you all may have lived beyond your means."

"He really liked to gamble, and apparently he did a lot of it. He really loved to play cards, and apparently he played real well, because he was always boasting that he won. He would say that he was real good at cribbage."

He must not have always won.

"I know that when they arrived here my mom had $5,000 in what they called US gold that was left to me for my inheritance and education. But he [Gene] was so much in debt. He owed back payments to his first wife for child support that he couldn't pay, and my mom bailed him out with that."

I had verified that earlier; court records in California proved that Crosthwaite had been late in child support and alimony and had been ordered by a judge to pay up immediately or face jail time. He came up with the money. Julia's money.

Tania said that her grandmother always turned over her paycheck from Birds Eye to Gene, and that her stepfather even kept all of her own earnings when she worked at an ice cream and coffee shop the summer before her senior year in high school.

"Mama got me a job in the coffee shop, and I rode the bus from Felton. I made $300 that summer and Gene took it. Grandma was so thankful to Dad that when she was working at Birds Eye she gave him her paychecks that helped build the house. Peter did all the cement work for free."

We moved on to the last three months of the purser's life, a time when he was increasingly moody and angry, struggling with the loss of Julia, worried about his future with Pan Am, and for whatever reasons always at odds with Tania.

There was at least one occasion when his relationship with Tania triggered something particularly strange.

"That's when I had that episode, for whatever it's worth. I don't know what it means. I don't know if it's bad or good. I didn't feel good about it, 'cuz I was afraid of him. One night when he was there, and I was in bed and the lights are all off and I thought he was in bed, all of sudden he comes in my bedroom, and I was just lying there acting like I was asleep. And then he sits on the bed and he put his hand on my back right here and he just sat there. Years later I thought maybe he was trying to tell me he was sorry or maybe he needed some kind of comfort or something, but I wasn't mature enough to do it, you know. I was only sixteen, and I was afraid of him. I didn't know what he wanted. He never hugged me or did anything, and I just pretended I was asleep. That's all he did, and he left. And that was all."

The next day he was just as weird.

"I don't know where I was going the next day, but I put on my skirt and I put on a sweater that was Mom's. It was a red sweater that we would wear back and forth, and I looked a lot like my mom. So, I came out with that sweater on and he was sitting there. Woo! He was so creepy, and he said, 'Get that sweater off right now!' And let me tell you, I looked at him and I went back, and I got that sweater off. He was one furious character."

Crosthwaite's behavior became even more bizarre in the following weeks.

"He's doing some crazy stuff now, and then later on, I don't know where I was when he did this, he got all of Mama's clothes and then they were gone. He even went in my closet and took what he thought was Mama's, but a lot of that was mine and he left me without hardly any clothes."

Tania didn't know it at the time, but the grieving Gene was chasing another woman and had given her Julia's clothing and her expensive perfume in an attempt to win her love.

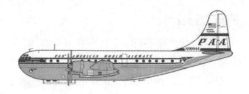

18

TANIA'S CONFESSION

GENE CROSTHWAITE was a very troubled man. Anyone who had contacted him within the final weeks of his life could tell you in a heartbeat that he was off-his-rocker nuts. One person, in addition to the Santa Cruz County juvenile officer, was convinced that he was mentally unstable.

That person was Tamara Shankoff, a Russian girlfriend of Tania's mother, and she telephoned first Tania and then her grandmother soon after Julia's funeral with some very disturbing information.

"Anyway, he used to bring Mama perfumes from France, Chanel Number 5 bottles, and all these expensive things, and he gave them away to this Russian girl. He wanted her to marry him."

This startling disclosure from Tania came from out of nowhere, and if true, would lend further credence to the idea that Crosthwaite was mentally imbalanced.

"She called us and said, 'What's wrong with Gene?' He showed up at her house and brought her perfume, Mama's clothes, and stuff that he really should have given to me."

"Wait a minute. How soon was this after your mother died?" I asked.

"I'll have to think on that. Anyway, he told Tamara that he really liked Russian women and didn't know how he could live without Julia, and he said he wanted to marry her 'cuz he wanted a Russian wife."

"Where did you hear this?

"From Tamara herself. T-A-M-A-R-A. I can't remember her last name. Anyway, she was my mama's girlfriend."

"He did this soon after your mama died?"

"That's what shocked all of us. I told Grandma and said that Tamara just called me, and she said, 'She talked to me, too.' Grandma said, 'He's just lost his mind, Tania. He's just beside himself. You'll have to forgive him. He doesn't know what he's doing. He's in grief. He doesn't know what he's doing.' I understood that because that's the way I was, too."

"After he gave the perfume away and the clothes away, when he wasn't there I didn't care because I was scared of him. He was acting so crazy.

"Anyway, she turned him down when he was asking her for marriage, and she kept saying no. He kept saying he wanted his Russian wife back, and then he was bawling and asking her for marriage. She said she felt so awful. She was so uncomfortable, and she felt he was just in a crazy state because of losing his wife and she turned him down."

Gene's unwanted advances to Tamara continued for several weeks.

"She kept telling him there's no way and he kept pressing her. 'Why? Why? What's wrong with me? Why can't you marry me?' And I mean she said she was afraid. She said she didn't want to bring more heartache to him, but she turned him down and she felt she had to tell us what happened. We were in such a quandary about it, and Grandma was so upset. There was so much going on. She said, 'He's just gone plum loco, Tania. He doesn't know what he's doing.'

"Yeah, he did that, and that other thing he did, too.

"That other thing?"

"Our house was on a hill and we had a big round driveway and as you came up the hill like this, and it's like, 'Whoop,' and he had a sprinkler on in the middle of the driveway. So Grandma is asking him, 'Why are you watering the driveway, Gene?' and he says, 'You know Julia don't like dust. She don't like dust and I'm just making sure there's no dust in the driveway.'"

Tania explained to me that her mother had been a stickler for cleanliness.

"You could eat off the floor. She did not like any kind of dirt. And then I thought, you know, well, he's right, but I thought, 'What difference does it make now? Mom's not here, and when she was alive, he never watered the driveway.' So he just left and we turned it off, 'cuz the water is running down the driveway."

Let's talk about that last week, I suggested.

"He wasn't home."

That was strange, I thought, because he was not flying and had been visiting people in the Bay Area, including the juvenile officer in Santa Cruz.

Tania said that her stepfather was away from home most of the final week of his life, and to this day she doesn't know where he stayed. That wasn't unusual, she said, because after her mother had died, he disappeared for days at a time with no explanation.

"He was missing after Mama died and Grandma was in shock and I was in shock."

"Where do you think he was staying?"

"Well, we don't know where he was staying at when he wasn't in Felton. I don't know. He could have been at his daughter's. Apparently, they developed a relationship."

Tania admitted that some things that happened after her mother's death were now a blur, so I refreshed her memory about one strange incident that had occurred in Gene's final week.

I read from her sworn statement to CAB investigator Schonberger in 1957:

"Four days before leaving on his last flight he gathered many of the papers in his desk and dresser and burned them. My grandmother, by protesting, prevented him from burning my adoption papers. . . ."

"OK, I remember that now. Yeah, I had forgotten it because I was so stressed. But yeah, when you said that I remember Grandma grabbing stuff from him."

I decided to test her memory a bit more and asked her to tell me about the desk and where it was in relation to the rest of the room in which he had burned the papers.

"It was a bright-red Chinese, a Chinese-American desk. It was in the front room in the corner."

She gestures: "Here's the fireplace and here is the red desk and it was at that desk, that's where the phone was, and, uh, I remember Grandma grabbing the papers, but, uh, he was burning stuff in the fireplace."

"What did you do?"

"I don't think I hung around, 'cuz he made me a nervous wreck."

"Do you remember what you told the CAB man about Gene working in his basement workshop and always tinkering around with something down there?"

"I just remember the two days prior [to the crash], but you know, I don't go down there. I don't want to be around him, so I couldn't tell you what he was doing, you know. I just figured as a man he was trying to keep busy, but I couldn't tell you what he was doing."

"What about the dynamite?"

"I do remember for some reason there was an issue with dynamite, some kind of dynamite, and he was gonna blow up some kind of stumps."

"What do you remember about that?"

"I just remember that he bought it and then Grandma was scared. And Grandma said, 'Do you know that your dad has bought dynamite?' I go, 'Dynamite? What for?' And she said he said he was going to blow up the stumps, and I just went, 'Oh,' and her and Peter were just like, 'He don't know anything about blowing up stumps. He could blow up half the yard,' and I thought, 'Well, that's true,' but that was it."

"They [investigators] couldn't find the dynamite," I reminded her.

"Yeah, they went down there, but they didn't find anything."

Now we were finally getting somewhere.

I asked her to tell me specifically what she remembered about how Gene acted the last two days before the crash.

"He spooked me because he just would sit in that chair by the window, the bay window. He didn't talk. He would just glare at me. So I pretty much stayed downstairs with Grandma."

"Did he watch TV?"

"No, he didn't have a TV. Grandma did. He was just very despondent. He just stared all the time. He was so gloomy. He would just sit in that chair and stare out that window, and so I figured he's in grief and wants to be left alone."

It was time. Long past time to find out what I needed to know and what I hoped she really wanted to tell me.

"Tell me about that last night and the morning he left for the flight."

"It was the final, final thing he said which I have thought about so much," she said. "That last day."

She hesitated to go on, but once again I decided not to fill the silence with my own words. I waited.

"And then I went to sleep that night and he was already in bed with the door closed, and I was glad. And in the morning, he, he was up, uh, getting ready and so, you know, I got up in the morning and I needed to go to the restroom real bad. So, the rules were: when Daddy's up getting ready for work stay out of his way. He doesn't want anybody bothering him.

"So, I went to the restroom and as I was coming out, and he just came out of the bedroom like he was going into the bathroom and he looked at me and says, 'Wait a minute!' I thought, 'Oh, Jesus!' You know, when you hear that voice, and I stopped, and I looked at him and he says, 'You really think you're something.' And I just thought, what? You know, I mean, and he points his finger at me and says, 'You're gonna find out some things. Some big things are gonna happen and you're gonna be shocked.'

"That scared me 'cause, you know, with his mean attitude. I try to figure out something that I'm going to find out bad, and I know it's not gonna be good coming from him. That was his last words to me: 'You really think you're something, but you're gonna find out big some things and you're gonna be shocked.' With his finger at me like that. 'You're gonna find out and you're not gonna like it.' I went into my room and just shut the door. I was shook up. He was mad again and I didn't know why."

That was it. This is what Tania had kept secret for more than sixty years. Gene had told Tania that "some big things are gonna happen" and that, in effect, he was not coming home alive. How else would she have been able to "find out some things?" When his will would be opened in a few days she would learn that he had excluded her unless she complied with his demands.

Gene would finally have control over Tania.

I decided I'd come back to his final words in a few minutes, but first, still in a bit of shock, I wanted to know how she had learned about the plane crash.

"I was in Santa Cruz. I think I had gone to a movie with a friend and I came back, and I was going upstairs, and I noticed the lights were on in the house. I looked in there and I saw a girlfriend of mine and her boyfriend—they were older than me—sitting there. So I come in and I said, 'What are you guys doing here?' 'Oh, we came to see you,' she said, and I said 'OK.' She said, 'Have you heard any news?' I said, 'No, I've been at the movies. I haven't heard anything.' She said, 'Well, come sit down. We've got some bad news,' and she says, 'Your dad's been in a plane crash and they are looking for the plane. They don't know if there are any survivors.'"

Tania said she was shocked beyond words when told of the crash. Her mother dead. Her stepfather likely dead. What would happen now?

Still reeling from what she had told me a few minutes earlier about her stepfather's final words, I asked her again, to see if her story was the same.

"He is leaving because I am still in my bathrobe. I hadn't even gotten dressed yet. I had just brushed my teeth. He turned around and started getting his stuff and leaving. And he points his finger and he says to me, 'You think you're something . . .'"

She repeats the same words. They have the same meaning.

"You know, he has to be dead for me to find out what he's talking about."

I needed to know more, and the search for my father's killer needed a conclusion.

"Looking back at this now, do you think he could have been involved in this? Do you think he did it?"

"Yep," she answered without hesitation.

"That was our secret, and Grandma said he just completely lost it. She said he was in such grief that he lost his mind. He couldn't handle Mama's death. She said he just wanted to be with her, and she says, 'I believe he did it,' and 'Tania, don't tell anybody, 'cause this could be big trouble. Big trouble.'"

Big trouble is exactly what Tania and her grandmother were afraid of when CAB investigators Claude Schonberger and Charles Collar started snooping around the neighborhood in the days after *Romance of the Skies* crashed. With no means of financial support, reeling from two deaths in three months and with neither understanding the US law enforcement system, they were scared to death. What if they said something wrong? What if Gene really did cause the plane crash? Would the government send them back to China? Those thoughts were foremost in their minds when investigators knocked on their door and started taking the place apart in a search for evidence.

"They took the pictures down and looked behind the pictures. I have no idea what they're looking for, and they went through the whole house. They took the pillows off the couch and looked there. They mentioned that they had followed me, that they've been following me, and that they've been asking questions. I remember Grandma saying. 'Do you know that there's some kind of people in town and that they say that they're FBI and they're detectives and they're asking questions about you and me and your dad and mom?' And I don't know; I hadn't heard anything about that.

"They went through the whole house. And then Grandma came, and she saw them doing this and she just wanted to know what they are searching for, and they just said they were looking. They never said what they were looking for. They just said, 'We're looking,' and whatever terms they mentioned."

Tania said she and her grandmother stood by in stunned silence as the federal investigators (she still believes they were FBI men) went through everything in every room in the house. Upstairs. Downstairs. In the basement, especially the basement workshop where Gene had been tinkering with something in his final days and where, presumably, the missing explosives might be found.

"You know, we were so horrified, so horrified by that, and then you know that FBI man says, 'Now I want you to be careful, young girl. And don't talk about this plane crash and about your dad and the FBI being here.' He said that we could be in danger.

"He says, 'You've got to realize how many people lost their families and their children. People can do funny things, and if they have suspicions that your dad had any involvement, that could put you in danger, because they would figure, 'Well, I lost my family and we're going to get you.'

"What that man said, that's what kept me afraid all those years."

That was the end of the federal investigation of sabotage suspect Oliver Eugene Crosthwaite. Tania and her grandmother never saw or heard from anyone involved in the crash investigation again. The FBI never raised a finger to help solve one of the greatest unsolved mysteries in American commercial aviation history.

Tania and her grandmother kept their little secret. They rarely talked with each other about the crash and never told anyone about the federal investigators' search of their house. They never mentioned that Tamara had repeatedly turned the grieving Gene down for marriage and never uttered a word about that strange day when Gene watered the driveway because "Julia don't like dust."

They never spoke a word about Gene's final, chilling promise that something big was about to happen, or their belief that he caused the crash.

"Did you ever have suspicions of your own that maybe Gene blew up the plane?"

"Yeah, yeah, after I knew what happened to the plane. After they couldn't find the plane and everything and it was missing. You know, I thought about those words. Those words have troubled me. . . . You know, that's where I just would like to know, what did he mean? You know, I basically, like, somehow he was trying to get me by doing that will thing, you know, or was it even further than that? Boy, you know, 'You're going to find out something big here.'"

I asked her this:

"Specifically, what do you remember your grandmother saying about Gene having done it?"

"Her words were: 'He went crazy at your mom's death and he went crazy. Crazy, and he's done this.' That's what her words were. And I believed her because of, seeing what I saw, how he acted, the words he said, the depression, just sitting there in that chair and going to his room . . . with the thing locked, and I couldn't stand it. I was afraid. All his behavior was very unnatural. I know he was not a happy father and that his behavior after Mom's death was so considerably worse than he ever was."

And how about stepgrandfather Peter, the man who had told the investigators about the missing explosives? Did he also believe Gene destroyed the plane?

"I do know that he was in total agreement with Grandma about that."

So, the three people who knew Crosthwaite best in the final months of his life—Tania, her grandmother, and her stepgrandfather—all believed he had destroyed the plane.

"Do you really think he was capable of blowing up the plane?"

"Yep."

"Why?"

"Because of his meanness. The way he looked, and his voice. I could actually see him plotting it when he was sitting in that chair looking so gloomy.

"Oh God, I know. I constantly put it out of my head for years because I thought, well, it made me mad, 'cuz I would think, 'How could he do that to all those people,' you know? But, Lord Almighty, he was that mean."

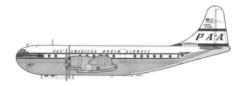

19

THE PROBABLE CAUSE

THE CONVERSATION WITH TANIA and her insistence that her stepfather had "changed" after he had contracted tuberculosis two years prior to the crash sent me once again back into my extensive files as soon as I returned home. How could this farm boy from Colorado have been turned into a suicidal murderer? Was the death of Gene Crosthwaite's wife three months prior to the plane crash enough to send him off the deep end or was something else involved? Was there something in his psychology or medical history that might provide the answers?

And what about that startling revelation that he had been bawling and begging some woman named Tamara to marry him soon after his wife's death? That should have raised the eyebrows of even the most novice of investigators.

While studying my Crosthwaite files I came across a page near the back of the notes I had received decades earlier from CAB investigator Schonberger. There, at the top of the page, was this: "Tamara Shankoff. Close friend of Julia. At least 40. Born in Shanghai. Was bridesmaid at wedding. Saw last at Julia's funeral."

There really was a Tamara. She really was Julia's close friend. Tania was telling the truth. Schonberger's notes supported Tania's story, but what intrigued me most was one brief sentence Schonberger had written about Tamara: "Gene didn't like her."

Gene didn't *like* her?

So not only was Schonberger totally unaware that Gene had been begging Tamara to marry him, but she had outright lied to the CAB investigator and said that Gene did not even like her. It made me wonder: What if she had told him the truth? What if she had told him that Gene had been repeatedly pestering her to marry him and that she had turned him down? What if she had told him how depressed he was when she had rejected his marriage proposal? Would that have pushed Schonberger to dig deeper into Crosthwaite's life and mental state and perhaps have helped persuade the higher-ups to deploy more resources into what turned out to be an inadequate investigation? And what if Tania and her grandmother had told Schonberger about Tamara or had told him about that last-minute warning that something "big" would soon happen?

I again reviewed Schonberger's notes from his interview with Santa Cruz County juvenile officer Johnson, and they further supported the idea, at least in my mind, that Crosthwaite was mentally imbalanced:

"Suffering from pre-occupation . . . badly disturbed . . . ill at ease . . . twitching . . . possible paranoid . . . very rambling in conversation . . . retire to room and cry . . . more frequent depression periods since wife's death . . . crew against him and trying to get rid of him."

There was also this short, cryptic statement in Schonberger's notes, which seemed to somewhat strengthen the possibility that Crosthwaite had sabotaged the plane:

"Stump gun. Wedge-shaped. 2"x12" long. Cap needed on one end of fuse. Black blasting powder. Electric fuse or?"

Schonberger died in 2015, so it was impossible to get any clarification from him at this stage of my investigation, and his fellow investigator, Charles S. Collar, died in 1998. Instead, I moved on to someone else who might provide answers about Crosthwaite: his only surviving sibling, Harold Richard "Dick" Crosthwaite, his ninety-three-year-old brother, living in rural Winnemucca, Nevada. For years I had maintained a Facebook friendship with his daughter,

Madonna, and she had been urging me to talk with her father, who, she had assured me on numerous occasions, was loaded with all sorts of important information about Gene, the crash, and "that nut" Tania.

"He knows a lot about that day, Ken. You need to talk with him," she insisted. "His mind is sharp as a whip."

I had purposely put off talking with Gene's brother, having decided that I wanted to learn everything I could about Gene before I talked to someone who was not only unaware of just how guilty his brother appeared, but who also might be his greatest defender, unwilling to accept the idea that he could have committed suicide and murder. But the clock was running out: Dick Crosthwaite wasn't getting any younger, and now that I had finally talked with Tania the time was right to approach him.

I called him one evening in November 2018, and although he was eager to talk, I was disappointed in just how little the tough-talking cowboy knew and how much he didn't seem to care. He bounced from one thought to the next in a pattern of disjointed sentences and disconnected thoughts. After a few minutes it was obvious that it was going to be very difficult to get him to concentrate on anything for more than a few seconds. It's not that he seemed mentally impaired in any way. I didn't think so then and don't think so now. That's just the way he was, a grizzled old codger like the western film star Gabby Hayes.

I asked him to tell me about his brother, to describe what kind of person he was.

"He was a very strong individual personally. Hell, he was not wishy-washy or anything. He was a very strong-willed person. He had his shit together. He treated me awful good; he didn't commit suicide."

That was strange, I thought.

I had never even mentioned suicide.

"He had the ticket and everything for him and my mother to go to Hawaii for a week. There's no way in the world he would have disappointed her and committed suicide. I think a prop went through the side. That son of a bitch [Stratocruiser] was eating props and engines. I still say it was the prop, the props on that bastard."

He told me about Gene's failed marriage to Thelma Lou and his years working as a steward with Matson.

"His wife had left him. She told my mother that she never got along with him being away. He made big money with Matson on those luxury liners. Anyway, in 1938 he come to Arizona and told my mom he was leaving Matson. He said, 'I don't want to go swimming. Those goddamn Japs. I don't want to be on a ship and for them to sink it,'" he said.

"One day the sheriff knocked on the door. He was eating dinner at his house in Belmont. The sheriff says, 'I have a summons for you,' and Gene says, 'What for?' The sheriff says 'Divorce,' and Gene says 'OK,' and that was that."

I needed to understand more about Gene and Tania's relationship and just how much Dick really knew about his brother in his final years.

"The last time I seen Gene alive was when we drove over to Felton and spent the night. I didn't see anything different about him. He could handle life as well as anybody else," he said.

I asked him if he was aware of Gene's personality changes after TB treatment and in the months before his death.

"I wouldn't know. The last time I seen him he was just like he always was. Julie was still alive. She was in good health when we were there, but you can't tell when cancer strikes a woman, a man, or a dog for that matter. I thought Julie was a pretty nice woman. Very polite. Courteous. She and Gene were both in love with each other. She was something you dreamed about. He was really happy with Julie."

Julie? Julie? He said that twice. Her name was Julia, with an "a." I was beginning to wonder just how much he really knew about his older brother's life. His next words told me:

"Me and Gene never talked much. I never seen him after that. I don't even know where he's buried."

So the man who supposedly knows everything about Gene, Julia, "that nut" Tania, and the plane crash that took his brother's life never talked much with his brother and doesn't even know where he is buried?

"What about Tania?" I asked him. "What was Gene's relationship with her?"

"I never did pay any attention to the girl."

"What about the comments that Gene made to others that she was out of control, a demon?"

"There was hearsay—it might have been from my sisters—that she was a little on the wild side. It's just my opinion. He never talked to me about her. This is just hearsay after the death."

"Did you ever meet Tania?"

"No, I don't think so," he admitted.

Dick's daughter had made a point several times through the years of letting me know that his mother, Mary, had received a phone call from Pan Am president Juan Trippe in the hours very soon after the plane had been reported missing because Gene was such a valuable, longtime, and loyal employee. That was further proof, she insisted, that Gene had nothing to do with the crash, but neither she nor Dick had a clue that Gene's job with Pan Am was on the line back in 1957.

"They talked for over an hour," Madonna stated.

Dick's story was the same.

"My mom was out here when the plane went down. It was on the TV. I think that's where we heard about it. Anyway, he called her and talked for one hour. One hour."

"What did they talk about?"

"I don't know what he said, but Gene was his oldest crew member on the plane."

"Did your mother tell you what he said in that one-hour conversation?"

"No, don't believe so."

That was odd, I thought. His mother had a one-hour conversation with the president of Pan American World Airways about a missing plane with his brother aboard and she never told him a single word about the conversation?

Trippe may have called Crosthwaite's mother, but it was unlikely to have been on the night the plane went missing. He may have been a compassionate man, but surely the president of the biggest airline company in the world had other things on his mind that night than calling and consoling the mother of a purser. Also, there is no way—with the time difference, if for no other reason—that a TV station in Nevada would have broadcast the news of the missing plane that same night. The following night, maybe.

I don't doubt that Trippe spoke with Crosthwaite's mother in the days following the disappearance, but I wonder if he might have been on more of a fishing expedition than a mission of consolation. Maybe Trippe had called Crosthwaite's mother to learn something more about the man who was fast becoming Pan Am's No. 1 suspect in the crash of the airplane.

"Did anyone from Pan American, the Civil Aeronautics Board or anyone with the investigation ever ask you any questions?"

"Not a damn word."

The interview was going nowhere, but as is often the case, the final comments may have been the most important. Out of the blue he added credibility to the notion that his brother had lost his mind after Julia's death and lapsed even further into depression after his amorous advances had been rejected by Julia's Russian friend, Tamara, a few weeks before the plane crash.

"He said he would never marry another American woman. Never."

Days later I reread every letter, email, and note that I had accumulated in decades of research about Gene Crosthwaite's life. I spent hours putting together a timeline not only for the last weeks of his life, but as far back as the 1930s, when he had worked on cargo ships in the Orient. I tracked his comings and goings with Pan American for ten years before the plane went down and documented every trip he made across the Pacific during that time.

What had happened to Gene Crosthwaite? Based on statements from his wife, his stepdaughter, his colleagues, and his friends, the angry, depressed, paranoid man who poured cocktails in the downstairs lounge on the Stratocruiser that fateful day in 1957 was not the same man who just a few years earlier had worked so diligently and faithfully to bring his foreign-born family into a new world with hoped-filled lives in California.

I had only a few notes about his medical history, but they began to fill in the blanks, and I dug into every research document I could find about tuberculosis and its effect on a patient's mental health. What I learned put another piece of the puzzle into place, but it also led to another possible reason for Crosthwaite's unexplained behavior.

Tuberculosis has been with mankind since ancient times, and its symptoms have been recorded since the days of the Old Testament. It is a painful disease that attacks the lungs and causes bloody, "graveyard" coughs, fatigue, fever, and, sometimes, death. Evidence of TB has been discovered in Egyptian mummies, and for centuries it was nearly always fatal. Even as late as the early 1900s nearly fifty percent of those who contracted tuberculosis in the United States died from the disease.

I discovered that three of its victims had been Gene Crosthwaite's aunts: sisters Hazel, Vivian, and Gertrude Mae, all of whom had suffered from the disease for months before passing away in the prime of their lives. Crosthwaite had more than the usual reasons to be depressed about TB and to fear its possible recurrence; he had a strong family connection to the killer.

The emergence of powerful medicines in the late 1940s and early fifties brought new hope to those afflicted with what was once called "consumption" and "White Death," and by the time Crosthwaite checked into the San Mateo County sanatorium in 1955 a TB diagnosis was no longer considered a death sentence. It was a treatable and even curable disease, although still considered by many, especially those of far Eastern European and Asian backgrounds, a shameful one, stigmatizing for life. Many family members and coworkers were fearful of "catching" TB, which is a contagious disease, and some patients felt not only guilty and lonely during their confinement, but also dirty, like "lepers" of olden days.

Two of the first drugs to be effectively used in the treatment of TB were isoniazid (INH) and iproniazid, both accidentally discovered by a Swiss pharmaceutical company experimenting with leftover Nazi V2 rocket fuel. By the 1950s INH was being prescribed to nearly half of those affected with TB in the United States. It was cheap, easy to administer, and effective, especially with TB patients who were confined to sanatoriums for months at a time, where medical staff could ensure that it was properly taken.

Gene Crosthwaite hated having TB. He hated being confined to the sanatorium and he hated not being able to be with his beautiful Russian wife and to fly across the Pacific. He hated the routine, the daily regimen of rest and required nutrition. He missed grilling steaks in his backyard, drinking his hard liquor, gambling, and playing cribbage. One of his doctors said he had been a "moderately difficult patient," but because he so desperately wanted to get out of the sanatorium, he did what he was told when he was told and how he was told. That was unusual for the strong-willed and independent Crosthwaite, who preferred doing things his own way.

Doing what he was told when he was told included taking 100 milligrams of the "miracle drug" INH twice a day for more than two years. He was taking INH until the day he died.

While the treatment of TB made considerable progress in the 1950s, psychiatry was still an evolving medical field, and the intersection of TB treatment with psychiatry was full of contradictions. Some TB patients developed psychiatric conditions, including major depression, anxiety disorders, delirium, and personality changes, likely a result of sanatorium confinement. Meanwhile, while "talk therapy" was still the primary treatment tool of psychiatrists, new drugs were emerging, and they worked nicely in treating both TB and resulting mental issues. One of those drugs was INH; doctors quickly learned that it was not only effective in treating TB, but also had a side effect as a mood enhancer in treating depression.

But INH also caused troubling neuropsychiatric side effects in some patients, including severe mood swings, depression, sleeplessness, emotional instability, irritability, and obsessive-compulsive neurosis, sometimes triggering suicide attempts. Patients older than fifty and those who drank alcohol had a higher prevalence of INH-induced psychoses, and weight gain was noted in many cases.

Those side effects fit Crosthwaite to a "T." He drank alcohol to excess. He had gained sixty pounds. He was deeply depressed. He was irritable. He had severe mood swings. He couldn't sleep. He was unstable to the point that the Santa Cruz County Sheriff's officer had described him as "psychotic."

Going back through my decades-old notes, I found an investigator's statement, attributed to Dr. James Bodie of the San Mateo TB hospital, that Crosthwaite "had paranoid tendencies" during his hospitalization and described him as "a rather strange fellow with a chip on his shoulder."

Dr. Bodie stated that Crosthwaite was "hypercritical of others and has a cynical attitude."

Grief controlled his life after his wife's death, and while it is true that only three months had elapsed since her death—likely not long enough for him to fully recover from his loss—it must be remembered that he had been mentally out of balance ever since his release from TB confinement, more than a year before she died, and likely even before that.

His bursts of anger, meanness, and instability had troubled his wife so much that just a few months before she had been hospitalized with cancer she had called his doctor at the sanatorium in a plea for help.

Medical experts had suspected the rare but documented INH-psychoses link for many years but were unable to prove it until more than twenty years after Crosthwaite began taking the drug.

By then it may have been too late. The misery may have already been spread. From Gene to Julia and from Gene to Tania. Could it also have been spread from Crosthwaite to the families of forty-three innocent men, women, and children who died on *Romance of the Skies*?

That seemed a plausible explanation for Crosthwaite's irrational and mean-spirited behavior and could have been the trigger for him to destroy the aircraft and kill everyone—including himself—but something else began nagging at me: What about that fall from the burro when he was only three years old? Could the fall that knocked him unconscious for a week also have played a role in what may later have developed into adult mental illness?

A few scribbled notes in a file I had received from CAB investigator Schonberger made me even more interested in that possible angle:

"At 3 yrs. age, brain concussion left violent headaches for years afterwards.

"Riding burro in Pueblo, Colo. Pulled from burro & struck head. Unconscious 5 days.

"Bad headaches. . . back injury. . . vertebrae damaged.

"Walked after several weeks after only one chiropractic treatment."

Unconscious for five days? Bad headaches?

Crosthwaite's fall from a burro as a child was not something to be ignored or dismissed then or now. He received no medical treatment, other than one visit to a chiropractor, and his five days of unconsciousness today would be considered a traumatic brain injury requiring hospitalization and expert medical care. When a person suffers sudden external trauma to the head to the degree that it renders the person unconscious for that long, the brain suffers damage that may not be noticed for many years to come.

The young Crosthwaite didn't just pass out when he fell from the burro; he was out of this world for nearly a week. Could his brain injury have been a contributory factor in a mental disorder later in his life?

In 2003, one of the most extensive studies of the relationship between traumatic brain injuries and mental illness determined that persons with traumatic brain injuries were an astonishing 439 percent more likely to suffer from mental disorders. That study of 1.4 million Danish citizens found that traumatic brain injury victims were 65 percent more likely to develop schizophrenia, 59 percent more likely to develop depression, and 28 percent more likely to develop bipolar disorder.

Equally interesting is the fact that most of the people in the study did not even have severe traumatic brain injuries like Crosthwaite. Many had mild concussions that required only a brief visit to the emergency room, aspirin, and bed rest.

Something else to consider: The brain of a three-year-old is still developing. A 2006 study published in the Indian Journal of Neurotrauma gives another clue as to how Crosthwaite might have been affected by the fall from the burro: "Clinical studies clearly show the benefit of a more enriching socioeconomic environment in the recovery after pediatric TBI."

A small child's hardscrabble life on an isolated Colorado farm in 1914 is not exactly an "enriching socioeconomic environment."

My theories about Crosthwaite made sense to me, but I needed input from an impartial outside professional, so I began researching forensic psychology, a specialty that has gained popularity in recent years primarily because of crime films and TV shows. I studied the backgrounds of numerous forensic psychologists and determined that the person I wanted to help me was Dr. Jeff Kieliszewski, a forensic psychologist in Grand Rapids, Michigan, whose expertise seemed to fit my needs.

Dr. Kieliszewski has spent decades studying the criminal mind and is often called as an expert witness in state and federal courts. I reached out to him in the hope that he might help me make sense out of not only Crosthwaite, but also the passenger and lodge owner Payne. What I needed was his professional evaluation of their mental frames of mind at the time of the crash and their potential for sabotaging the airliner. Dr. Kieliszewski graciously agreed to take on the challenge and immediately began to delve into the backgrounds and minds of my two primary suspects.

While Dr. Kieliszewski invested his time and expertise in developing what is called a forensic psychological autopsy, I returned to the University of Miami's Otto Richter Library and spent two days scouring Pan Am's records to see if I had missed anything in my two previous research visits or if any new information had been archived. I wanted to make certain that I wasn't leaving any angle untouched. While I came up with some interesting new information, there was nothing of significant material value, and I returned home and waited for the psychologist's reports on Crosthwaite and Payne.

Months later, Dr. Kieliszewski's report and professional conclusions helped me finally bring the lifelong search for my father's killer to an end.

In a detailed report, the psychologist outlined how he had examined the evidence and reached his conclusions.

About Payne, he noted that there was no information that he had ever suffered from any known mental health problems and no evidence of significant medical issues.

"Payne had interpersonal and possibly legal problems while living in California. He allegedly shot a firearm at individuals he was in conflict with on two occasions. He also had conflicts with a county government agency. Payne reportedly caused damage to public roads including the use of explosives to blow a large hole in a public road. He apparently was ordered to pay money for the damage, but he did not pay and did not show up in court.

"There is also information in the investigation records and through collateral interviews that report Payne had significant financial difficulties just prior to the plane crash. The hunting lodge he owned and operated was up for sale and reportedly heavily mortgaged.

"The information in the investigation records as well as collateral records describe Payne as having great affection for his wife and in a very close relationship with his mother. There is also information that Payne's wife may have had tendencies to become involved with men outside of their marriage.

"Information from the investigation records and information obtained through numerous collateral interviews describe Payne as an outgoing individual who often had tendencies towards being moody or a 'hot head.' Information provided through collateral interviews report he may have had periods where an alcohol abuse problem was operating. There is also information that describes Payne as often becoming quite jealous due to his wife's attention from other men. Also, there is consistent information about Payne being quite close with his mother. Reportedly, Harriet and Payne's mother did not have a good relationship. There is also information and collateral interviews that describe Payne as lacking in healthy or effective assertiveness and having difficulties coping with stressors. Information describes Payne as typically becoming easily overwhelmed with problems and deferring to his wife in order to deal with issues or stressors that arose. The information in the investigation records and collateral interviews also describe a man that oftentimes was not easy to get along with. Payne is also described as often quick to emotion and anger, particularly if stressed or overwhelmed.

"From a historical perspective, faking one's death in an attempt to collect insurance money was known to occur in the 1950s. Also, purchasing life insurance policies from airports prior to boarding flights was not that uncommon. One investigator presented an observation that it appears Payne organized his affairs in a manner one would expect if death in the near future was anticipated.

"One point in theory that can be argued is that, given Payne's circumstances, there was adequate motivation and readily available means for him to fake his death in order to obtain financial benefit as well as relieve himself of obligations. However, the question becomes whether Payne was a man of enough gumption and mental sharpness to devise and pull off a plan where he would fake his own death for financial gain," Dr. Kieliszewski reported.

"The available information and evidence suggest a psychological profile of an individual with deficit-coping skills, difficulties and deficits in deploying effective assertiveness, and an individual who may be prone to impulsiveness. There was also evidence to suggest an individual who may not have had the best business acumen, and in a sense, created situations for himself that led to interpersonal problems. The data does not suggest an individual with tendencies toward interpersonal or social manipulation. This is an individual who has more tendencies towards being reactive rather than scheming."

That made perfect sense. Everything I had learned about "mama's boy" Payne had indicated that Harriet wore the pants in the family, and that while he sometimes often acted strangely, he seldom made major decisions on his own.

"An important factor in analyzing Payne and his situation is his wife, Harriet. The limited data regarding Harriet's psychological functioning suggest tendencies towards being the type of person who could be interpersonally manipulative and scheming. There's also data that suggests she likely had some degree of manipulative power over Payne. And the theory of Payne faking his own death for financial gain would need to involve Harriet, the beneficiary.

"In my opinion, the data does not strongly support the notion that Payne alone devised a scheme to fake his own death and could carry it out and kill dozens of other passengers in the process. Also, of note, there are very few questions about Harriet's whereabouts and activities after the plane crash. There is established information regarding her whereabouts, interpersonal functioning and lifestyle. If Harriet mysteriously disappeared, appeared to have died in an accident, or her whereabouts were unknown after the plane crash that supposedly killed her husband this would add some credence to the theory that Payne faked his own death for financial gain and was assisted in this endeavor by Harriet. However, another interesting theory could be that maybe Payne with the help of Harriet was in the process of planning his own fake death when he came to an untimely demise. In other words, did

Payne get his affairs in order and possibly want to fake his own death when he was in Hawaii but never had the opportunity?"

Based on what was known about Payne, Dr. Kieliszewski determined that Payne likely was not responsible for the crash of Pan Am Flight 7.

Crosthwaite, however, was another matter entirely.

"In regards to social history, Gene was born December 13, 1911, in Bennington, Kansas. Crosthwaite's family history and upbringing are quite relevant. Also, many of the documented behaviors of his father are relevant as well. Crosthwaite's father, Herb, moved the family frequently across several states while Gene was growing up. His father had successful businesses that it appeared he would abruptly sell and geographically move the family and go on to other ventures. The information obtained suggests some degree of impulsivity with his father that resulted in the entire family being uprooted frequently. Crosthwaite's father died in May 1927 due to a construction accident. Gene was 16 years old.

"The information indicates Crosthwaite was employed with Pan Am for several years but on several occasions was close to being fired and his union had to intervene. Some coworkers describe Crosthwaite as being very angry with his employer in general and he was viewed by some as a rather vindictive character.

"In 1955, Crosthwaite is diagnosed with acute glossitis and underwent extensive treatment in Hong Kong. The family then returned to California. In October 1955, Crosthwaite is admitted to a sanatorium and diagnosed with active pulmonary tuberculosis. He remained in the sanatorium for approximately six months. After being discharged from the sanatorium, he was not immediately cleared for flight duty until August 1956 with the restriction that he could not fly in confined areas. Information indicates Gene was not happy with this determination and was angry Pan Am did not want him to fly due to his medical issues.

"Crosthwaite began flight duty with restrictions towards the end of 1956. He also began flying lessons. Reportedly, Crosthwaite was treated with isoniazid and para-aminosalicylic acid as maintenance therapy to prevent reemergence of tuberculosis during this time.

There is information to indicate Crosthwaite began to exhibit erratic behavior and angry outbursts. The records indicate Julia talked with Gene's doctor about these issues and the doctor informed her it may have something to do with his medication.

"In August 1957, Julia died in San Mateo. It was later determined she died from stomach cancer. There is information from multiple collateral sources that describe Crosthwaite as not coping well with his wife's death. The medical examiner for Pan Am remarked that Gene was not coping well with his wife's death and began to develop a significant fear of his tuberculosis returning. A month after Julia's death, Crosthwaite met with an attorney to make a will.

"In the fall of 1957, Crosthwaite began to exhibit more emotionally laden and erratic behavior. The collateral information indicates he became quite focused on trying to convince a Russian friend of his deceased wife to marry him. His relationship with Tania also began to deteriorate. Collateral sources reported he attempted to burn Tania's adoption papers but was stopped by Julia's mother. Reportedly, Crosthwaite made contact with a juvenile law enforcement officer to complain about Tania. The officer described his perception of Gene as psychologically unstable. In interviews, Tania described her stepfather in the weeks before his death as being quite despondent and spending hours at a time in a chair staring out the window.

"During the week prior to the Pan Am crash, Crosthwaite exhibited more differences in his behavior. He apparently began to visit several people that he had known throughout his life. He also had an appointment with his doctor who informed him he needed to continue to take his medications to prevent his tuberculosis from reemerging. There is also information during this time that Crosthwaite became more paranoid and was convinced that Pan Am was looking to terminate him. There also is a report from a collateral source (his stepfather-in-law) that Crosthwaite showed him some type of explosive powder.

"Tania described her perception of Crosthwaite's temperament and character as changing over the years she knew him. She claims she observed a difference after his bout with tuberculosis. She described him as being much more angry and moody after his tuberculosis. She said there were even instances where Gene and Julia had physical altercations. Tania explained that her mother would be aggressive with Gene as they would fight over his alcohol abuse. There is also a report from Tania that Crosthwaite told her in the weeks prior to his death that some type of 'shock' would be coming soon.

"After the Pan Am Flight 7 crash, Crosthwaite's body was discovered. His car was parked at the airport. His newly drafted will was in the glove compartment. Also, his and Julia's wedding rings were found in a safety deposit box, wrapped in one of Gene's necklaces."

Dr. Kieliszewski's report was detailed but focused a great deal on information I already knew. What I was most eager to learn was his professional opinion about the possibility of Crosthwaite being a suicidal murderer.

A few paragraphs later he gave me the answers.

"Crosthwaite's family history, consistent information from various collateral sources, and the investigation records suggest a remarkable clinical picture. His family history suggests Gene's father, Herb, may have had mental health difficulties. The reported history suggests an individual who may have had some issues with mood disturbance, impulsivity, and a somewhat erratic approach to life. Mental health conditions manifested in these types of behaviors can be inherited or passed down to children.

"There is a lot of evidence to suggest that Crosthwaite himself suffered from some level of mood disturbance. He had some long-standing patterns of a problematic behavior at work that resulted in a downturn in his upward occupational mobility a few years after being hired at Pan Am. There is also further evidence from multiple collateral sources and investigation records that Gene's mental status deteriorated more after his diagnosis and treatment for tuberculosis. He also maintained a medication regimen to prevent reemergence of tuberculosis. One of the medications (isoniazid) is associated with mental status disturbance as a side effect. There is also evidence from multiple collateral sources that suggest Gene's mental health further deteriorated after his wife's death," the psychologist reported.

"One theory concerning Crosthwaite's potential involvement

in the crash of Pan Am Flight 7 is that he orchestrated a suicide by sabotaging the plane that also resulted in the deaths of 43 other people. In my opinion, the evidence is overwhelming that Gene suffered from mental illness and exacerbated mental status decompensation in the months prior to the airliner crash. The data would suggest his mood disturbance was acutely active and directly impacting his behavior. Just prior to the airliner crash, Gene was also acting in a manner that would be consistent with an individual who is contemplating or planning their own death. He got his affairs in order and for no other known reason, made a will. He also used this opportunity to make a will to play out some hostilities towards his stepdaughter. Gene also began to visit old friends in a rather unusual manner. It is also significant and of note that Gene put his and his wife's wedding rings together and in a safe place.

"At the time of Crosthwaite's death, he was 46 years old, had recently lost his wife to illness, was coping with the effects of a chronic severe disease himself that had killed relatives in the past, and demonstrated an exacerbation of a likely long-held mood disturbance. Frankly, these factors would support the notion that he could have indeed become suicidal and took steps to produce his own demise. The data would support a notion that Gene had lost reasons to live. The data support that Gene could have easily developed a sound motivation to end his life.

"Also of note, if Gene indeed ended his life by sabotaging Pan Am Flight 7, he would not only kill himself but also attempt to inflict some type of retribution on his employer, Pan Am, by orchestrating a crash that took multiple lives, potentially to the embarrassment of his employer. Given his increasing aggression and anger, along with the mood disturbance towards the end of his life, committing suicide in this fashion would fit the clinical picture," the psychologist determined.

"Another question involves whether or not Crosthwaite had the means to sabotage an airliner in order for it to crash. Given he had worked in various capacities within the airline industry for 17 years, it is very plausible he had special knowledge and the potential requisite knowledge in order to know how to effectively sabotage a plane and orchestrate a plane crash."

Dr. Kieliszewski pointed out that psychological autopsies are "limited and do not produce unequivocal answers to questions about an individual or a situation. However, it is a powerful tool to help understand an individual's frame of mind at the time of an event."

He also stated that "because the cause of the crash of Pan Am Flight 7 was never determined, there is a relevant and arguable theory that this particular airliner was suspect to technological difficulties that could result in a crash similar to what we know about this tragedy."

Point well-taken. Stratocruisers had flown hundreds of thousands of miles with no issues, but the airplanes did crash, and when they crashed the results often were fatal.

Dr. Kieliszewski then turned his attention to the possibility of human involvement in the crash of *Romance of the Skies,* the angle I had been working on for most of my life, the angle that I believed federal investigators should have devoted more time and resources to back in 1957.

"However, the theory about sabotage resulting in the airliner crash is also relevant and arguable, given the information we have about the suspects in question.

"In my opinion, the data and evidence strongly supports the notion that Gene Crosthwaite was experiencing a debilitating emotional decompensation, had the motivation to kill himself and attempt to cause embarrassment to his employer, and likely had the means to sabotage the airliner to result in a crash.

"The evidence to suggest or support a theory of Gene Crosthwaite sabotaging Pan Am Flight 7 is much more plausible, and fits with the clinical and sociological picture as compared to the possibility that William Payne orchestrated and caused the tragedy in an attempt to collude with his wife to fake his own death."

And what did Dr. Kieliszewski think about my theory that Crosthwaite's childhood fall from a burro and resulting unconsciousness might have been a factor in the purser's mental health as an adult?

"I think the brain injury (unconscious for five days - definitely a brain injury) could have contributed to the development of mental illness later in life. Absolutely," he told me in a post-report interview. It almost certainly was one piece of the puzzle in Crosthwaite's development of mental illness, he said.

His professional opinion matched my own theory.

In US criminal law there are three aspects of a crime that prosecutors must establish before they can hope for a conviction: means, motive, and opportunity.

Oliver Eugene Crosthwaite had all three. William Harrison Payne had all three. In some ways, Pan American World Airways had all three.

For Crosthwaite the means would have been the blasting powder that investigators could never find, despite turning his house upside down, and the fact that he had been secretly making something in his basement workshop in the days prior to the crash.

The motive? There were many: the recent death of his wife; the rejection of his amorous advances on her Russian girlfriend; the ax he had to grind against Pan Am; and a stepdaughter he perceived to be out of control.

Add to those the brain injury from his childhood fall, his adult mental illness, the abuse of alcohol, and the possibility of drug-induced paranoia resulting from his treatment for tuberculosis and you have all the ingredients necessary.

The opportunity? He was scheduled for Flight 7 more than a week prior to its departure. He was the first crewman to board *Romance of the Skies*, and no one would question what might have been in his two suitcases that likely were stowed with the rest of the crew's luggage in the forward cargo department beneath the cockpit. He also was carrying a gladstone travel bag, a small, carry-on suitcase popular with airline crews and not considered luggage that must be stored.

As purser, he oversaw the downstairs cocktail lounge/bar and had full access to every section of the plane, including the cockpit, where one of his duties was to ensure the crew had plenty of hot coffee. He also knew when the airplane would make radio reports and at what point it would be the farthest from land, and therefore unable to return to San Francisco because of fuel limitations.

Plenty of opportunity.

Tania said her stepfather had made this prophetic statement not long before his final flight:

"Gene said if he was to die, there was only one way he wanted to die, and that was in the aircraft he was flying on. He didn't want to die of any sickness, but in the plane."

And Payne? His means was his frequent handling of dynamite, his expertise in blowing things up, and his easy access to explosives, sometimes with homemade, timed devices.

His motive? Financial distress and huge life-insurance policies, the proceeds of which either ended up entirely in his widow's hands or were split between a "grieving" widow and her husband, who had escaped to a new life outside of the country.

Opportunity? Little or no security while the plane sat for two days away far from the passenger terminal, with no passenger security screening before boarding the aircraft itself.

Many troubling and unanswered questions remain about Payne; curious circumstances and coincidences involving him and his family in the last months of his life are still unexplained. But there is nothing to indicate that he might have been suicidal. More importantly, not a single shred of evidence has arisen in more than sixty years to indicate that he was alive after November 8, 1957. Payne as a lone saboteur is an interesting story, but nothing more.

The final suspect, Pan American World Airways, was a magnificent and justifiably proud airline company that opened the world to travelers from all walks of life. It would not deliberately destroy its own airplane and kill innocent people, but it certainly had the indirect means to do so with questionable maintenance and cost-cutting inspections.

The motive would have been money, because Pan Am's Pacific-Alaska Division was bleeding it in 1957. Airplanes in maintenance hangars don't make money; the only way they can help generate a profit is to be in the air as much as possible.

The opportunity? Any plane at any time during that period was an accident waiting to happen, according to CAB investigators, and to the union that insisted Pan Am was operating unsafe aircraft.

Stratocruisers were plagued with mechanical issues, most of them easily and inexpensively fixed, but there is absolutely no proof—not even a shred of evidence—that *Romance of the Skies* was unfit for flight on November 8, 1957.

Possible. Plausible. Probable.

All three suspects were possible and plausible killers. But what was the probable cause?

After my lifelong search for my father's killer, all the available evidence and my extensive research leads me to one conclusion: the bereaved and mentally unstable purser Oliver Eugene Crosthwaite deliberately caused the crash of Flight 7, killing himself and murdering forty-three innocent people in the process.

How he did it we likely will never know.

Until the plane's wreckage is found at the bottom of the ocean and physical evidence proves otherwise, the lifelong search for my father's killer has ended.

I have kept my promises and now I can sleep.

See you on the next flight out, Dad.

SATURDAY, JUNE 11, 1955

"Dear Mom and Boys:

"It's a letter from your old Dad again. I don't know anything special to write about but maybe you would like to know that I am still kicking. Don't know for sure when I'll be coming home, but maybe we'll know something soon.

"It wouldn't surprise me if they sent me home any day. It wouldn't make me mad, either. I miss you all so much. I know you don't miss me nearly so much as I miss you, but then you don't need me as I do you. Well, I'm going to make you need me when I come home. I'm going to smooch you until you turn purple with passion and then I'm going to sleep.

"You know that I am insanely happy, and the only reason is you. You are all I live for. You and my boys. The boys might be so big when I get home, they might not know me. Tell them to eat and get really big for me. . .

"Ten million years from tonight, whether I'm lighting stars in Heaven or clinking chunks of coal down there, I will be loving all of you with all my heart and soul as I do tonight.

"I love you always and always and always

"Your Dad."

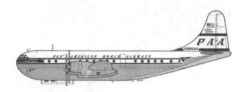

ADDENDUM

Tuberculosis remains one of the leading causes of death and illness in the world.

My mother, Ronnie Everette Fortenberry, remarried after I was grown but died from complications of Alzheimer's on June 25, 2010, at the age of 85. She was still in love with her grumbling and devoted Bill.

Tania Crosthwaite didn't inherit a penny from her stepfather's estate, and the house in Felton was sold at a public auction to settle her stepfather's financial affairs.

When Katherina Pavlichenko, purser Gene Crosthwaite's mother-in-law, left China in April 1951 for her new life in the United States, she was a passenger on *Romance of the Skies* for the Honolulu-to-San Francisco segment of her trip. She died in the 1970s.

Harriet Avah Hunter Theiler Payne Isaac Power died on September 5, 1997, at the age of 81. Her fourth husband, George T. Power, died three weeks later. They lived in Sonora, California.

Siskiyou County Sheriff Allen B. Cottar, the officer who convinced Scott Bar Postmistress Jessie Payne not to talk with Western Life Insurance investigator Russell Stiles in 1958, resigned from office in

1975 after a grand jury accused him of accepting $500 a month from a land developer, and submitting fraudulent bills and destroying public documents.

After being retired from commercial service, most of the remaining Boeing Stratocruiser fleet (Stratocruisers were Boeing's last propeller-driven airplanes) was sold as scrap for about $9,000 each. A few were converted into "Pregnant Guppies" and used as military and commercial cargo haulers for many years.

BODIES RECOVERED AND CAUSES OF DEATH

ONLY 19 BODIES FROM *ROMANCE OF THE SKIES* WERE RECOVERED. HERE ARE THEIR NAMES AND AUTOPSY SUMMARIES:

Robert Spencer Alexander, 38, Los Altos, California, pulmonary congestion and edema. Other conditions: fracture of upper sternum with mild hemorrhage.

Margaret Alexander, 33, Los Altos, California, probable drowning. Other conditions: fracture of right ribs, three, four and five.

Judy Alexander, 9, Los Altos, California, probable drowning

Yvonne Lucy Alexander, 26, San Francisco, probable drowning.

Gordon H. Brown, 40, Los Altos, California, undetermined.

Other conditions: fracture of sternum, left ribs 3 through 11, left clavicle (marine life evisceration and avulsion).

Mrs. Tomiko Boyd, 36, Baltimore, Maryland, asphyxiation due to drowning and/or fracture of hyoid bone.

Mrs. Ann Carter Clack, 35, Tokyo and Midland, Michigan, multiple compound rib fractures, massive internal hemorrhage, dislocated neck.

Scott Clack, 6, Tokyo and Midland, Michigan, probable drowning, fracture of left clavicle.

Commander Gordon Cole, 36, Alexandria, Virginia, extensive basal skull fracture and multiple rib fractures.

Oliver E. Crosthwaite, 45, Felton, California, probable drowning. Other conditions: subarachnoid hemorrhage.

William Homer Deck, 24, Radford, Virginia, subdural and subarchnoid hemorrhage. Other conditions: extensive decomposition avulsion of skin and subcutaneous tissue over left forehead and left calf.

Edward Ellis, 45, Hillsborough, California, transection of thoracic aorta and fracture, dislocation of neck.

Dr. William Hagan, 37, Louisville, Kentucky, subdural hematoma, left occipitoparietal (brain) region.

Robert Halliday, 38, New South Wales, Australia, fractured cervical vertebrae with spinal cord and basal skull fracture.

Nicole Truchy LaMaison, 34, New York City, probable drowning.

Thomas McGrail, 52, West Roxbury, Massachusetts, multiple injuries, fracture of ribs, right ankle. Other conditions: Ruptured left kidney and spleen.

Philip Sullivan, 59, Arlington, Virginia, fractured sternum and ribs and other damage.

Cassiqua Soehertijah Van Der Bijl, multiple cervical vertebrae fractures, other fractures.

Toyoe Tanaka, 50, Tokyo, undetermined, probable drowning. Other conditions: fracture of right ribs, 3, 4 and 5.

BODIES LOST AT SEA AND NEVER RECOVERED

David Alexander, 11, Los Altos, California

Marion Florence Bluim Barber, 49, Shaker Heights, Ohio

Fred Choy, 31, San Mateo, California

Bruce Clack, 9, Tokyo and Midland, Michigan

H. Lee Clack, 36, Tokyo and Midland, Michigan

Kimi Clack, 7, Tokyo and Midland, Michigan

Nancy Mariko Clack, 2, Tokyo and Midland, Michigan

Melih Dural, 25, Ankara, Turkey

William Holland Fortenberry, 35, Santa Clara, California

Norma Hagan, 34, Louisville, Kentucky

Sergeant David Hill, 21, Pink Hill, NC and Honolulu

Commander Joseph Jones, 33, New York City

John (Jack) King, 42, San Francisco

Hideo Kubota, Tokyo

Robert LaMaison, 41, New York City

Marie McGrath, 26, Burlingame, California

Soledad Mercado, 52, Phoenix, Arizona

William H. Payne, 45, Scott Bar, California

Ruby Quong, 29, San Francisco

Albert Pinataro, 26, Belmont, California

Louis Rodriguez, 53, San Francisco

Helen Rowland, 60, Springfield, Vermont

Bess Sullivan, 58, Arlington, Virginia

Major Harold Sunderland, 37, Miles, Montana, and Sacramento, California

William P. Wygant, 37, Sausalito, California

INDEX

121-123, 126, 135-137, 141-144, 158, 168, 170-171, 173-175, 189-190, 196, 212, 282-283, 310-311

Felton, California 10. 119, 127-129, 131-132, 201, 294, 297, 299, 302, 306, 316, 336, 339

Ferguson, Dick, viii, 60-61, 89

Fortenberry, Craig H. viii, 60-61, 74, 92, 139-40, 148, 229, 273-274

Fortenberry, Jerry H. viii, 19, 50, 63, 67-68, 70, 74, 139-140, 148, 150-151, 273-275, 285

Fortenberry, William H. 3-5, 16-18, 48, 50, 61-63, 67-68, 71, 78, 83, 273, 341

Fortune, Norvin B. 27, 30-31

Frankfurt, Germany 34, 70, 73, 151, 186

G

Gaffrey, Lt. Lee J. viii, 87

Garcia, Frank Jr, viii, 269-270

Gillespie, Hal 69

Goodman, Judge Louis Earl 178-179

Graham, Jack Gilbert 111

Guisness, Earl 168-169, 170, 214

H

Hagan, Dr. William and Norma 43, 339-341

Halliday, Robert 37, 78, 93,340

Hansen, Lawrence 220, 224-225, 227-228

Herken, Dr. Gregg vii, 267-269, 271-272, 277-278, 290

Hickam Field 75

Hill, Sgt. David Anderson 42, 340

Hillsborough, California 71, 253, 339

Holloman, F.C. 109-112

Honolulu, Hawaii ix, xi, 3-5, 10,18, 24, 27, 29-30, 32, 35, 36, 39, 42-44, 46, 50, 54, 56, 59, 62, 66, 68, 76, 79, 82-83, 88, 99, 108, 117, 127, 154, 162, 169, 174, 184, 197, 217, 224, 227, 229, 255-256, 273, 336

Hoover, J. Edgar x, 85, 98-99, 104-109, 111-114, 118, 121-122, 126, 135-136, 141, 144, 174-175, 189-190

Hoover, Isaac 159-160

Hostutler, Ray 107, 111

Houlgate, Deke 85, 88, 90-91

Huang, C.H. 24-25

Huston, John 124

I

IBM computers 28, 45, 160-165

Ice, Phil 101, 157, 163

136, 144, 172, 173, 175, 177, 179, 185, 189, 197, 207, 210, 214, 222, 227, 2355, 252, 272, 278, 281, 311, 314, 329-330
Salaz, Joe 12-13
San Diego, California 71-72, 165
San Francisco Chronicle 192, 194, 271, 276
San Francisco Examiner 75, 171-172, 174, 193-194
San Francisco International Airport 23, 27, 30, 112, 179, 223, 271, 273
San Mateo, California 9, 17, 29, 35, 42, 71, 117, 119, 129, 133, 138, 201, 268, 272, 319, 321, 327, 341
Santa Clara, California 16, 19, 26, 50, 61, 67, 78, 148, 272, 274-275, 341
Santa Cruz, California 6, 29, 116, 119-120, 126, 130, 132, 142, 196, 130, 132, 142, 196, 292, 294, 300, 304, 306, 309, 314, 320
San Mateo Times 71
Sasaki, Masako 39
Saucedo, Pedro 12-13
Scanlon, Jim 126
Schmidt, Ronald 257-259
Schonberger, Claude M. 122-135, 306, 310, 313-314, 321
Scott Bar California 23-25, 79-81, 165-167, 171, 173, 191, 208, 213-215, 218, 220, 222-223, 229, 282, 336, 342

Shanghai, China 129, 133, 200-201, 247, 313
Shankoff, Tamara 304-305, 311, 313-314, 318
Sharpe, Major John H. 261, 263
Sherman, Don 28
Sherman, John D. 215, 218-222
Siskiyou County, California 23, 79, 173, 210, 216, 218, 336
Sizoo, J.A. 141, 143
Smith, Dr. Angela Thompson 233, 235-237, 240-243
Snipes, Les 75
Sohn, Fred 149-150
Sorensen, Emil Jacob 136-137
Sovereign of the Skies 102, 197, 268-270
Spartanburg, South Carolina 18, 147
Sputnik 16, 26, 61, 253-254
Stanley, Lt. John N. 87
Stokes, James 15
Stiles, Russell viii, 156, 172, 174, 180, 190-194, 204-227, 336
Stratocruiser, Boeing ix, 3-5, 18, 24-25, 28, 30-33, 35, 41, 44, 47-50, 53-54, 57, 60, 65, 66-67, 76-78, 84-85, 88, 93, 99-100, 102-103, 107, 113, 140, 150, 159, 172, 183, 233-234, 236-238, 240, 252-253, 256, 267, 269-270, 278-280, 315, 318, 330, 333, 337

ABOUT THE AUTHOR

Ken H. Fortenberry is a nationally recognized investigative journalist and author who has earned more than 200 state, regional, and national awards for excellence in reporting and writing.

Millions of Americans were introduced to the author when he was featured on the CBS's *60 Minutes* and NBC's *Today* show and in *The New York Times* for his courageous coverage of a corrupt county sheriff in South Carolina. His first book, *Kill the Messenger*, tells about his family's trials and tribulations — including death threats and bombings — during that investigation, and was optioned for a television movie.

The retired newspaper editor lives with his wife, Anna, in the mountains of North Carolina, where he is working on a new book, *The Field on Hanging Tree Road*, a coming-of-age novel set against the backdrop of the Vietnam War and the civil rights era in the South.

Ken is a member of the Nonfiction Authors Association and The Authors Guild. For more about the author and his works go to: www.kenfortenberry.com.

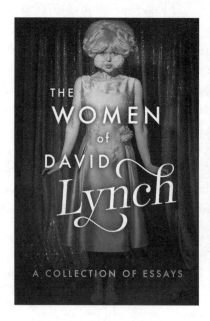
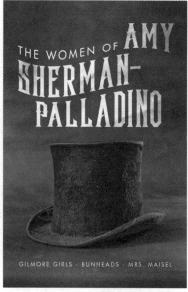

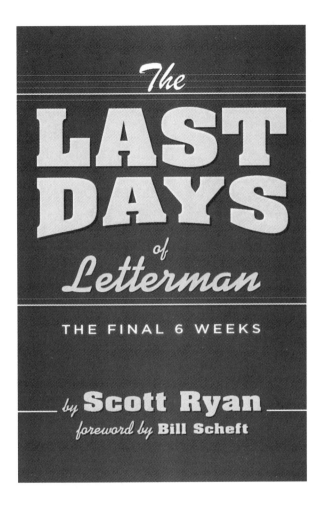

Read an inside look at the final 6 weeks of *Late Show with David Letterman,* all told through the words of the staff that wrote, directed, and produced those iconic last 28 episodes in 2015. *The Last Days of Letterman* by Scott Ryan

ISBN: 9781949024005

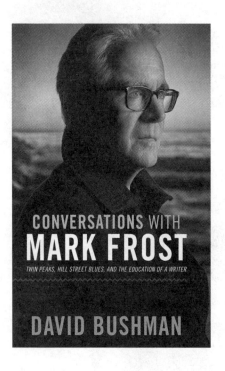

Mark Frost cocreated *Twin Peaks*, wrote for *Hill Street Blues*, and has written novels and nonfiction books. Learn about his life, his craft, and his career in this new book by David Bushman.

ISBN: 9781949024111

The Massillon Tigers: 15 for 15 is the powerful tale of one of the most storied high school football programs in the country and its magical 2019 season, as told by award-winning author and journalist David Lee Morgan, Jr., who enjoyed unlimited access to the players, coaches, and families through his role as running-backs coach. Foreword by former Buckeye Coach Jim Tressel.

ISBN: 9781949024166

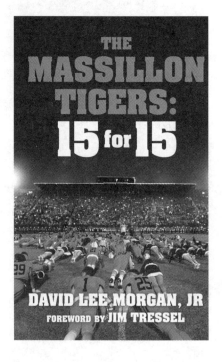

COMING SOON

Laura's Ghost: Women Speak About Twin Peaks by Courtenay Stallings
(August 28, 2020) ISBN: 9781949024081

Moonlighting: Cases, Chases and Conversations by Scott Ryan
& E. J. Kishpaugh (2021) ISBN: 9781949024128

A Diva Was a Female Version of a Wrestler By Scarlett Harris
(2021)

More information at FayettevilleMafiaPress.com